DE'LURE PUBLICATIONS PRESENTS

TAKE MY BREATH *Away* 2

WHEN LOVE CALLS

TAKE MY BREATH AWAY 2

DE'LURE

INTERNATIONAL BESTSELLING AUTHOR

DE'LURE

De'Lure

Publishing

Take My Breath Away 2
When Love Calls
All Rights Reserved.
Copyright © 2015 De'Lure
De'Lure Publishing
Cover Image by Edifyin Graphix

PRINTED IN THE UNITED STATES OF AMERICA

Author Quotes

"If you already know your greatness half the battle is already won...
Now you need only show your greatness to the world!!
De'Lure

"You defeat and discount a terrible past by willfully illuminating
your present as it blossoms into your future...
De'Lure

"I will die a dreamer... A dreamer with the heart and the talent to
realize their dream is more powerful and blessed than the richest man
on the planet..."
De'Lure

"Once you recognize the fact that **NOTHING** *in your past be it lies*
or truth, can discount your present accomplishments, or the things you
will achieve in the future, life becomes much simpler."
De'Lure

"We are taught to believe that our names and our images are everything...
If so that's a good thing because we are in control of all of the above..."
De'Lure

"To read my work... is to peek inside of my very heart and experience my
vivid rainbow of imagination"
De'Lure

*"When people can't compete with your **present**, and they fear your **future**,*

they have no choice but to bring up and attempt to distort your past"
De'Lure

"We are not who THEY say we are… but exactly who we choose to be"
De'Lure

"If we let the ghosts of our past affect our present and our future… well then, we were much better off dying, along with those nagging ghosts of long ago…"
De'Lure

Dedication

This book, my third published novel is dedicated to me. I worked extremely hard on this project, day in and day out for four straight months. During that time, evil people who don't really know me, attempted to torment and destroy me, but I made it through and like the late great Maya Angelou, "Still I Rise". This novel like all of my books is also dedicated to all of my dreamers out there, and also the ones that are scared to dream. I'm living my dream every day, and with everything I've been through… if I can do it so can you.

"If you're scared of becoming great just attach yourself to somebody who already knows how to fly. You'll never learn how to soar until somebody shows you how to grow your own wings…"

M.L. De'Lure

Acknowledgments

First and foremost, I thank GOD for giving me the drive and the strong mind to stay focused long enough to bring yet another project to completion. Mentally I'm still in a good place, and I know I'm doing what He created me to do. I don't have a clue where these stories come from, but they are so real to me. When I create, I don't sit down at my lap top with an outline or a writing plan. I just start typing and let my characters tell their stories themselves. This has always been my writing style. I thank God, every day for the feeling I get when his hand is upon me, as these stories bleed out through my fingertips. I also want to acknowledge my God Mother Carole Burton, my friend Valerie Olivier, and my friend Twaneshia Powell who all worked tirelessly on the editing of *"Take my Breath Away Too"* (When Love Calls). Ladies, I thank you, and I love you all.

These events and the characters you are about to read about are all fictional. The things I write about are always born through pure imagination.

Chapter 13
Back in the Game

(Kel)

Today is a magical day for me. My name is Keldrick Jermaine Cole Sr., and I'm writing this letter to let the world know that dreams really do come true. This marks the end of one rocky chapter in the book of my life, and the beginning of a new wonderful chapter. With all the charges my brother Lance has pending against him, he will never see day light again. I used to say I would never wish prison on anybody because I know how bad prison is first hand. But Lance tricked the mother of my child into falling in love with him, and then he tried to kill her. He also kidnapped my daughter and hid her in a dark dusty old storage shed for days, and then he shot her at our family reunion.

Both of my girls made full recoveries, and they're doing well. My baby will carry that scar on the right side of stomach forever but that's okay, I told her the scar gives her character. She has a story to tell her friends when she's older, and they'll all think it's cool that she survived a gun shot at such a young age. So, my baby has learned to embrace her battle scar. Whitney has been working extra hard to be the perfect wife and mother. I haven't brought that day up again, and I'm not going to punish her for it. It's my fault too. If I had been there for her she never would have entertained Lance. I haven't seen Cam since the family reunion.

I saw on Facebook awhile back that she and Ty had a house together in Atlanta. Then we found out my father Paul was an even bigger hoe than we thought before. It turns out Tyrone is my half-brother.

After Cam found out, she left Ty and disappeared. Nobody has seen her since. I wish her the best though. Dr. Sanchez quit his job at the hospital, and word is he's off traveling the world, trying to mend his broken heart. Mama Cole has been perfect. She nursed both of my girls back to full health. She helped us get moved into our new five-bedroom house in Miami as well.

That's right baby, "Big Daddy" brought his talents to South Beach. I'm the biggest thing to hit the city since the king LeBron James. The Miami Dolphins had been scouting me throughout high school up until my injury, after that I kind of fell of the map. They wrote several letters of interest over the years, stating that they wanted me to attend some camps over the summer.

I always ignored the letters because after I healed physically, I was still crippled mentally. Then after I got locked up, I was sure they would lose interest. They never did so finally Whitney wrote them back expressing interest in their programs. I didn't have a clue what she had done. She just cooked a huge dinner one day, and asked me to dress nice. We had dinner with the Dolphins Offensive coordinator Mike Sherman. It was nice, and after hours of video, actual play diagrams, and talk about a sizeable signing bonus I was sold.

I immediately started secretly training with the coaches. They saw my potential and decided to go ahead and give me the opportunity to walk on and play for them. I signed on the dotted line, deposited my three hundred thousand dollar signing bonus, and started practicing in full pads the next week. At that point, nobody knew but my mom. I didn't want to get anybody's hopes up, because I still had my doubts that I could continue to perform at the level they expected me to.

If I failed to deliver, I knew that with the stipulations in my special *contract I would owe the organization every penny back. So far everything*

has been lovely though, I'm slowly becoming the face of the franchise. They need a new face after the huge scandal they just went through with Richie Incognito.

My mom also lives with us at our beachfront home, she has her own room and she takes care of Jaze for us, and our new son Keldrick Jr. Mama's happy because I'm happy, and she's finally living the life she deserves. We had to go through some extensive family counseling, but we're good now. I think everybody is good now, Jaze loves her baby brother, and Whit seems to be finally in her comfort zone. I don't think we'll have any more problems like we had in the past. Our wedding will be next month.

We decided to get married right here on the beach. Our wedding colors are white and pink. I wanted blue but my baby is an A.K.A. so I had to let her have that. It's her day anyway. I want it to be her, dream day come true. The honeymoon is all me though, I want a sexy private exotic island getaway for just my queen and I. To all my fellas out there if you're ever lucky enough to find a woman that you know you can't live without, don't hesitate to treat her just like that. And ladies if you ever find a man who treats you like a queen, if you continue to act like one, he will continue to treat you like one.

Epilogue
"Island Get Away"

Whitney left home early this morning to catch her plane. The flight was long and peaceful. She didn't sleep at all. The anticipation was too much for her to doze off even for a second.

She's been waiting her entire life for a real moment like this. A weekend getaway on an exotic island in the Quirimbas Archipelago near Pemba in northern Mozambique; is the perfect engagement present. He's already been on the island for a day or so waiting for her to arrive. Whitney had never even heard of the gorgeous island before she received the ticket he had delivered to her. Stepping   off the small plane Whitney feels as if she's stepping into a new chapter of her life.

The driver was already there waiting for her when the plane landed. He got all of her luggage and loaded it into the back of the brand new fiery red Rolls Royce. She's at a loss for words when they arrive at the exquisite Ibo Island Lodge. She can't believe any of this is real, and she's so happy guilt doesn't even cross her mind. "Right this way Ms. Powell," the driver says, "he's waiting for you."

A couple of young men from the island begin to carefully grab her luggage and follow her and the driver inside the luxurious hotel. Walking along the pristine halls of the lodge Whitney feels as if she's having and outer body experience.

She's being lead down each hall by her own personal chauffeur, and being followed by ruggedly handsome local island men carrying her brand-new Hermes luggage set. He picked it out for her a week ago and had it delivered to her house. She feels like a powerful island queen headed to her royal chamber in her stunning castle. She's lost in her own personal fantasy.

As they approach the door to her room she can hear her heart beating fiercely in her ears. She reaches up and tries to make sure her hair is still perfectly in place. Nervously she grabs the driver's arm before he can open the door. Then she takes a small mirror out of her honey orange Hermes clutch.

Holding the mirror up in front of her face she truly believes she's looking at perfection. After placing the mirror back in her clutch, she nods at the driver giving him permission to open her door. He immediately takes his hat off, opens the door and stands to the side as she slowly steps inside. Her heart is no longer beating in her ears because it has now dropped to her stomach.

The room is even more breath taking than she could have ever imagined. Almost every wall is pearly white, except for the accent wall behind the bed in the bedroom. This wall is a pretty pale green color, the exact same color as the perfectly hand stitched comforter on the bed. As she enters the bedroom she can hear the shower running. She figures she must have arrived a little earlier than he planned, and he must still be getting ready for her.

The wildly flowing white cloth canopy on the bed is swaying methodically as a nice warm breeze is wafting in from the veranda. There is a small antique lamp sitting on a small table on each side of the bed. The hardwood floors have been buffed to perfection. The soft air smells like fresh mango fruit.

On the right side of the bed a gorgeous red Alexander Wang summer dress with a white floral print on it has been laid out for her. As she reaches out to carefully feel the material she feels a sudden

chill and her arm is covered in tiny goose bumps. Whit sighs happily as the gorgeous dress is made of pure silk.

Below the dress on the floor beside the bed is a light brown Christian Louboutin box. She can hardly wait to see what's inside the box. She quickly kneels down to take the top off of it. Inside she finds a pair of exclusive red and white Christian Louboutin pumps with tiny rhinestones all over them.

She can no longer contain herself. She begins squealing joyfully like a small child on Christmas. Lying to the right side of the dress is a small Chanel box. Inside the box she finds a luxurious Chanel jewelry set, containing a thin gold watch, bracelet, anklet, and two diamond earrings.

As she looks around the room she realizes the driver and bag boys have been gone for quite some time, she's all alone. She sits down on the bed. "I wonder why he chose to buy so many different designers instead of just sticking to one." Whit says to herself. "Because," a voice says near the door, "you're going to acquire so much clothing and jewelry for the rest of your life… if you don't learn to mix them all up you'll probably never get around to wearing them all."

"Carlos," Whit says smiling from ear to ear, "where have you been?" He smoothly struts towards her, never taking his eyes off her. Picking her up off the bed, she wraps her legs around him, as he kisses her deeply and passionately. He allows her to lean back in his arms so he can look at her.

"You know Carlos," she says, "you're going to have to work a lot harder to keep me now." Carlos furrows his brows "Why is that?" He asks. "Because K.C. is rich too now, so you have to find other ways to excite me." "So, you're saying you want something different," Carlos says, "something exciting, a twist, right?" "Yes, baby yes!" She tells him, as she hugs him tightly.

Carlos puts her down. He sits down on the bed with a mischievous smile on his face. He looks towards the bathroom door and

claps his hands. Moments later the shower cuts off. Whitney can hear movement in the bathroom. Frozen, where she stands Whitney awaits curiously for Carlos' next move.

The bathroom door opens. A woman walks out in a bright red Chanel bath robe, drying her hair with a velour towel. Sitting down next to Carlos on the bed, the lady looks through the soft towel with a smile and says. "What's up boo?"

"Cam…" Whitney says.

"The one and only…" She replies. "Is this a good enough twist for you?" Carlos says laughing out loud.

"Ladies I'll be back." He says kissing them each on the lips.

"Make yourselves look like the queens you are," he continues, "tonight… we start living the way we were born too." With that, the good doctor leaves the room.

Whitney continues to stare at Cameron. "I can't believe we're both here in the same room together." Whit says. "Well believe it girl," Cam replies, "girl, Carlos bought the hospital on this island. The man owns an entire hospital. I understand that Kel is playing football now, but that little NFL money is only a drop in the bucket of what Carlos is worth.

This island is my home now Whit. And I'm hoping you decide to stay too." "Wait, how long have you been here," Whitney asks, "I can't stay here… with both of you. Carlos told me I would be his wife." Cameron smiles at Whitney. "You will be his wife boo," she says, "we both will. Come sit next to me. It's time we get to know each other." Whitney obediently does as Cam asked her to do.

"Your hair is gorgeous girl; it always has been." Cam says as she softly runs her fingers through Whit's blonde highlights. "So," Whitney says enjoying her scalp massage, "you knew I was coming, and you didn't mind? You don't see anything wrong with this… at all?" "Girl," Cam says with a real smile, "this is 2015 nothing surprises me anymore.

Wait, weren't you and Love living with another man?" Whitney puts her head down as her face starts to turn red. "Girl pick your head up," Cam says, "don't be ashamed. When I heard about ya'll little situation I was jealous. I was like that girl had two men all to herself, damn."

They share their first laugh together ever. "Look Whit," Cam says, "I'm saying just relax while you're here. If you decide to stay cool, if not Carlos and I will miss you but we'll understand." Whitney turns to look at Cam. "What do you mean Carlos *and I* will miss you?" Whit asks. Cam starts to blush herself. "Girl, are you serious," Cam says, "Whitney you are *fine as hell*. I never wanted to be with a woman until the very first time I laid eyes on you." Whitney kisses

Cam softly on the lips.

(Five years later)

Cameron and Whitney are still living on Dr. Carlos Sanchez's island with him. K.C. is the star of the Miami Dolphin's football team, and he's taking the NFL by storm. Ty and Jay are moving home to Orlando from Atlanta. Mama Cole lives in K.C.'s Miami mansion. Jaze is in fifth grade now, and she's is the woman of her father's house, and the primary caretaker of her baby brother K.J. Love is still in prison with a life sentence and no chance of parole.

Prologue

(Love is talking to a psychiatrist at a prison in Orlando)

Lance Orlandis Cole is sitting in a hard iron chair in a cold office near the infirmary, inside of the Central Florida Reception Center, a large prison facility in Orlando Florida. This is where he has lived for the past five years. Lance is in the middle of a conversation with one of his psychiatrists, Dr. Granger. "How do you feel today Lance…" the doctor asks.

"The same…" he replies blankly. "When you say the same what exactly does that mean Mr. Cole?" Love looks at the aging doctor and replies with malice in his eyes.

"I told you **Kevorkian**,my name is Vinson, and I am not a Cole." "Don't call me Kevorkian, Lance. You don't have to be disrespectful." the doctor replies.

"Don't call me Cole, respect goes both ways or not at all. Do I not deserve respect as well as you do? You and I are not the slightest bit different Doc." Love says with a sick smile on his face.

Dr. Bruce Granger removes his glasses calmly and asks, "What are you referring to Cole?"

"My name is Lance Orlandis Vinson. I'm not going to correct you again verbally." Love tells him.

"Is that a threat Lance?" Dr. Granger asks. "Check my record Doc I don't make idle threats," Love says, looking as deep as he possibly can into the frightened eyes of Dr. Granger. "Where did the name Love come from," he asks," that's what you call yourself right Lance?"

"You've never met Lance Doc," Love replies, "and you don't want to meet him. So, it's best you leave him out of this conversation, because I like you Doc, I really do but Lance doesn't feel the same

way." "But you are Lance Mr. Co…Mr. Vinson I mean. You *are* Lance
so why do you speak of yourself in third person?" Dr. Granger asks. "I am not Lance Dr. Granger. "He is here though, and he is a part of me but our thinking patterns contrast in a way that the two of us could never truly co-exist. When he's here… Love is not."

"I see," the doctor says, "so what do you think caused your initial break down?" "Why so many deep questions today Doc…" Love asks through his sadistic smile. "This is the most talking you've ever done in one session," Granger looks intently at him, "so I'm hoping for a brea…"

"You want a breakthrough Doc, is that what you want?" Love stands up quickly. Dr. Granger flinches in fear. Love smiles, then he walks slowly towards a wall in the doctor's office filled with various awards in the medical field he has been given over the years.

With his back to the doctor he begins to speak. "Fine Doc… here's your breakthrough. From a very young age, I was alienated by my entire family because they thought they saw something in me that I eventually accepted as well to be true." "What did they think they saw?" Dr. Granger asks.

"Don't interrupt me again Doc." Love stares a whole through him.

"Like I was saying before you broke my thought…They thought I was unusually feminine for a little boy. I was unsafe in my own home. I was molested and raped repeatedly by my brother's father and… one other person. So, for years they told me I liked boys, that I was a faggot, and a little red sissy." Love laughs silently to himself. "But look at me Doc, I'm all man. I run this damn prison. No moves are made in this camp unless they go through me. Looking back I don't think I was ever gay."

"Son, you had a boyfriend… Corey. You were definitely gay." Dr. Granger assures him.

"Sex makes you gay, not companionship you idiot. The first time I ever had sex as a grown man was with my ex Whitney Powell."

"So, you and Corey Lewis never had sex?" Dr. Granger asks.

"Never," he replies, "not even once. Living a life that wasn't mine was destroying me. But I'm doing much better now over all Doc, which is as good thing since I'm getting out soon. I'll be able to use my new-found skills to be successful out in the free world."

"Getting out…" Dr. Granger "Love…You have a life sentence without parole. You're never leaving here."

"Oh, but I am Doc," Love replies, "and you have the keys I need to do so."

"What are you talking about boy?" the doctor asks. Love turns to face him.

"Don't ever call me boy again, you disgusting pedophile!" Love screams.

"What are you talking about Vinson?" the doctor asks standing up from his seat. "Sit back down right now." Love demands with finality.

Love begins to pace back and forth in front of the doctor. "Were you born and raised in Orlando, Doc?" he asks. "I was but…" the doctor starts. "And did you ever own a private practice on Orange Avenue?" Love asks.

"Yes, but how…" the doctor tries to speak again. "You used to drive a beat up old station wagon. It had a cracked windshield and a spare tire on the front passenger side. Inside it always smelled of cigarettes and old rotting fast food dinners."

Dr. Granger stands up again.

"Wait… how did you know…?" Dr. Granger is cut off again as Love rushes around his desk and grips his throat as tightly as he possibly can. Love puts his angry lips close to Dr. Granger's fat face as he continues to squeeze his throat.

"Shhh… just, be quiet Doc," Love loosens his grip briefly, "I'm not going to kill you… even though I should. But I'm not because you're going to redeem your sins by getting me out of here next week."

"Look son," the doctor says struggling to breathe, "I don't know what's going on, and I don't know how you know all those things about my past but I am not helping you escape this prison." Love releases his neck and forces him to sit back down.

Walking around the desk Love takes a seat himself facing the doctor.

"Escape," Love says smiling at the doctor, "oh no, no, no Doc. There will be no need to break the law… we've both done enough of that for a lifetime. No, you're going to write Judge Whatley and have her release me based on your evaluation of me."

"I have **never** broken the law." the doctor claims standing up yet again. Love stands up and pounds his fist on the doctor's desk.

"Rape is against the law Bruce, or Brucie that's what you used to like me to call you right?" Love licks his full pink lips, and then smiles his sick but handsome smile.

The doctor holds his hand over his mouth with his eyes bulging out of his head. Slowly he sits back down. Love walks around the desk. Standing behind the doctor he begins to run his fingers through his thin graying hair.

"You remember me now Doc," Love smiles that sick smile, "I never told a soul. My mother Linda brought me to you, so you could fix me. See in her mind I needed fixing, I was a strange and disturbed little kid." Love laughs snidely.

"Hell, after my step father sexually abused me for all those years, I think I deserved to be a little disturbed, don't you? So, then… then she brought me to a shrink. But not just any shrink, the great Dr. Bruce Granger, born and raised in Orange County.

xix

Yeah, Linda left it up to you to fix her disgusting little baby boy. But you had other plans for me didn't you Doc? How many little boys did you do this to Bruce?"

The doctor feels completely numb he can't even feel the rough scalp massage Love is attempting to hurt him with.

"This can't be real." the doctor says. Love laughs. "Oh, it's very real Brucie. So now the ball is in your court, are you going to write that letter, and ultimately right your wrongs to me, or do I have to ruin your entire existence?" Love asks.

"No, no, no… you can't…" The doctor starts. "I can't what Bruce?" Love asks. "You plan to ruin me," he replies, "I can't lose my license, my job… and my wife, what about my poor wife Rachel?" Love laughs loudly.

"What about Rachel…I can honestly say Bruce; I don't give a damn about Rachel!" he screams. "I'm about to be late to chow call," he continues, "You need to let me know something now, because I don't plan on missing out on the fried chicken and mashed potatoes. I'm sure Rachel has a wonderful meal waiting on you at home." Dr. Granger stares briefly into the eyes of the convicted inmate who holds his entire life in his very hands.

"What exactly do you want?" Dr. Granger asks. "The letter Bruce," Love looks deep in the old man's eyes, "all I want is Whatley to get the letter and then you walk away free. You can remain in your comfortable fairytale life without a worry in the world." Love exits Granger's office confidently.

Alone in his office, Granger tries to calm himself. Inside the pocket of his polo button down, he finds a small faded blue handkerchief. Trying to steady his shaky hand he wipes the sweat beads from his face and forehead.

"What's done in the dark…" he mumbles nervously to himself. After refreshing his laptop screen, he begins to delete all of the child pornography videos he's downloaded, and made himself over the years.

After the last video is completely gone from his computer, Granger tries to gather his thoughts about what exactly he plans to put in this letter to Love's judge. One thing's for sure it will be the most well posed letter he's ever written in his life.

(Shadows)

In the middle of the night Love wakes up and he can't move. He can barely breathe and he can see absolutely nothing. He tries to lick his dry lips, but he can't find them, and he can't touch them. He squirms in panic. A cool breeze floats across his body chilling him to the bone. He shivers. His body is completely naked.

I must be in Hell he thinks to himself. Is this how bad Hell is? You can't move, talk, or breathe. I can't even touch or see myself. And it's cold here, how is that possible. Hell is nothing like I imagined, I knew one day I would reside here, but I pictured it much differently. Wait, how did I die?

A cold gloved hand is running down his perfect stomach. Now two hands are running up and down his thighs.

SMACK!! Someone or something slaps him hard across the face. He can feel some of his senses returning to him. He can feel his legs more now. He's standing up, and has been for quite some time. His legs must have fallen asleep.

Somebody is biting his left thigh softly. Now they begin kissing it as they make their way up towards his private center. As it begins to fondle him, he closes his eyes tightly. Love has no idea who or what is teasing, and tormenting his body right now, but it's been so long since he's been touched he really doesn't care at this point.

The violator engulfs him with its large, warm, wet mouth. Moving its head in a winding motion it slowly causes Love to become fully **awake**. Love knows now what must be going on. Officer Patterson did what he said he would. He allowed some death row inmates to come into his cell late at night to torture him, and do with him whatever they want.

Love tries not to be aroused mentally by the awesome feeling this thing is giving him, but his mind is not strong enough to do pull this feat off. It reaches around and palms his buttocks to push Love further down its throat.

Now there's light. He's not blind after all. Someone had put a thick bag over his head. Love can see a bright light blinding him from straight ahead.

He looks down at his body to assure himself that he is completely naked, and he's not he does have on one holy sock. Love looks to his arms above either side of his head to see that he is hand cuffed to a wall.

His feet are tightly restrained to the same wall as well. In the darkness, he can see two maybe three shapes. As the dark figures walk closer to him he can see they are two masked women with their breast out wearing only panties.

"I heard you get out in four days." one of the ladies says. "Yeah," the second agrees, "so we had to give your pretty, yellow, ass a going home present. He tries to, but he still can't speak. There's something salty stuck in his mouth preventing him from making any noise.

Down on their knees in front of him now they take turns kissing, biting, licking, and sucking him. Love moans silently. Both women are taking delicate care of his body from head to toe. One of them stands up, takes off a glove and begins to run her long fingernails along his chest and stomach, while the other one can't seem to stop feasting on his throbbing member.

The one who is standing up takes her time to pull of her own panties. Then she rubs them across Love's face. The orange thongs are completely soaked and they smell of crushed apples. She throws them down to the floor, and then pulls her mask up high enough to expose her lips and kiss him. The kisses feel innocent to him at first, and then she begins kissing him as if she *needs* him inside of her. She looks down at the other woman and then joins her back on her own knees biting Love's thighs again.

The lady who was standing before grabs hold of Love taking him away from the hungry one. Stroking him quickly and then slowly she lifts the bottom of the other woman's mask and begins kissing her. Now they're sucking each other's breast. Love is ready now. This private performance he's witnessing now is something he has dreamed about for over four years now.

The one who kissed him stands up and faces him. She steps closer now and bites his full bottom pink lip. "Out there in the free world," she says gripping his behind, "you would never look at me twice. Hell, you would never look at me period."

Love doesn't respond because he can't. She opens a condom and then grabs him in her right hand to roll it on him. Then she carefully climbs up on him, wrapping her legs and arms around him.

The second woman helps put Love inside of her. She begins to bounce on him wildly. Her screams are even louder than he expected them to be as she starts to go harder in an attempt to take even more of him.

The second woman grabs the wet orange panties off the dark floor and stuffs them in her friend's mouth to shut her up. "Girl, be quiet," she whispers to her, "you're going to get us caught bitch. And hurry up we only got like five more minutes. I gotta get mine too…" She bites down hard on her wet panties as she grinds on him pushing herself to her own climatic eruption. He can feel her nails going deeper in his back. Her body locks up;

she begins to shake.

Her head falls forward on his solid chest.

The other woman, a much larger woman helps her down off of Love's body and is ready to take her turn with him. Standing in front of him she tries to figure out how to climb up on him, like her much smaller friend just did. Love realizes what she's thinking and begins shaking his head in protest as his eyes triple in size.

She decides that may not be the best way, instead she turns around in front of him and bends over. Her friend steps towards Love and spreads the woman open from the back to help Love enter her body.

Once he's in, she allows the bigger woman's behind to collapse on him. Back and forth, the full-figured woman continues to thrust herself back on him. Love closes his eyes, she is so wet and incredibly tight. He wants to take her as long as she can take him, because he doesn't know what they might do to him if they don't both get a chance to finish.

She's pushing back hard on him now grinding slowly. Her moans are amazing; the sound of her voice is turning Love on more than anything else. He won't last much longer.

Damn it. Love can't take it. Up on the tips of his pale white toes, he can feel his entire body tensing up. "Oh no you didn't." the woman growls. She turns around with a hand on each hip staring at him.

"Come on Peaches," the smaller woman says putting her clothes on, "we gotta get him backed locked up before the Captain gets in." "I know Lacy, damn." the bigger woman groans making her way towards her own clothing. She reaches inside her pants pocket to get

something out.

Then with her pants still in her hands she approaches Love. She snatches the black tape off his mouth, and then he spits out the small salty rag that was stuffed in his mouth.

"Swallow this." she tells him placing a smallish pill on his numb tongue. Love can't even feel his mouth so he really doesn't know if he swallowed the pill or not. Minutes later everything goes black.

(Three days later)

Love hears a knock on his cell door early in the morning. "What…" he yells. "You got visitation Cole." the guard tells him.

"I ain't got no visitation," Love replies, "so, leave me alone and stop fucking with me." "What?" the officer asks. "I ain't had a visit in over four years." Love tells him.

"Well you got one now," the guard insists, "it's some old preacher." "Pastor White." Love whispers to himself. "Hey Officer Patterson," Love says, "Give me five minutes, and I'll be dressed for that visit."

"You got it kid," the officer replies, "hell, take your time… you're gonna die here anyway."

He walks off laughing. Love joins him in his laughter. "No worries Officer Patterson," Love says, "your time is coming soon. Just remember when Love calls you better answer mother fucker. I hate being ignored."

The officer walks back to Love's cell door. "Look kid…" he says, "I've never had a problem with you, but you ain't in no situation to be calling shots. Don't feel special I treat all you mother fuckers the same, like shit." Patterson laughs again.

"News flash Patterson," Love smiles, "I'm getting out in a few days, and not even God can save you from me." Love laughs loudly in the officer's face. "In fact," Love continues, "you will be my very first victim."

"Yeah whatever..." the officer replies, "If I could legally refuse you this visit I would, you sick prick. And I heard about how you used to get raped as a kid. Reminds me of when you first got here, and the other officer's and I, beat you to a pulp just for fun." Patterson laughs at Love again.

"I'll tell you what," Patterson continues, "how's about I let two of the death row crazies in your cell late tonight, with nothing but Vaseline, a pillow case, and some rope?" Patterson stands up on the tips of his toes, to better see Love's face through the cell door.

Love looks up at the officer, with pure hatred in his eyes and soul. "If you ever put anybody in my cell with me late at night," Love explains in a dark tone, "including you and God, I will gut you all like fish with my bare hands, and then slowly eat your raw remains."

Patterson involuntarily grabs hold of his mouth and stomach. "Cole, just put on your damn visitation uniform and get your ass out here now." Officer Patterson says trying not to vomit on himself.

Visitations at the Central Florida Reception Center are usually public, out on the "yard" with the other inmates and their visitors. But Patterson explained to me that members of the clergy have the option of having private visitations with the inmates they come to visit.

This is the longest walk of my life; my feet feel so heavy. I'm nervous for the first time since my first prison fight. Everybody who goes to prison has to fight at least one time. It's the nature of the cage and the animals it holds captive. That first fight separates you from being a man or a boy. You can lose the fight, but you must stand your ground, because if you don't soon you won't even be able to shower in peace.

There will always be several inmates standing around you while you try to bathe, with their dicks in their hands, gunning you down every time you set foot in the shower. The prison term "gunnin' you down," means being the obvious object of someone's masturbation focus. After they start gunnin' you down, it won't be long before they have you arching your eye brows, wearing Kool aid lip stick on your lips, and sporting fish net stockings made of old cut up laundry bags. Glad I stood my damn ground.

I'm curious as to why my childhood pastor has come today, to pay me a visit. I mean I've been stuck in here for almost five years and he just now decided to acknowledge that I'm still alive. Inmates usually only get visits from members of the clergy if they are getting out soon or if they have requested spiritual counsel. The only other reason clergy randomly visits inmates, is to break the news to them that one of their family members has passed. If someone in my family has passed away, hopefully it wasn't my mother... Mama Cole is my problem to correct.

From down the hall Love can see his apparent visitor speaking to Dr. Granger. But whoever the man is, he's definitely not Pastor White. Dr. Granger shakes hands with the man and then walks in the opposite direction. The short white guy who was speaking to Granger turns around and knocks on the window of the room behind him. He holds both of his thumbs up, and then walks off in the same direction Granger just left in.

Now close enough to look in the window, the man was knocking on, Love can see the man inside the room is Pastor White. As Love steps into the private visitation room, he tries to hide his emotion but looking at the aging pastor, he can't help but to feel like that little boy again, sitting in the back row of his old church every Sunday morning. "Lance," Pastor White says, "How are you son?" Love hesitates to respond. Pastor White is one of the only people that he will allow to call him Lance. "I'm doing good pastor," Love says, "How are you?" "Well now son," the pastor starts, "my heart is conflicted."

"Now why is that pastor?" Love asks as he surveys the room.

"I've had several dreams about you lately son," Pastor White explains, "it's always the same dream for the most part, but it never ends the same way."

"Tell me about the dream Pastor." Love says leaning forward attentively. "Um…" Pastor White hesitates, "it's not that simple son." "Of course, it is Pastor White," Love smiles a dangerous smile, "this dream, is one as you said you have had several times. So, if that's the case, telling me about the dream shouldn't be a difficult task at all. Now… studies show that we forget ninety percent of our dreams after we wake up but I just want that ten percent you do remember pastor."

"Okay I'll try." Pastor White replies. "Well now, that's all I ask Pastor White, just try." Love grins with mock appreciation.

"Lance," Pastor White starts, "I've known you all of your life. I prayed for you… the second you came from your mother's womb, I later christened you at my old church, and I was there at your high school graduation. I know terrible things that happened in your past, and I also know tragic things that will transpire in your future."

"What the hell is this Pastor White," Love laughs, "are you a fortune teller now?"

"No son," he replies, "I have come to prophesy to you about your life. You have a great demon resting on your back even as we speak son. You call him Lance; you even speak to him as if he is an actual person outside of yourself. If you are not careful that demon is going to devour you, from the inside out. You did not create it, but it has been with you for many, many years. Many times, you have allowed the demon to speak, and act for and through you. This cannot be son, or your destruction is unavoidable. Your hatred and blood thirst for mankind is growing by the second. At this point you are not strong enough to fight the demon yourself. But with my help, you can rid your life of its evil

xxviii

forever. Pray with me son." Pastor White reaches out for Love's hands.

Love pulls his hands back away from the pastor. "If you allow Lance to continue to control you, you are going to ruin a lot of lives in a very short time son…" The pastor tells him. "You know pastor," Love starts, "up until about six months ago I would have agreed with you, on most of what you've just said. I might have even said a few false prayers with you, just to pacify you…"

"But now…" Pastor White interjects.

"Now," Love says through a crude smile, "now I, you… well we can no longer blame Lance. I have gown, and evolved. I am the demon you speak of."

"No son," the pastor leans forward, "Never claim, that on your life. I rebuke that in the name of Jesus Christ our Lord and Savior." "I am my only lord and savior," Love says, "God ain't never saved
me."

"He has Lance," Pastor White assures him, "and he's trying to now son, if you'll just let him…"

"Thanks for stopping by Pastor." Love stands up and walks towards the exit. "Wait Lance," he calls out, "the child can save you. You will love the child."

Love pretends to ignore the Pastor's final words to him, as he heads back to his cold, dark, lonely cell.

Pastor White falls to his knees from his chair, and begins praying fiercely, for everybody who will cross Love's path while he is still tormented by the evil spirit.

Chapter 1
Free at Last

(Love)

    The morning of release... Any man or woman, who has ever been to prison, will forever remember the morning of their last day of incarceration. A lot of the things we take for granted in the "free world", are dearly missed by inmates who are intelligent enough to notice.

    I miss touching, smelling, and seeing things that you will never see inside this cage. I haven't been genuinely touched in over four years. Just to be touched, by someone... anyone. Inside the cage sometimes we purposely make a mistake and bump into each other, just to feel another human body.

    The last morning of incarceration almost feels like Christmas morning to a naïve child. Every Christmas morning as children most of us believed in an old white man named Santa Clause, and the idea that he snuck into our home's during the night and left us toys that we specifically requested. Being released from prison is similar to that notion in the sense that most inmates believe upon release from their facility of incarceration they will have a new lease on life with their new-found freedom. Freedom can be a very, very dangerous thing.

    Freedom though, is the most beautiful gift and idea God ever created. But God didn't grant me my freedom, a pedophile named Bruce Granger, and a racist judge, one Catherine Whatley gave me my freedom back. And one day I will kill them both.

    It's 7:30am. I'll finally be free from the Central Florida Reception Center, in less than twenty minutes. I'm just waiting on the last of my paperwork to be completed, and to receive my walking papers. I'm actually hoping they stall a little bit longer, because that

asshole Officer Patterson gets off at 8am. I want to taste his blood before I leave this God forsaken parking lot.

"Lance Cole..." a soft vaguely familiar voice says.

"Yes." Love replies. "Here are your release papers," the pleasantly attractive dark skin officer says, "just follow me and I'll show you the way out."

As Love follows her, he can't help but watch her perfect shape from the back. She presses several buttons, and then Love can hear the large mechanical door unlocking from the inside.

"Here you go love," she says, "welcome back to your life. Please don't waste it sir." Love stands in the doorway, staring back at the woman. "Did you just call me Love?" he asks.

"I call everybody love," she tells him through a cute smirk, "don't look at women like that either Mr. Cole. You are a gorgeous man,

but that look in your eyes right now is slightly creepy." They share an uncomfortable laugh together.

"Thanks for the compliment Miss..." he hesitates. "Officer Pruitt," she says, "hell you're free now just call me Lacy."

"Perfect," he smiles, "can you do one more thing for me Ms. Lacy?" "I can't give you my number here..." she starts. Love laughs softly. "No not that," he blushes slightly, "I was wondering what time it is."

"Oh," she laughs nervously looking down at her cheap watch, "Its 8:03." "Really, damn it I'm late. Thanks for everything Lacy." he says, as he starts to run towards the parking lot.

"Oh, one more thing Mr. Cole..." she calls out. "Yeah..." he says walking a few steps back towards her. "My friend and I really had fun with you the other night." she whispers. Then she smiles and winks before closing the large door in his face locking it behind her. Love smiles and then rushes back out towards the huge parking lot. He soon notices even the air in the free world smells different than

the air inside the cage. As he finally reaches the parking lot, he can see Officer Patterson driving off.

Love continues to watch the tiny brown Honda Civic. Instead of

2

heading down the street out of his reach, the car pulls into the gas station right across the street.

"Oh God wants you dead Patterson..." Love whispers to himself licking his dry lips in triumph.

Love quickly discards all of the prison nonsense he walked out with in a nearby trash can. He leaves everything from his legal release papers to his Bible, right there in the filthy old trash can. The only thing he does keep in his pocket is his complimentary bus ticket.

By the time Love makes it across the street, Patterson's car is empty, and the gas pump is still pumping gas into his raggedy old car. The driver's side window is down and his radio is blasting some local rapper's terrible auto tune filled monotonous song.

Love balls up his bus ticket, and throws it down on the ground.

Next, he climbs in the back of Patterson's car and crouches down behind the driver's seat. Under the seat he finds a tiny mountain of molding French fries, old ketchup packets, a few skittles, and an empty can of Red Bull. The nauseating smell is reminiscent of an old sweaty high school football locker room.

Patterson's music selection doesn't surprise Love at all, because most of the officers at the prison sadly think they're cool. While he waits on his victim, Love reminisces about some of the other officers he encountered during his trying prison sentence. He remembers how the majority of them were using their jobs to live out their teenage fantasies.

He truly believes that many correctional officers were unpopular in school, and the inmates they now control are some of the cool kids who use to bully and torment them back in school. So of course, they use their new, man given power to take revenge on their childhood tormentors.

As Officer Patterson returns to his vehicle, he can't stop smiling. Life for the thirty-four-year-old, balding, college dropout is perfectly, routine. There are no real changes or variations in his day to day life. He knows exactly what to expect every single day, or at least he used to. Bobbing his head to the nonsense blasting from his shaky old radio speakers, Patterson places the gas nozzle back on its holder. Then he jumps in his car without a worry in the

3

world.

As he drives off slowly, he has no clue as to how much pain and hatred is riding along with him. Love reaches in the front seat and cuts the officer's radio off.

"What the hell?" Officer Patterson screams. "Pull the car over Patterson." Love says calmly with a large smile plastered on his handsome yellow face.

"Hell no," Patterson screams, "do you want to go back to prison you idiot? I'm going to press charges on you, you faggot!"

"Wrong word..." Love says slapping the officer hard in the back of his head. "Ouch!" Patterson exclaims holding the back of his

throbbing head. Love laughs menacingly at his pain. "Keep on faggot," Patterson yells, "the charges are just piling up. Just keep right on. Let's see now that's stalking, harassment, attempted grand theft auto, battery…"

"Funny thing Patterson," he says slapping the officer again, "I've never seen a dead man press charges before… pull the car over now!" "Hell no, Cole," Patterson says, "this is a catch twenty-two, I'm damned if I do, damned if I don't. If you're gonna kill me, you gone have to do it while I'm driving you pussy!"

Love spies a dull pencil on the filthy floor in the back of the car. He quickly grabs it, and with one hard stab he plunges it deep into the side of the officer's neck. Choking, and now shaking in shock, Officer Patterson desperately pulls his car over on the side of the road sealing his dark fate.

(Two Days Later)

    Today is almost a normal day at the Orlando Police Department, but not quite. But then what is a normal day at a police station? You never really know what kind of crazy is going to come along with each new day. Today's crazy came in the form of a new unknown dangerous serial killer on the loose in central Florida.

    The news broke last night about the body of a corrections officer being strangled to death in his own car in Orlando, with a shoe lace. The killer is believed to still be in the Orlando, Orange county area. Half of the city is in an uproar; the other half is lost and frozen in panic.

    A young hardnosed detective, O. Blue is sitting outside of Orlando Chief of Police Marcel Tiago's office waiting to be briefed on a new case. Detective Blue born and raised in central Florida, is the product of two police officers, and decided to follow proudly in their footsteps. Being an only child Blue was alone a lot growing up,

    and never really developed good people skills. So, in turn the detective has always been a loner and a complete hard ass.

    Blue is undeniably attractive, but sadly because of childhood insecurities, has no social life, or even a life outside of the police force whatsoever. At just thirty-one years old, Blue is one of the most decorated detectives the Orlando police force has ever seen.

    "Blue!" Chief Tiago yells through his thick door. "Yes, sir Chief!" Blue yells back. "Get your ass in here!" Chief says. "Yes sir…" Blue mumbles stepping confidently inside the Chief's large office.

    Chief Marcel Tiago, who looks like a tall, rough, Mexican cowboy is originally from Houston Texas, and has been the active Chief of Police here in Orlando for the past ten years. With his deep southern drawl, when he speaks he almost sounds like an old white plantation owner.

    "Damn it Blue, we've really got our asses on the market this time." Chief says. "Um… I have no idea what that means, but whatever you need me to do Chief, you know I'm there." Blue

replies.

"You're a good kid Blue," Chief admits, "you remind me a lot of your father God rest his soul." Blue's eyebrows wrinkle tightly. "My father didn't die chief... he just retired from the force alongside my mother." Blue reminds him.

"I know they're not dead Blue..." he says, "but in my mind once you take off the badge, put down your gun, and walk away from the force it is a form of dying. They are dead to the ongoing fight against crime." Chief waits silently for a reaction as if he has just imparted some golden, age old wisdom on the young detective.

Blue doesn't respond, obviously unimpressed by the thoughts of the aging chief. "But like I was saying Blue," Chief continues, "you remind me of your father because you don't really get in the mix with the other detectives and officers, but you would die for anyone of them just the same. I like that, and you're accomplished but not a glory hog."

"Thanks for the kind words Chief," Blue says, "but am I here for a new case or a promotion?" "Oh, hell no," Chief replies quickly, "I love you like my own child Blue but you're too damn young for another promotion. I'd probably have half the precinct trying to report me, and the other half would go on strike if I promote you again."

"That's not fair Chief," Blue frowns hard, "You know I deserve it. These old farts here don't want to see me promoted again because I'm young and because I'm..."

"Just stop it detective," Tiago interjects, "Damn it Blue, now I lost my train of thought." "I'm sorry Chief..." Blue apologizes.

"Oh, I remember now," Chief cuts Blue off, "I said all of that about who you are... to tell you that you are going to have to become even less than what you portray yourself to be now."

"I'm sorry Chief I don't follow." Blue replies.

"Close my door would you Blue," Chief says, "This is some top-secret shit."

Blue closes the door to the Chief's office as instructed. After sitting back down Blue leans forward to take in with certainty every shred of sensitive information the chief is about to give   out. "That C.O. from that prison that died the other day," Chief Tiago starts, "he was killed by an inmate. The problem is the though Blue... the inmate never existed."

"What the hell does that even mean Chief?" Blue asks leaning back in total confusion. "I told you," Tiago whispers, "This is some top-secret shit. Only one inmate was released from the Central Florida Reception Center, the morning of the murder."

"Then he's our guy right," Blue asks, "What's the perp's name Chief?"

"That's the thing," Tiago explains, "nobody inside or outside of the prison knows. The inmate's name has been removed from all records. There is no date of arrest, no record of the release, no name no picture... nothing Blue."

"What about a paper trail inside the prison," Blue asks, "I used to work at that prison Chief, so I know they have to have a filed copy of the inmate's walking papers that he was given before they walked him out of that front door."

"Blue," the Chief stresses, "I am telling you there is nothing. It's as if the entire prison has amnesia, or they've all been sworn to some kind of secrecy. I think they all fear they may be next on this guy's hit list. I wish I knew who his judge was, because only a judge could make an entire case file disappear like that."

"Damn it," Blue says, "So what the hell do you want me to do Chief?" "You... are going to quit the force." Tiago tells Blue.

"What the hell Chief," Blue yells, "never!"

"Calm down kid," Tiago says, "don't make a scene. You're only going to quit the force for show, you're still getting paid. I just need you to get down in the gutter, and go bag me that sleaze bag ASAP. No one is going to be able to get close to this guy but you. It's your killer instinct kid, you have solved every case I've ever given to you, and I know you won't fail me now. I know sometimes I kind of take credit for some of what you do... but I swear to God it's never been personal it's just the politics of it all. It just looks better with the chief being the top dog... you follow me Blue?"

"I follow Chief," Blue says holding back obvious angry sentiments, "but how the hell do I catch a dangerous murderer who has no face, no name, and no known motive? It's like I'm hunting a ghost, hell for all I know the killer could be you Chief."

Chief Tiago pulls a thin manila folder out of his top desk draw, and hands it to Detective Blue. "This is the file I have created for you with the little information I was able to obtain myself," Chief Tiago tells the young detective, "now good luck Blue, and get the hell out of my office."

Blue leaves the chief's office with no idea where to start. It pains the passionate young detective to know that the only lead will present itself once the killer strikes again. Deep down, Blue hopes Chief Tiago is on the murder's wish list.

The detective's father never particularly liked the Chief's rude demeanor, public credit stealing ways, and biased antics. Blue didn't truly understand until after joining the force, but the apple usually doesn't fall too far from the tree.

Next, he climbs in the back of Patterson's car and crouches down behind the driver's seat. Under the seat he finds a tiny mountain of molding French fries, old ketchup packets, a few skittles, and an empty can of Red Bull. The nauseating smell is reminiscent of an old sweaty high school football locker room.

Patterson's music selection doesn't surprise Love at all, because most of the officers at the prison sadly think they're cool. While he waits on his victim, Love reminisces about some of the other officers he encountered during his trying prison sentence. He remembers how the majority of them were using their jobs to live out their teenage fantasies.

He truly believes that many correctional officers were unpopular in school, and the inmates they now control are some of the cool kids who use to bully and torment them back in school. So of course, they use their new, man given power to take revenge on their childhood tormentors.

As Officer Patterson returns to his vehicle, he can't stop smiling. Life for the thirty-four-year-old, balding, college dropout is perfectly, routine. There are no real changes or variations in his day to day life. He knows exactly what to expect every single day, or at least he used to. Bobbing his head to the nonsense blasting from his shaky old radio speakers, Patterson places the gas nozzle back on its holder. Then he jumps in his car without a worry in the world.

As he drives off slowly, he has no clue as to how much pain and hatred is riding along with him. Love reaches in the front seat and cuts the officer's radio off.

"What the hell?" Officer Patterson screams. "Pull the car over Patterson." Love says calmly with a large smile plastered on his handsome yellow face.

"Hell no," Patterson screams, "do you want to go back to prison you idiot? I'm going to press charges on you, you faggot!"

"Wrong word..." Love says slapping the officer hard in the back of his head. "Ouch!" Patterson exclaims holding the back of his throbbing head. Love laughs menacingly at his pain. "Keep on faggot," Patterson yells, "the charges are just piling up. Just keep right on. Let's see now that's stalking, harassment, attempted grand theft auto, battery..."

"Funny thing Patterson," he says slapping the officer again, "I've never seen a dead man press charges before... pull the car over now!" "Hell no, Cole," Patterson says, "this is a catch twenty-two, I'm damned if I do, damned if I don't. If you're gonna kill me, you gone have to do it while I'm driving you pussy!"

Love spies a dull pencil on the filthy floor in the back of the car. He quickly grabs it, and with one hard stab he plunges it deep into the side of the officer's neck. Choking, and now shaking in shock, Officer Patterson desperately pulls his car over on the side of the road sealing his dark fate.

(Two Days Later)

Today is almost a normal day at the Orlando Police Department, but not quite. But then what is a normal day at a police station? You never really know what kind of crazy is going to come along with each new day. Today's crazy came in the form of a new unknown dangerous serial killer on the loose in central Florida.

The news broke last night about the body of a corrections officer being strangled to death in his own car in Orlando, with a shoe lace. The killer is believed to still be in the Orlando, Orange county area. Half of the city is in an uproar; the other half is lost and frozen in panic.

A young hardnosed detective, O. Blue is sitting outside of Orlando Chief of Police Marcel Tiago's office waiting to be briefed on a new case. Detective Blue born and raised in central Florida, is the product of two police officers, and decided to follow proudly in their footsteps. Being an only child Blue was alone a lot growing up,

and never really developed good people skills. So, in turn the detective has always been a loner and a complete hard ass.

Blue is undeniably attractive, but sadly because of childhood insecurities, has no social life, or even a life outside of the police force whatsoever. At just thirty-one years old, Blue is one of the most decorated detectives the Orlando police force has ever seen.

"Blue!" Chief Tiago yells through his thick door. "Yes, sir Chief!" Blue yells back. "Get your ass in here!" Chief says. "Yes sir…" Blue mumbles stepping confidently inside the Chief's large office.

Chief Marcel Tiago, who looks like a tall, rough, Mexican cowboy is originally from Houston Texas, and has been the active Chief of Police here in Orlando for the past ten years. With his deep southern drawl, when he speaks he almost sounds like an old white plantation owner.

"Damn it Blue, we've really got our asses on the market this time." Chief says. "Um… I have no idea what that means, but whatever you need me to do Chief, you know I'm there." Blue replies.

"You're a good kid Blue," Chief admits, "you remind me a lot of your father God rest his soul." Blue's eyebrows wrinkle tightly. "My father didn't die chief… he just retired from the force alongside my mother." Blue reminds him.

"I know they're not dead Blue…" he says, "but in my mind once you take off the badge, put down your gun, and walk away from the force it is a form of dying. They are dead to the ongoing fight against crime." Chief waits silently for a reaction as if he has just imparted some golden, age old wisdom on the young detective.

10

Blue doesn't respond, obviously unimpressed by the thoughts of the aging chief. "But like I was saying Blue," Chief continues, "you remind me of your father because you don't really get in the mix with the other detectives and officers, but you would die for anyone of them just the same. I like that, and you're accomplished but not a glory hog."

"Thanks for the kind words Chief," Blue says, "but am I here for a new case or a promotion?" "Oh, hell no," Chief replies quickly, "I love you like my own child Blue but you're too damn young for another promotion. I'd probably have half the precinct trying to report me, and the other half would go on strike if I promote you again."

"That's not fair Chief," Blue frowns hard, "You know I deserve it. These old farts here don't want to see me promoted again because I'm young and because I'm..."

"Just stop it detective," Tiago interjects, "Damn it Blue, now I lost my train of thought." "I'm sorry Chief..." Blue apologizes.

"Oh, I remember now," Chief cuts Blue off, "I said all of that about who you are... to tell you that you are going to have to become even less than what you portray yourself to be now."

"I'm sorry Chief I don't follow." Blue replies.

"Close my door would you Blue," Chief says, "This is some top-secret shit."

Blue closes the door to the Chief's office as instructed. After sitting back down Blue leans forward to take in with certainty every shred of sensitive information the chief is about to give out. "That C.O. from that prison that died the other day," Chief Tiago starts, "he was killed by an inmate. The problem is the though Blue... the inmate never existed."

"What the hell does that even mean Chief?" Blue asks leaning back in total confusion. "I told you," Tiago whispers, "This is some top-secret shit. Only one inmate was released from the Central Florida Reception Center, the morning of the murder."

"Then he's our guy right," Blue asks, "What's the perp's name Chief?"

"That's the thing," Tiago explains, "nobody inside or outside of the prison knows. The inmate's name has been removed from all

11

records. There is no date of arrest, no record of the release, no name no picture… nothing Blue."

"What about a paper trail inside the prison," Blue asks, "I used to work at that prison Chief, so I know they have to have a filed copy of the inmate's walking papers that he was given before they walked him out of that front door."

"Blue," the Chief stresses, "I am telling you there is nothing. It's as if the entire prison has amnesia, or they've all been sworn to some kind of secrecy. I think they all fear they may be next on this guy's hit list. I wish I knew who his judge was, because only a judge could make an entire case file disappear like that."

"Damn it," Blue says, "So what the hell do you want me to do Chief?" "You… are going to quit the force." Tiago tells Blue.

"What the hell Chief," Blue yells, "never!"

"Calm down kid," Tiago says, "don't make a scene. You're only going to quit the force for show, you're still getting paid. I just need you to get down in the gutter, and go bag me that sleaze bag ASAP. No one is going to be able to get close to this guy but you. It's your killer instinct kid, you have solved every case I've ever given to you, and I know you won't fail me now. I know sometimes I kind of take credit for some of what you do… but I swear to God it's never been personal it's just the politics of it all. It just looks better with the chief being the top dog… you follow me Blue?"

"I follow Chief," Blue says holding back obvious angry sentiments, "but how the hell do I catch a dangerous murderer who has no face, no name, and no known motive? It's like I'm hunting a ghost, hell for all I know the killer could be you Chief."

Chief Tiago pulls a thin manila folder out of his top desk draw, and hands it to Detective Blue. "This is the file I have created for you with the little information I was able to obtain myself," Chief Tiago tells the young detective, "now good luck Blue, and get the hell out of my office."

Blue leaves the chief's office with no idea where to start. It pains the passionate young detective to know that the only lead will present itself once the killer strikes again. Deep down, Blue hopes Chief Tiago is on the murder's wish list.

The detective's father never particularly liked the Chief's rude demeanor, public credit stealing ways, and biased antics. Blue didn't truly understand until after joining the force, but the apple usually doesn't fall too far from the tree.

Chapter 2
Mama Jaze

(At K.C.'s Miami Beach front mansion)

A pretty little girl around ten years old is watching a reality T.V. show on a seventy-inch flat screen T.V. in her father's bedroom. She's all alone of course but it's okay, she's used to that now. She has on hot pink sweatpants, purple socks, and a baby blue tank top.

Her long light brown hair is curled to perfection. Lying across the foot of her father's California king bed with two strawberry pop tarts, Jazemene Cole doesn't have a care in the world.

Her mother rarely crosses her mind anymore, but the pain is still fresh whenever her name is brought up, or if she accidentally stumbles upon an old picture of her. Deep down she knows she will never be completely rid of her mother's ghost, because she sees her every time she looks in the mirror. The older she gets she looks less and less like her dad, as she's becoming the spitting image of her beautiful estranged mother Whitney Powell.

Jazemene is an extremely observant child, so the downward spiral her father has been caught in since her mother's disappearance is really taking a toll on her. Her father is all she really has left; she knows if she loses him everything she's already dealing with now will only be amplified. She can't handle much more.

The problem is K.C. has lost focus again. Whitney's disappearance really threw him for a hard loop. Laying there on his bed the musky aroma of her dad's favorite cologne comforts Jaze when she's alone. Losing all interest in the television she begins to think to herself.

My mother is killing my father, and she's not even here. If she knew, I wonder if she would care. I don't know if my mom is dead or not, but she better be dead. If she ever came back, I would never forgive her for leaving me and my Dad. And my kid brother K.J., what did he do to deserve this? He couldn't walk or even talk when our mom left.

Damn it, I sit outside my father's door many nights listening to him cry out for her... or somebody. I'm never really sure if he's yearning for my mother or my old baby sitter, his ex-girlfriend Cameron Jiles. I'm old enough now to understand that my father loves both of them. I'm also old enough to realize he's beginning to sabotage his own life again.

He brings a different woman home every night, sometimes two or three at the same time. I wake up early each morning and put the women out myself. I always freak them out by telling them my mommy just called and said she's on her way home. If I ever have a problem with one of them I just go get Mama Cole, and she changes their minds quickly. And I can deal with all of that but the look in my daddy's eyes is just not normal anymore. My daddy needs help... or maybe he just needs love.

Jaze had to mature much quicker than she should have because of her mother's absence. Mama Cole used to help out a lot around the house but with all the new money flowing into the household she has begun *"living her life"* as she puts it. Ten-year-old Jaze does the bulk of the cooking, cleaning, and house management all by herself.

"Jazemeeene..." a cranky five-year-old boy says as he walks into the room. "Good morning K.J., what's wrong?" Jaze asks. "I'm hungry." he whines.

"I know, you're always hungry," she smiles down at his cute curly head, "what do you want to eat?"

"Where's my Mommy?" he whines. "Keldrick Jermaine Cole

15

Jr." she screams,

"I already told you we do not have a mother. If you want a mommy so bad then I'm your mommy, now what do you want to eat?" He looks up at her with those unmistakable green eyes unsure what to do or say next.

"Cinnamon Toast Crunch," she says, "it's your favorite. Now come on so you can wash your teeth and brush your face."

K.J. giggles. "You said *wash my teeth… and brush my face.*" he tells his bossy big sister. "Oh, shut up you little yellow *smurf,*" Jaze snaps, "You know what I meant, now come on."

Little K.J. follows behind her obediently still tickled at her simple mistake. Once inside their nice sized bathroom that connects to both of their bedrooms, Jaze cuts the light on. As she looks in the mirror a young, tired, angry Whitney stares back at her. She exhales deeply before turning the water on. Holding her tiny yellow hands beneath the faucet she waits until the water is warm enough. In the closet behind her she finds a small orange face towel. She wets it and then lathers it with a bar of white Dove soap.

"Come here K.J." she commands. He steps forward hesitantly. Jaze massages his small face with the soapy towel, and then she cleans out his tiny ears. Holding the towel back under the faucet she rinses all the soap out of the towel.

After wiping all of the excess soap from her baby brother's face and neck she puts some kid's Colgate toothpaste on his Gator Boy toothbrush and hands it to him. After a few quick strokes K.J. tries to hand it back to her. Looking up into her disapproving eyes he knows better. She doesn't have to say a word, that look is enough. K.J. finishes brushing his teeth and after he's done Jaze rinses his tooth brush out, hangs his towel on the rack, and wipes the extra water off the sink top they head to the kitchen for some Cinnamon Toast Crunch.

(Key Point Academy)

Jazemene attends a prestigious elementary school by the name of Key Point Academy in South Miami Florida. She's in the fourth grade now and already comfortably at the top her class in every facet. Without her mother and father in her life as much as she would like Jaze puts all of her focus on school, basketball, her baby brother K.J., and making sure the house is in order from top to bottom. All of her teachers love her, and often show her favoritism. This of course doesn't help her popularity with her fellow classmates.

Jaze tries hard not to notice how much all the other kids don't like her. Some of them are jealous of her because her father is a super star, others don't like the fact the she's the prettiest girl in the school, other just hate her because it's the popular thing to do at Key Point Academy. Jaze knows she only has and needs one friend in the whole school, the ever-loyal Josiah Bell.

Jazemene's favorite teacher is Ms. Bell. Ms. Bell, who is originally from Orlando, was also Jaze's kindergarten teacher back in the O-town. Cidra Bell, a thirty-three-year-old single mother of two has known Jaze since she was five years old, and has been close to her family ever since.

She and her children visited Jaze and her mother quite frequently in the hospital, after Love almost murdered them both in one afternoon. It's been five years since that dangerous barbecue at Mama Cole's house.

Cidra has one son, ten-year-old Josiah. Josiah, is in Jaze's class. Jaze developed a strong crush on him over the years, but refuses to admit it, even though the whole school can tell... everybody except for Josiah that is. Josiah and Jaze are the best of friends, and that's more important to young Jaze than her crush. At least for now it is.

(Tyrone)

Ty used to always want to go to the local **Starbucks restaurants** in Orlando when he was younger. His mindset was so warped, he believed because he was poor and black they wouldn't allow him to even come inside and sit down. Now that he's older, even though he still doesn't have much money, he has better clothes, manners, and he just plain knows better period.

"Blood of Jesus today is not my day!" Ty exclaims.

"Wow," a pretty white woman in a pant suit giggles at a table nearby, "yeah the coffee is supposed to go in your mouth not on your shirt."

"First off lady," Ty snaps, "this is a Venti Cinnamon Dolce Latte, never is it a coffee."

"Well aren't you just the **Renaissance man** today." she scoffs. "Don't patronize me lady." Ty replies.

"Wow," she says again, "I never realized black men were so sensitive."

Ty pauses for a moment to look at the woman. "Wait, wait, bitch did you just play the race card with a black person?" he asks. "Ah...

the five-letter word," she smiles, "that is how **you all** refer to your women isn't it?"

"You all," Ty repeats, "lady, are you serious right now? Why are you so confident while being so completely racist?" Ty leans forward and notices the small woman has a gun resting just inside her open purse.

"Now I see why yo white ass is bumping your chest like you **Wonder Woman**," Ty says, "or some damn fictional great white hope. What is it that you do lady, because I'm sure you do something?"

"Nope I'm actually unemployed." she replies.

"Now that surprises me," Ty crosses his legs in his thin linen polo pants, "so what's with the gun and the attitude lady?"

"Well as far as my gun," she starts, "Orlando the beautiful, as I'm sure you know can be a very scary place sometimes. And attitude, I have no attitude."

"Seriously," Ty replies, "You just sat here and basically called me a clumsy, rude, chauvinistic porch monkey in softer terms."

"It was all in fun *my brother*." she winks at him.

"Yeah," Ty starts, "just stop *all* of that. It's not cute or cool. I don't know where you're from but…"

"I'm from right here in the O-town, *my nigga*." she interjects.

"Damn it that's it…" Ty stands up. The lady holds her hands up in protest as she laughs uncontrollably.

"Sit down sir," she laughs, "I'm sorry. To be honest I'm intrigued… okay no I'm obsessed with black men and the essence of your culture."

Ty sits back down reluctantly.

"Our culture," Ty asks, "What the hell is the culture of the black man to you lady? I gotta hear this."

"Okay first my name is Osiana, what is yours?" she asks. "Tyrone." he responds dryly.

"Okay Tyrone," she starts, "to me black men are the most unappreciated species on our planet. Now, this is just me speaking off the record of course…"

"Sure." he agrees.

"To me…" Osiana continues, "Black men have the potential to do so much more than what they have already accomplished. In every field from the sciences, to athletics, to other forms of entertainment, to religion, there is at least one black man near the top of almost every possible field. But… there could be and should be a lot more."

"And that's all?" Ty asks. "And," Osiana continues, "don't take this the wrong way but it's my firm belief that black women, and the

19

black community are the cause of so many black men not becoming the societal giants they could be."

"Mmmm, how so…" Ty inquires.

"Well think about it Tyrone," she explains, "Most children grow up believing they can be anything they want to be at first, but then the older they get their belief systems alter themselves. They begin to see what they perceive to be reality, and they now believe they can only go as far as their parents have gone, or their friends, or even their neighbors. If a lot of young black boys were snatched from the womb and whisked away to some top-notch school programs in other countries, those same little boys who would have been destined to die on the street they grew up on, would become so academically inclined and successful they would shame Barack Obama himself. Gorgeous man by the way, Obama is an absolutely perfect specimen."

"Wow…" Ty leans back.

"So now you're taking my favorite word huh?" she asks playfully. "No, but I think I'm in love with your mind Ms. Osiana," Ty gushes, "Did I say that right?"

"You did my love, you said it perfectly."
she replies.

"No, I'm not your love, not yet anyway," Ty flirts, "but listen, can I take you out tonight, I'd love to pick your brain some more. Dinner, maybe a movie…"

"I'm sorry," she looks down at her watch, "I can't…"

"Oh," Ty blushes, "my mistake, I misunderstood you. When you said you were obsessed with black men, I didn't realize you meant just from an analytical stand point. But I understand you can't take me seriously, that's fine I…"

"Tyrone…" she says between laughs.

"What?" he asks.

"Shut up," she tells him, "I was going to say, I'm sorry I can't stop staring at that huge stain on your Polo shirt. But I would love to go out with you tonight. On one condition though."

"What's that?" he asks.

"I'm paying." she smiles.

"Blood of Jesus..." Ty smiles back.

(Jacody)

The self-proclaimed new king of southern rap has taken time to reevaluate his life goals and plans. The last thing he wants is to follow in his father's footsteps and join the military. He loves and respects what his father has done, and who his father is as a man, but his dream is not the same as his old man's dream was at his age.

Jay can't help but acknowledge the fact that his father and mother have done very well for themselves because of all of the obvious advantages the military has afforded them over the years. This fact alone is what's making the military still an extremely viable option for the lyrical beast.

Music is, and has always been his passion since he stopped playing basketball his sophomore year in high school. At this point he really doesn't care what part of the music game he ends up excelling at he just wants to be a part of it, and in turn make his parent's truly proud of him.

Five years later since the last time he was home in the O; Jay has toned his style down considerably. No more bright colored temp fades and flamboyant exclusive clothing. He's more a jeans and polo kind of guy now. But don't get it twisted, musically he still knows how to take it back to the streets and get dirty with raw rap verses filled with clever placed analogies and punch lines.

Now that Jay has moved home to Orlando with no job and a limited amount of cash in the bank, he's forced to do some real soul searching. It's rough but he knows somehow some way the Lord is going to provide for him. He always has, and He won't stop now.

Chapter 3
Fantasy Island

Dr. Carlos Sanchez's mansion is unusually quiet tonight, and all of the lights are off throughout the house. It's been days since she's been available to him. Her body tastes amazing to him right now. Her natural juices taste like crushed apples and sweet mango fruit.

To him this moment feels like the very first time all over again. As his long dark dreads accented with blood red tips lay flat on his back, his fingers are fiercely massaging her taught yellow thighs. The guest bathroom floor is cold beneath his strong knees. Now he stretches out to try to lie down flat as he hastily eats her body.

After kicking an empty beer bottle out of his way he finally finds a semi comfortable position. As his tongue caresses her soft wet flesh, his senses begin to leave him. He can't see or hear anything, his entire being is numb. A bright pink glow is somehow engulfing his entire body and soul. The pleasure of being with the woman of his dreams with absolutely no restrictions is almost too much for any man.

He pauses briefly. Looking up into her eyes he says, "Perfection only shows its face to you once in a lifetime." She smiles her perfect smile. After licking his own wet lips slowly, he dives back in, to him nothing exists beyond Whitney, and her pleasure.

(The Next Morning)

It's raining softly outside on the Veranda. Carlos forgot to close the veranda doors before climbing into bed between his two queens last night. None of the maids have been in the master bedroom this morning so the evidence of the night before is still splayed out across the floor and the foot of the gigantic bed.

Carlos moved them both into his biggest beach house just last year. A distant aroma of cigar smoke and *Amberella* wine still linger in the air. As the bed sways back and forth, the smooth sultry sounds of TGT's song "Explode" are kissing Whitney's warm wet back, through the surround sound speakers. Biting her lip, she continues to hold on tight to the top of the headboard with one hand, and desperately grip a large red pillow with her other hand.

The black China doll, Cameron Jiles carefully kisses his hard stomach as he strokes. Then wearing nothing but a bright purple thong, she crawls towards Whit and begins licking the sweet sweat from her neck and face. Sliding beneath Whitney's tense body Cameron reaches around behind her and unfastens her white lace Victoria's Secret bra. Then she begins to kiss and suck Whitney's heavily aroused nipples. Looking around Whit's perfect body, Cam looks up searching for approval in his eyes. Then as Cam bites Whit's left nipple, she simultaneously reaches down to rub her clitoris just the way she likes it. Whitney starts to shake, even more than before.

"Oh my God…" she screams out. Sitting up straight, still beneath Whitney, Cameron kisses her as if she loves her. Then she caresses her as if she's *in love* with her. Whitney opens her eyes to stare into Cam's eyes with unclear intent.

She pushes Cam down to the bed on her back and forces her to scoot up towards the headboard. Spreading her dark chocolate thighs with her hands, Whit buries her face in Cam's wet pinkness. She begins rolling her tongue in and out of her as if she trying to speak another language, she strategically elevates Cameron to several quick orgasmic explosions.

Wiping her wet face off on Cams left thigh, Whit glances back at Carlos who's been positioned behind her for thirty minutes straight, giving her long hard back shots as deep as he can humanly go inside of her. The look of ecstasy in his eyes lets her know he likes what he sees. Carlos loves when his girls play nice with each other. Whit turns back around, arches her back just a little bit more and resumes pleasuring Cameron.

Cam grows bored with Whitney's fatiguing tongue and decides to slide from beneath her and make her way back to Dr. Sanchez. Cameron rises up on her knees and begins kissing him as he continues to give Whitney straight back shots. Cam has one hand gripping the back of his head and her other hand is slapping and caressing Whitney's perfect ass.

Cameron kisses him once more, and then she kneels down to put her face right there in the middle of the action. Cam begins to lick Carlos' strong shaft as it enters and exits Whit's warm wet body. Then Cam pulls him out of her completely and begins sucking and licking all of her juices off of him from his tip to his sack. Then she slowly stuffs him back inside of Whit. As he enters her body
again, Whit and Carlos both moan loudly in unison.

After five or six more powerful strokes, Cameron pulls him out of her once more. This time she strokes all of him in one hand while she eats Whitney's gorgeous body from the back. Cam greedily licks up and swallows all of Whitney's stray passion juices. Then Cam puts three fingers in Carlos' mouth, after he wets them thoroughly for her she slides them inside of Whitney, while staring in Carlos' steel gray eyes. With a perfect twist of her wrist Cam continues to penetrate Whit as she takes all of Carlos in her mouth and throat.

25

Carlos stares down at his beautiful Cameron and smiles at just how in tune she is with all of his sexual desires. He quickly grabs her by her hair and snatches her up to his face and licks all the wetness he caused from around her mouth.

Then he plunges his large tongue inside her mouth. Cam accepts his sweet tongue as she explores his mouth with her own. Carlos notices that Cam is still fiercely fingering Whitney. He can barely hear Whit's moans over the sultry sounds of the *TGT* album still playing loudly though the speakers on repeat.

Carlos reaches down with his left hand and snatches Cam's hand out of Whitney. With her hair still tightly grasped in his right hand he continues to kiss Cam for a few more seconds. Then he forces her to turn around.

With his grip on her hair still perfectly intact Carlos enters Cam hard from the back. He has both of his queens bent over side by side, a vision of supreme loveliness. He stares at both of their asses trying to decide which one of them he should cum on, or in for that matter.

As he strokes deep inside of Cameron, he points towards the table on the side of the bed. Whitney follows his eyes and finger and crawls towards the table to retrieve the long dark red candle and its solid gold holder.

Then she crawls back to Carlos and hands the candle to him. "Bend over." he tells her. Whitney obeys. She crawls right next to Cameron and bends over just as she was positioned before. As she waits for Carlos to make his next move she kisses Cameron on the cheek twice. Cameron turns towards Whitney and starts kissing her lips before Whit can kiss her cheek a third time.

Carlos decides to start with Cameron. With the candle holder held high above her back he begins to tilt it slowly. The beautiful deep red wax begins to drip on and down the sides of Cam's unsuspecting back. Her dark chocolate flesh is very complementary to the bright red tones of the steamy hot candle wax. "Carlos…" she moans. Then she bites Whitney's bottom lip softly.

Carlos holds the candle holder above Whitney's body now as he continues to run in and out of Cameron's wet center. He allows the wax to flow freely on her strong yellow back and neck. The warm wet wax beating down on her back sounds like constant rain tapping on a sturdy windowsill.

Whitney screams, but she doesn't dare move from beneath the hot candle wax because the pain is way too good to her. "That's my girl…" Carlos moans as the music continues to leave them all lost inside of this unreal moment of erotic perfection.

(Charlie Breeze)

Carlos' right hand man on the island is Charlie Breeze. Charlie stands 5'10 tall, he weighs 170 pounds, and his body appears to have been sculpted by the hands of God himself. His long black dreads, adorned with blood red tips hang down to his lower back. From the moment he laid eyes on Whitney he vowed to make her his own one day.

His loyalty to Carlos is definite, but his attraction to Whitney is unforgettable no matter how hard he tries to ignore it. She avoided him for years, because the way he felt for her was so obvious it was dangerous. His eyes tell Whitney anything she wants to know, and everything she fears. If Carlos ever found out how Charlie feels about her, he would surely kill them both.

The days around the mansion have gone from routine to redundant. The girls constantly endure long boring nights and even longer boring days mostly locked inside of Carlos' castle. By the time they wake up each morning Carlos is already gone to run his hospital.

The cooks make both ladies whatever their hearts desire for breakfast, and then they exercise together in the private gym at the back of the mansion. Carlos insists that the girls stay in perfect shape at all times. He says they are an extension of him so they should look just as flawless as he does.

Whitney has grown tired of Carlos' overbearing tyrant attitude. Cam on the other hand is just happy to have so much alone time with Whitney. She believes she could endure all of Carlos' foolishness forever, right here on this island as long as she has Whitney with her. Whitney is hell bent on making a way to escape Carlos and his beautiful Island prison.

(Whit)

Outside the bathroom window Charlie is watching her closely. Whitney is sitting in one of the Jacuzzis, in one of the mansion's many bathrooms. She's finally alone, just thinking to herself. The relationship between Carlos' two queens is a strange one, but it has evolved slowly and steadily over the past five years.

Why is Cameron so attached to me? I don't understand it. The woman single handedly ruined my life almost five years ago now she's my best friend, or my girlfriend…I don't know, whatever the hell she is. When this all started it was nice, and exciting. Doing so many things with both Carlos and Cameron that I fantasized about doing for so long gave me life. Hell, it still does, but I want more than just fantasy. I want some reality too. I want someone…just one someone to call my own. I used to like choosing in the middle of the night if I wanted to cuddle up next to Cameron's soft breasts, gripping her round behind, or if I wanted to back it up on Carlos and feel his perfect stomach on my back as his strong arms held me tight. It was very nice but now I want more… so much more.

Charlie Breeze… now that man is something special. I held out as long as I could but his presence is so undeniably overpowering. That man could charm an angel out of her robe and wings. And I still remember the very first time I saw him. I had heard Carlos speak

28

his name before but never had I actually seen him until that day on the beach. I was minding my own business collecting gorgeous seashells close to the water, and then I heard his deep voice.

"Perfection only shows you its face once in a lifetime." he said. I was startled because I didn't even notice him as he was swimming in the ocean not far from where I was collecting my shells. When I turned in the direction his voice came from I died instantly, and then he gave me life all over again honey. His swagger was impeccable.

Every step he took he seemed to be growing harder, and stronger. His perfectly sculpted six pack abs and chest were glowing in the glorious ambiance of the sunlight, and his beautiful white teeth were shinning forth like real pearls. He licked his lips once and I became wetter than ever before. His long dark dreads were hanging loose, and the blood red tips of them were being perfectly illuminated by the thirsty beams of the sun rays.

"You are even prettier up close aren't you…" he said. I blushed. Not long after I began to stutter out a response Carlos stepped out onto the

mansion balcony completely nude with Cam hugging him from the back and beckoned for me to come back to the house. Carlos must have known then how much of a threat that man was already. I did as I was told, but I dreamed about that man something awful that night, and needless to say my portion of the bed was still soaked when I awoke the next morning.

Later that day I was down on the beach again, this time with Carlos and Cameron. We were all just laying out on soft afghan blankets enjoying the sun when he came striding toward us, shirtless of course. His perfectly twisted dreads were tied up in a spiral on top of his head.

He had in his hands a large stained-glass platter covered with assorted fruits. There were fresh berries, slices of watermelon, grapes, lemons, mangos, pineapples, and even kiwis. We all ate of Charlie's fruit but deep down I knew he was attempting to cater to me.

29

The entire charade was executed just for him to prove to me that he wasn't scared of Carlos, and that there were ways around his deadly island rules. As I watched Charlie bite into a large yellow piece of succulent mango fruit I was at a loss for words.

My throat went dry as my eyes began to water at the corners. His lips and tongue were so skillful. I couldn't help but imagine the sweet mango fruit was my body that his wet, hungry mouth tasted, and was dying to devour… before swallowing me whole in unforgiving satisfaction.

I knew one day soon our time alone would come, and with God as my witness I knew he was going to fall in love with me like no one ever has before. Our chemistry and connection to each other is so powerful you can actually smell the fire between us in the air when we're near each other.

"Whitney…" Cam calls out from down the hallway, breaking Whit's perfect concentration on her delightful daydream.

"Oh, there you are girl," Cam peeps her head inside one of the many guest bathrooms, "I've been looking everywhere for you girl."

"What's wrong Cameron?" Whit asks.

"Nothing, I'm just missin' my girlfriend actually." Cam flaunts her seductive smile.

"That's sweet." Whit replies returning Cam's gorgeous smile. Cam sits down on a padded white marble bench near the door. She takes off her custom blue and purple retro five Jordan shoes, and then her white and purple Jordan socks. Next, she stands up turning her back to the observant Whitney and slowly pulls her extra short white shorts down to her ankles exposing her bright blue boy short panties.

Over the past five years, Cam has really filled out; she's thicker than Whitney now. Staring at Cam's perfect round behind Whitney can't help but lick her voluptuous pink lips. Turning back towards her, Cam slowly pulls her purple tank top off over her head and

30

tosses to the side. Then she shakes her head a few times to reposition her freshly sewn-in hair. Walking towards the large Jacuzzi with model precision, Cam unfastens her matching blue bra, exposing her perky bosom.

After dropping the expensive bra carelessly on the floor, she steps into the warm water close to an anxious Whitney. With the bright purple scrunchie she has on her left wrist Cam pulls her hair up into a comfortable ball on top of her head, as not to get her hair wet while making love to her sexy girlfriend.

Whitney stares up at Cam's grown woman physique in awe. "Cameron, baby you are the *archetype* of a perfect African Goddess." Whit tells her without a shred of doubt in her eyes or voice.

"Aw." Cam blushes as she covers her mouth with both hands, still standing above Whit in the Jacuzzi.

"What you waitin' on..." Whit bites her bottom lip.

"I don't know," Cam blushes even more now, "after five years you still make me nervous bae. I know it's crazy but I can't help it."

Making her way down into the water, Cam lays her body plush on top of Whitney's. Gripping Cam's perfect behind Whit pulls her woman as close to her body as she possibly can. As they kiss each other's passionate lips nothing else on the planet seems to matter.

Caressing and massaging Whit's face and neck, Cam continues to kiss the only woman she has ever loved. Unbeknownst to Whitney, Cam's attraction to her is three-fold. Cam sees Whitney as the supportive mother she never had, the light skin home girl she always wanted back in high school who isn't mean to her, and the best lover by far that she has ever had.

Cam's hands make their way down to Whit's supple breasts. Whitney's breasts are very sensitive and her entire body is tingling outrageously as Cam squeezes them, and then her hard nipples. Trying to take her mind off her sexual explosion that is near, Whit

31

enters Cams body from the back with two strong fingers.

"Cameron baby..." Whit moans. "Yeah bae…" Cam responds softly. "When did you start loving me? And why?" Whit asks. Cam giggles.

"Are you serious?" Cam asks.

"I wanna know." Whit says continuing to kiss the perfect black china doll.

"Um," Cam starts, "to be honest you had me gone from the moment I laid eyes on you. I'm sure I've told you this story a hundred times bae, but whatever. The reason why I fought you so hard in that hospital is because in my mind I could never compete with you. I had spent months believing I was the only woman in Keldrick's life. Then Carlos broke the devastating news to me that I was not the only woman… and then once I saw what you, the other woman looked like, I knew I was going to lose in the end. So, I had to fight and try to show him, how much I loved him. But you… were so gorgeous I really just wanted to talk to you, know you, touch you… and be close to you."

"Wow," Whit can't help but blush herself now, "Kiss me again baby girl."

The two of them enjoy hours of pleasure like this quite often during the day while Dr. Carlos is away.

(Hours later)

Whitney is awakened by the sound of the front door slamming shut. She jumps up and surveys her surroundings to be sure her personal room is in order.

"Wake up Charlie," she nudges the sleepy dread head roughly, "Carlos is home." She tries not to panic as she looks back towards her bedroom door.

Charlie rolls over and kisses her quickly, before jumping from

32

her comfortable bed to her soft carpeted floor. He pulls his jogging pants on first, then his socks, and lastly his shoes. He rarely wears underwear or a shirt at all, he doesn't find them necessary. Charlie enjoys above all else feeling free within mind, body, and spirit.

After slipping his second Nike shoe on he climbs out of her window, and masterfully scales the roof of the second floor towards the ladder that will lead him safely to the ground.

Whitney scrambles around quickly, fixing the edges of her bed sheets, because Carlos likes everything to be just so when he comes home from work or else. Then she rushes into her bathroom grabs a clean towel from the closet and begins to wet it with warm water from her bathroom sink. After lathering the towel generously with her Dove facial soap, she wipes her body and face vigorously, in attempt to clean Charlie's essence off of herself.

After the soap has been scrubbed into her skin from her delicate center up to her forehead, Whit begins to rinse the excess soap out of the warm towel. Once the water from the towel is almost running

clear and free of soap suds as she wrings it out, she begins to wash all of the soap off of her gorgeous body.

After she is satisfied with the smell of herself she hangs her damp towel on a rack to the left of the sink, and then returns to her towel closet to get a bigger towel to dry off with. Then Whit quickly rushes back to her bed to lie down, and at least try to steady her pounding heartbeat.

"Rise and shine sleepy head." Cam barges into Whit's room sporting a new evening gown and colorful glistening jewelry.

"You scared the shit out of me Cameron." Whit says still trying to steady her now erratic heartbeat.

"I'm sorry boo," Cam approaches her bed, "I was going to wake you up earlier, but you had been in here for so long, I didn't want to disturb you. I figured you must have been really tired."

Whitney smirks at her girlfriend knowing exactly what that usually means. "So," Cam continues, "of course I pulled the covers down off of you… and made you cum in your sleep a few times before I went to my room to take a nap of my own."

"Was I loud?" Whit asks smiling coyly now. "It was amazing," Cam replies, "I don't know how in the world you didn't wake yourself up." They both laugh. Whit's just glad Cam didn't see Charlie Breeze hiding in her closet, when she came in and fondled her earlier. Whit wasn't asleep at all.

"Girl you have been around that man for way too long." Whit smiles at Cameron.

"Who Carlos?" she asks.

"Yes bitch," Whit laughs, "You are starting to turn into him. You better stop sneaking in my room unannounced molesting me, and sucking on my body like he does you. I mean don't get me wrong I always know it's you so it turns me on now, but I'm just saying… you might sneak in here one night and get more than you came looking for."

Whit gets out of her bed and walks over to her large window to see if she can spy Charlie Breeze in the distance on the beach. He seems to live in the ocean; Whitney believes that he was born to be one with the island elements. He's so comfortable out there, and he just looks like he belongs on the beach completely naked at all times.

Whit smiles to herself. Just before her mind is swept away into yet another sexy daydream about that man and his long gorgeous locks, Whit turns around to look at Cameron.

"I'm serious Cameron," Whit contends, "you better start being more careful." Cam laughs at herself trying not to blush.

"I can't help it," she admits, "he has changed me, and not just in good ways. And with you baby… every time we have sex alone you're always in control. But when you're sleeping everything goes

34

just the way I want it to go. But… do you really think I'm turning into Carlos though bae…"

"Cam," Whit studies her carefully, "the way you kiss, the way you talk, and even the way you hold your face at times is eerily reminiscent of him. You are the female Dr. Sanchez girl."

"Wow," Cam pauses, "that's crazy I swear I didn't even notice…" Whitney crawls back up into her comfortable bed.

"Oh, and excuse me miss *all dolled up dinner date Barbie*," Whit says playfully, "where exactly is it you think you're going looking like Gabrielle Union's sexy baby sister?" Cam looks down at her perfect gown.

"Carlos called earlier…" she says through an unsure smile.

"And said what," Whit climbs back out of bed once again her eyes wide open now, "Carlos called earlier and said what little girl?"

"You were sleeping bae." Cam steps back.

"So, the Hell what," Whitney yells, "that didn't matter when you were in here licking, biting, and sucking on me now did it?" Cam shakes her head silently.

"Oh, hell nawl," Whit screams, "Don't get all quiet and shy now

bitch!" Whitney pushes Cam's head with one strong finger, knocking her slightly off balance.

"Calm down baby before you make Carlos upset." Cam tries to hug Whit.

"Fuck Carlos," Whit growls staring a hole through her young lover, "Where are you going Cameron Jiles?"

"Just down to the other side of the beach..." Cam claims.

"Dinner on the beach," Whit frowns, "How could you? Huh Cam, how could you do this to me again?"

"I didn't plan it Whit, I promise." Cam tells her.

"How do you do that? How do you stand there and lie through your teeth… to *me* with a straight face?"

"Cameron!" Carlos beckons from downstairs.

"Coming Carlos..." she pleasantly yells back to him.

"We won't be gone long," Cam tells her, "he said he just wants to talk to me alone tonight. Baby it's just for one night." Without another word Cam kisses Whitney softly on the lips then exits her room just as quickly as she came. Whitney is left in her room all alone once again to ponder her strange life and the terrible, costly choices she's made. Whit shakes her head sadly as she climbs back up in her bed once again.

(Whit)

I know she does this on purpose. She has to be doing this shit on purpose because it's happening way too often now. At first Carlos would fly us both to Paris, or Milan, or Italy for endless shopping sprees and romantic getaways. But over the past couple of months I feel myself slowly being cut out of the equation. I don't understand it, I look better than I ever have in my entire life, my sex is great, and I'm fun to be around. Or at least I thought so. Damn it!

If I'm forced to stay here in this beautiful prison, and I know I am because I don't see any way for me to leave the island… Then things are going to have to change quickly. I am way beyond unhappy. I must be Carlos' only queen and Cameron can be my girlfriend and our joint sex slave. I have been passive and overtly submissive to this man for way too long. I am Whitney Michelle Powell… a strong, beautiful, intelligent, sexy ass black woman. I deserve to be treated like a real queen. I will tolerate nothing less. I would rather be dead and gone. This life for me has become excruciatingly unacceptable.

(Down on the beach)

The gorgeous blue waves of the evening tide are crashing upon

36

the golden shores of the island ever so calmly. The multi colored sea shells are being submissively swept back into the water by the dominant waves. The moon rising over the steady waters appears bright orange in the distance, and it's even more breath taking now than Carlos remembers it ever being. He smiles calmly at the moon's amazing splendor.

Cam's gown is a custom-made silver beach night dress made by Carlos' personal tailoring company. The dress almost the same color as Carlos' steel grey eyes is contoured to Cam's firm shape quite flawlessly. She wore matching diamond encrusted sandals this evening but has long kicked them off to the side to allow her toes to enjoy the soft sand. Her exclusive three-piece necklace and matching earrings are the perfect accessories to her stunning ensemble. The platinum charm bracelet on her left wrist was the first piece of jewelry Carlos ever bought her. She picked it out at a luxurious jewelry store in Paris on the very first surprise vacation he ever took her own.

Carlos is wearing silver linen beach pants, and a cool black linen shirt adorned with sterling silver buttons from top to bottom. He has grown his curly hair out considerably, but it still fits his regal face well. He is barefoot as well, having left the house without any shoes at all.

Carlos calmly takes a sip of his glass of *Amberella wine*, studying his younger wife closely.

"What's on your mind Dr. Carlos Sanchez..." she tries to seduce him with her big, bright, bedroom eyes.

"No ma'am Cameron Jiles," he says in that thick sexy accent, "we are here to talk about what you have on *your mind*. Tell me the truth, are you happy my dear?"

Sensing how serious the conversation is, Cam sits up straight before she responds. "What do you mean Carlos?" she asks. "What do I mean," he repeats, "well I mean me, you, Whitney... the grand scheme of it all. Are you genuinely happy here? And don't lie to me Cameron."

"Am I happy…" she repeats, "more than I could ever show or tell you Carlos." she responds with a confident smile and no hesitation. "Truth Cameron," Carlos looks deep in her eyes, "is always found
in a woman's body language, her eyes, and her diction… and almost never her actual words. By paying close attention to those three things any man can find and know any woman's real truth within."

"Enlightening…" Cameron gushes. Truly impressed by the thought of what Carlos has just described to her. "Then I'm sure," she continues, "that you know from observing me that my heart, body, and soul all belong to you."

"This is true and I'm glad to hear that," he looks down at the table, "but I'm saddened that Whitney doesn't share that sentiment. I'm going to have to… take her out soon."

"Take her out," Cam repeats, "What the hell does that mean?"

"Don't be so naïve Cameron," he smiles at her ignorant question, "it's no longer attractive, and you're much older now. So, I want you to act, think, and speak accordingly."

"Answer my question Carlos!" she demands. "I'm going to kill her very soon, and throw her body into the ocean. The fish will feed on her remains until she no longer exists in the physical sense." he tells her.

"In the physical sense…" Cam repeats, "Are you fucking kidding me? You sound like a freaking psycho Carlos." she tells him.

"Maybe I am…" he replies.

"What the hell Carlos," she screams, "you can't just kill her."
"Oh… I forgot you love her." he teases her completely void of emotion.

"You're damn right I love her," Cam admits, "but even if I didn't love her you still can't just go around killing people. It's immoral to kill people just because you don't like them Carlos."

"So, what." he sips more of his tasty wine.

"You cannot be serious Carlos," Cam pleads with him, "come on baby you can't just kill her in cold blood." Cam leans forward to caress his left hand.

"Oh, I can… and I will," he informs her, "You see this island and everything on it belongs to me. That includes the houses, the boats, all the people, and especially you and her."

"What happened to you Carlos?" she asks in genuine fear and concern. "What do you mean darling?" he says taking another sip of *Amberella wine*.

"You've changed Carlos." she insists calmly. "Have I?" he asks. "Yes, you have changed drastically," she tells him, "and I'm asking you why. What happened to you so badly that you became this… this beautiful monster?" He doesn't respond instead he just chuckles lightly to himself.

"Well," he grins, "all is not lost at least you still think I'm attractive. But to answer your pressing question, what happened to me that was so terrible… You happened, Cameron Jiles."

"Me, what do you mean *I* happened?" she asks.

"It's simple really," he looks towards the water, "you destroyed me. See when women meet good men, even if that man was not a good man to the women in his past, you as the current woman in his life can make or break him. And Cameron you broke me. I felt as though you actually shattered my heart, mind, and soul."

"Wait, wait, wait how the hell, did I break you?" she asks smiling nervously. "I wasn't just talking, while I was prancing around preaching to you in that hospital room years ago Cameron. I really know all of what I told you to be true. And I also know that since in your mind, I was never anything more than a fantasy…*I never really mattered to you*."

"That is not true Carlos," she says with conviction, "And you don't believe that." "Actually… I do my love," he replies, "and I gave you chance after chance to love me and me alone… but you never quite did. Did you Cameron?" he asks. Tears are now streaming down Cam's face as she stares into his demon-like eyes.

Chapter 4
Orange County
(K.C.)

*D*uring my breaks from football my mother Linda, my children, and I all reside at our comfortable home in Orlando. Miami is great don't get me wrong we all love Dade County, but Orlando will always be our home.

Jazemene is still doing exceptionally well in school and she's becoming quite the young basketball player. Going back and forth from city to city is never a problem because I have it set up so Jaze can attend class at her school in Orlando, and her school in Miami whenever we're in either city.

My baby girl is the starting point guard for the Florida Fire, youth traveling basketball team. They play every other Saturday in a different city in Florida. They've been undefeated since Jaze joined their team six months ago.

Basketball is good for Jaze it takes her mind off her Mom, me, and her baby brother for a brief while. One little girl should never have to endure as much stress as she is taking on with no complaints. She is truly a remarkable child.

My son K.J. still misses his mommy. The fact that he never really got a chance to know her doesn't seem to matter, he still wants her here. He'll start kindergarten this fall and he will eventually forget all about Whitney. Well I hope he forgets about her, because if not that pain will begin to shape his young life in a very negative way.

Mama Cole has been in her own little world for a while now. In Orlando, she's at home so she's at the house mostly, and she's all about her grand babies but in the 305 (Miami), we rarely ever see her at all.

(Universal Studios)

It's a bright sunny day in Orlando in March. The small breeze is cool and comforting. The parking lot at Universal Studios is packed to capacity today. Keldrick decided to come to the Universal Orlando Resort to watch the new movie "Phoenix Rain" written by De'Lure. He's the same writer from the "Onyx Cielo" series that Cam introduced to K.C. over six years ago. K.C has literally been a fan ever since. The new movie by De'Lure is already an enormous fan favorite worldwide. *"Phoenix Rain"* is the refreshing tale of a young white English Dr. Mr. Colin Byrd, his beautiful West African wife Lalani Byrd, and their undeniably gifted and gorgeous daughter Coliana Byrd.
Coliana's birth was threatened by a disease her mother contracted by drinking contaminated water.

While still inside her mother's womb, Coliana was miraculously cured when her father was able to directly inject the pure blood of black phoenix birds into her still developing body. As a result, her existence is elevated supremely. After her father is murdered in the streets of London in cold blood, Coliana's mother moves her away to America where she will soon become the crime fighting power bomb *"Phoenix Rain"*.

As Kel approaches the ticket booth he notices a familiar face working in the booth. He rubs his eyes roughly several times to try and correct his false vision. He knows he can't possibly see what he thinks he sees. He's next in line to buy his ticket and he can hear his heart pounding redundantly in his ears.

"May I help whose next?" Her voice sounds a little different now. But Kel is close enough now to see her face, and it's unmistakable. He tries to hide his face by looking down as he approaches her window.

"Yes, sir what can I get for you?" she asks. He looks into her comforting eyes for the first time in five years. He tries to speak but every word he has ever known has completely escaped his mind.

Strangely as she looks back at him, she doesn't appear to recognize him at all. He's bigger now of course, from all the NFL training he's been through. His skin is a little darker, and he has facial hair now, but all in all he still looks the same.

"Sir… what can I get for you?" she asks again.

"Oh, I'm sorry," he blushes, "let me get two tickets for *"Phoenix Rain"* please."

"Two," she says looking behind him playfully, "you must be meeting somebody here sir?"

"No," he smiles genuinely, "I was hoping you would quit your job and come join me…" K.C. pulls a large roll of cash out of his pocket. Her eyes bulge briefly and then she pretends to regain her composure.

"Um," she puts a hand on her hip, "Sir, I don't know what you think this is but we sell tickets at this booth *not ass*."

"Baby, why are you even here," he asks, "We're good now. You never have to ever work again."

"Sir I don't have a clue who you are or what you're talking about, but I have a line behind you and I'm not trying to lose this job… I just started working here last week."

"Love at first sight…" he smiles affectionately.

"Oh really…" she says noticeably unimpressed by the sentiment.

"Three times in just one lifetime… there's gotta be something to it." K.C. contends.

"Look sir," she reaches for the phone in the booth, "if you don't leave I'm going to call security…"

"And why do you keep calling me sir," he frowns. "It's me baby, Keldrick, K.C., your first… *everything*." he whispers.

"Oh my God," she puts the phone back down, "*it is you*."

"Yeah baby it's me," K.C. jumps up and down in obvious excitement, "you recognize me now?"

43

"Yeah, you're the new star football player for the Miami Dolphins, Keldrick "Kool Hands" Cole." she says.

K.C. stops jumping and drops his head. "No baby," he looks down, "Well yes I am "**Kool Hands**" Cole but it's me Cameron, your *ex*-fiancé. I miss you baby."

Her eyes begin to grow again. "Ooooh you're making a mistake," she claims, "I'm sorry…"

"You know what Cam," he looks down at his feet again, "I deserve this. Every single bit of it. Here's a hundred dollars just give me one ticket to "**Phoenix Rain**"."

"Here's your change." she attempts to hand him eighty-five dollars.

"Just keep it." he takes his ticket and heads towards the movie entrance without another word. She watches him curiously until he disappears inside the theater.

(Mama Cole in Miami)

Lord why should any mother ever feel the way I do, and the way I have in my past. I felt so alone in my own home for years. I had a man, but I'm sure he wasn't sent to me by you, Father God. Paul was never good for me, or my children, but at least from time to time he was there. Every woman wants at least a piece of a man in their house, and I'm no different Lord.

God, I was so lost when it came to my younger son. Lance was so different from his older brother and my brothers when I grew up with them. He always preferred to stay in the house and write, or draw instead of going outside to get dirty with the other boys and girls his age. He was always into art. And when he wasn't being artsy he was following me around trying to mimic my every move like a little red sissy. Damn it that boy was a fag at two years old Lord. It was not my fault or anything I did. But I couldn't help but feel like it was something I said, did… or maybe something I ate while I was

44

carrying him in my stomach that made him the way he was.

I never wanted to take the boy out anywhere in public with me. I was embarrassed. Okay Lord? I admit it. I was embarrassed to be seen with my young gay son Lance. Was I right? Hell no, I was wrong as could be. I realize that now, but it's way too late to fix it, or correct the damage that's already been done to him.

That boy is gonna die crazy and gay. He can fight it as long as he wants to God, but I know the truth that boy gone die crazy and gay just like his crazy gay daddy. The apple doesn't ever fall too far from the tree. I always knew Lance was gonna be a strange man when he got older, because he was such a strange kid. I said awful things to him as a child Lord, so many terrible things that I had no business saying to any
human being let alone my own child.

I take it all back right now Lord if you'll let me. I need to re... what is that thing when you apologize for your sins against other people? Repent... that's it I need to repent Lord for the way I tortured my son as a young boy.

My other son Keldrick... my son has finally made it Lord. I am so proud of him. I am happy for him but I can't help but feel like he owes me. I was the one who first put a football in his hands and played catch with him all those years ago. He is rich and I feel like Mama Cole should be just as rich as he is if not richer. Am I wrong, Lord? I want some of that spotlight too. Keldrick is an amazing ball player but I gave him life, what about Mama Cole...

I hope one day Keldrick understands why I'm doing the things I'm doing right now without his knowledge. Father God I repent to you right now for all the evil I have done, and will do before I leave this earth. And honestly... if I was Lance I would kill me dead. Because, I deserve to be dead, there's no doubt about that. Lord, please don't let my son out of prison... ever, because if you do I won't live long. Amen.

(Downtown Orlando)

The streets of downtown Orlando are surprisingly calm tonight. An almost eerie quiet has fallen over North Magnolia Avenue. Death is in the air. As he steps out of his taxi cab he surveys his surroundings briefly, not actually caring if anyone catches him in the act or not. This job is long overdue, and he's just man enough to do it.

How long can you truly hate someone before that hate turns deadly? Not long, but most of us are not blessed with a non-existent conscious, that allows us to be powerful beyond measure. This mindset results in the ability to focus with remarkable precision. The few humans who have lived with this rare ability have all been great. All geniuses in their own right, and whether they were a positive or a negative influence on our world doesn't matter it will never change the fact of their supreme intellects.

There's Hitler, Einstein, Steve Jobs, and Bin Laden to name a few. He's leaning more towards Hitler and Bin Laden, but it's not his fault, they made him this way. Tonight, he's dressed in all black from head to toe, walking calmly along the crowded street.

Walking a few yards in front of him is a tall thin Italian man. He's on the phone threatening a tenant that owes him two months' rent.

Inside *the killer's* long trench coat is a high-powered handgun. The silencer is already attached. 730 North Magnolia Avenue, the Courtyard by Marriott Hotel is the building the tall man walks in. Parked illegally across the street from the hotel is an empty light blue Camry. The owner of the Camry is already inside the hotel sitting at the end of the bar.

The man in the trench coat follows the tall man through the front door of the hotel. The tall man ends his disrespectful phone call and then steps up to the front desk of the hotel.

"I have a reservation for Ligetti." the tall man says. "Yes sir," the lady at the front desk replies, "room 435 is yours Mr. Ligetti."

"Cool," he looks down at his watch, "Hey is the hotel's bar still accessible this late at night?"

"Yes sir." she replies with a refreshing smile.

She hands him his room key. "Thank you," Mr. Ligetti says looking down at her from his six-foot seven view, "I'll just go put my things in my room and then come back down for a drink."
"Take your time Mr. Ligetti." the nice lady responds.

"You should join me," he continues, "I wouldn't mind spending a few bucks on a nice black piece of ass like you baby." Too arrogant to wait for her response he heads towards the elevator that will take him to his room.

The man in the trench coat watches Mr. Ligetti walk away with pure poison in his eyes. "May I help you sir?" the lady at the desk asks.

"Oh no ma'am I'm with that asshole." he points towards the tall thin man getting in the elevator.

"Oh," she smiles politely, "I'll stop him. Does he know you're here?"

"No ma'am that won't be necessary," the man tells her, "we're old friends and I have a score to settle with him."

"I didn't realize you two were together," she grins, "I can upgrade your room because the one you guys have only has one bed... *Oh* unless you *two are*..." She hesitates, waiting for confirmation.

His heart begins to race, and his body feels extremely tense now. He pulls the gun out of his pocket quickly, holding it down by his side where she can't see it.

"Unless we *are what*..." he hopes she says something... anything to give him a reason to do it.

"You know," she blushes, "together, *like partners*."

He raises his gun instantly and shoots her twice, once in the head and once in the chest. Looking around him, he makes sure no one saw what he just did. He quickly makes his way behind the desk.

47

Crouching down over her he realizes how tiny the woman is. Behind the desk he sees a large thick laundry bag in a big blue cart with wheels on it. He has no time to clean up all the blood on the floor, so he just hastily stuffs her limp petite body in the large bag and then rolls her out of the front door in the large blue laundry cart.

After disposing her body, he makes his way back into the hotel lobby as if nothing has happened. Sitting at the bar is the tall thin Italian man. The man in the trench coat approaches him from behind. He's close enough now to smell his cheap cologne. As soon as the bartender turns his back, the man in the trench coat reaches the gun around in front of the man sitting at the bar, and pokes him in the stomach with it, to make sure he can feel it. Then he leans down slightly and whispers in the man's ear, "When Love calls… mother fucker you answer."

He shoots him twice. The Italian man never saw it coming. Love closes the man's eyes for him and then leaves him with his head lying on the bar like he's sleeping peacefully.

"You're next Mommy dearest…" Love mumbles as he walks out of the front door of the hotel, with his gun back safely in his coat pocket. He feels much better now that Marco Ligetti, his old scum bag landlord is dead. Ligetti is the reason Love had to kidnap his niece Jaze years ago, and hold her for ransom because he couldn't afford the new rental rate mandated by Ligetti's rental company. As Love leaves the hotel, the owner of the light blue Camry isn't far behind him.

(Universal Studios)

The movie "Phoenix Rain" was damn good, but because Cameron was on K.C.'s mind the entire time, he wasn't able to really enjoy it. As he exits the theater he throws his popcorn container in the overflowing trash can right outside the theater door. Still agonizing painfully over Cam pretending not to recognize him K.C. heads towards the building's exit trying not to make eye contact with anyone. "Leaving without me?" a woman says from behind him. He turns around hesitantly, and there she is sitting down with her jacket on, clutching her large replica MK purse, and ready to leave with him. "Cam..." he smiles.

"I guess so." she replies. Walking towards him she studies his face hard. "So, Cam was really... I mean I was really engaged to you?" she asks.

"Well you turned me down," he looks out of his window, "but are you okay baby? Do you really not remember my proposal?"

"I don't," she takes his hand in hers, "but I'm sure you don't mind reminding me on our way home." Keldrick smiles at the thought.

"So, you're going to ride all the way to Miami with me... right now?" he asks. "Of course..." she replies. Then Keldrick happily leads the pretty black china doll to his expensive new sports car in the parking lot.

Chapter 5
Stranded

"*Lord, I know I don't pray often, and I damn sure haven't prayed in a long time. But I need you now God, more than ever. I don't know if you even listen to the prayers and cries of sinners… my mama always told me a sinner's prayer's never makes it any higher than the ceiling. But if we're all sinners then do anybody's prayers actually matter?*

I really don't understand, but I'm not going to question you. I'm not stupid. I know my lovers and I are living in sin. I also know death is around the corner. Carlos knows I'm not happy here, he can sense it. I truly believe before he lets me leave he would sooner kill me and hide my body.

I can't let the devil win. Through Jesus, I have to survive all of this for more than just me. I realize I've been gone a long time but my children still need me, without Cam there K.C. needs me, hell I need me. I have to leave Lord… I want out now."

"Then leave." Carlos says startling her from behind. "But first," he says approaching her with no detectable emotion on his face, "pay me back every penny I've ever spent taking care of you for the past five years."

"What?" she inquires. "You've been here for five years now," he

50

starts with one hand hidden strategically behind his back, "never lifting a finger to help do anything in any of my houses. What do you do Whitney? You don't cook, you never clean your sex is subpar…"

Whit stands up facing him with a defiant hand hard on her hip. "Seriously Carlos," she says, "Cam and I never lifted a finger because you told us not too. We would have done anything you asked us too Car…"

"Please call me Dr. Sanchez," he interjects, "and *don't* involve Cameron, she has nothing to do with this."

"Oh," she smiles at the floor, "I forgot she's your favorite, right?" Whit laughs.

"I don't blame you at all Carlos," she continues, "If I was a wealthy, aging man like yourself I would choose the young dumb bitch as well, as opposed to the slightly older, smarter, experienced woman. Less problems for you I understand completely."

"Less problems," he repeats, "for whom?"

"You sir," she smiles teasingly; "You always knew even five years ago at some point I wasn't gonna continue to go for the *Okie doke*." "The okie doke," he repeats, "I'm sorry I'm not familiar with the phrase." Whit laughs again. "You knew one day I would get tired of this superficial lifestyle you created for me." she tells him. He steps closer to her, his hand still hidden behind his back.

"I created more than just your lifestyle," he explains, "I created you. Before I brought you here you were the walking dead."

Whit laughs. "Don't make that mistake again." Carlos frowns harshly.

"And what mistake is that Carlos?" she asks. "Your laughter upsets me." he replies.

"*I don't give a damn what upsets you negro!*" she screams.

"I'm Puerto Rican, never have I ever been a Negro." he tells her. "Again," she screams, "*I don't give a damn*! See you were so perfect

51

before that bitch Cam ruined you. You are damaged goods Dr. Carlos Sanchez. And you really believe that you gave me life bringing me here…" she smiles. "Only one man ever gave me life," she continues, "and that was Love. But because I was too blind to see what he and I had the potential to become, I ruined him just like Cameron ruined you."

"Is that so?" he asks. "Men and women don't start off psychologically scarred for life," she says, "I don't have to tell you this Carlos you already know."

"So, you're saying what exactly?" he asks.

Whitney smiles again. "You *are* not good for me, and *this*… *this* situation is not good for me."

Carlos hits her hard across the face with his fist. With a long knife clutched tightly in the hand that was behind his back he slashes her hard on her left shin. Whitney screams out loudly. She quickly attempts to run away from him. He follows closely behind her.

"Waaaaaait Carlos…Wait! Please don't. Aaaaahh…" she screams out as he tries to cut her again. The door opens.

"Dr. Sanchez," one of the maids opens the door, "I heard screaming…"

His deadly glare silences her immediately. She closes the door and runs back downstairs. With only a few seconds to capitalize on, Whit grabs a nearby lamp and breaks it on the back of his head.

The good doctor falls to the floor seemingly lifeless. Whit quickly runs to the door and opens it. Looking back at his limp body, she easily changes her mind. Walking back to him, she stares down at him hating him with her very soul. She kicks him hard in the face.

"Damn it Carlos!" she exclaims. Again, she kicks him hard in the face, this time causing blood to begin leaking from his bottom lip. Whit kicks him in the head and in his face several more times before exiting the room.

With nothing but a bottle of water, a couple of bananas, and Carlos' knife, Whit flees the mansion without a clue how she's going to find her way back home to Florida.

(Downtown Orlando)

"Keldrick only has maybe three or four good years left in him, and then he's done." a short balding white man says.

"We both know that Jerry," his client agrees, "we're not here to discuss whether or not "Kool Hands" can last longer than three more years. I'm asking you how much are we talking?"

"We've made over two hundred million dollars together over the past four years," the short man recollects, "you know K.C. better than anybody else on the planet, that's obvious. So, I trust you and I'll go as far as I can, because I know the well is going to run dry soon on Mr. Cole."

"Damn it Jerry how much?" the client asks. "$450,000..." Jerry says with finality. "Fine," the client replies, "and "Kool Hands" will never know what hit him." "You are a despicable person," Jerry tells his client, "but, so am I. And that's why we work so well together."

(In a cave on the beach)
(Whit)

How can such a beautiful place become so frightening and cold? It's getting dark now, and no one has come looking for me yet, not even Cam. I can't go back to that house. Damn it! I might have killed Carlos, and if I didn't he's gonna kill me for sure if I return. I know I'm going to die in this cave all alone. But so be it...I know I deserve it. I left my kids and my fiancé, my high school sweetheart without even saying goodbye. I deserve to die here alone. If I had the courage, I would probably just kill myself now...

53

Damn it. Am I cramping? Tell me I am not cramping… not now. This can't be happening. I'm stuck in this tiny cave and my cycle is coming on. It's never heavy but damn it, I don't have any meds, or tampons, I don't even have any soap to clean myself with. I deserve it I know I deserve it all.

Whit drops to her knees in the cold sand. *"God, I don't blame you for turning your back on me again… but I swear on everything I am or will ever be that if you show me your face just one more time I will never leave your side ever again. Amen."*

(Back at the mansion on the Island)

Cam is sleeping peacefully in her California king bed. Carlos is standing at her door watching her as she sleeps. He does this often. He doesn't really know why. The only time he ever feels something close to true peace is when he's watching her sleep. He knows his sentiments for her run far deeper than mere obsession.

What a beautiful idea that one person can love another to the point of desperate dependency, although the feeling is pure insanity. As she moves in her sleep his body begins to tingle. He approaches her bed careful not to make a sound. At the foot of her bed he begins to pull the covers down off of her slowly. "Keldrick… baby is that you?" Cam moans in her sleep.

Carlos punches the foot of her bed with both fists startling Cam out of her sleep. "Carlos," Cam says wiping her eyes, "What's wrong babe?" she asks him.

He looks away from her. "Carlos, what did I do now?" she asks.

"It's always something, isn't it?" he walks towards her bedroom window.

"I can't read your mind Carlos." Cam climbs out of her warm comfortable bed. The cold tile floor is unpleasant to the touch of her feet, but pleasing her man is far more important to her than her own comfort. This would be a wonderful notion if he deserved such treatment.

Walking up behind him she throws her loyal arms around his waist. With his hands planted firmly on the windowsill, he doesn't react to her obvious display of affection. Carlos holds his head down.

"Damn it." he whispers. "What is it baby?" she asks.

"Why couldn't you just…" he starts. Cam turns him around towards her. Searching his eyes desperately Cam softly caresses his face.

"Why couldn't I just what…" she asks.

"Why couldn't you… be this?" he asks. "Be what Carlos," Cam furrows her brow tightly, "I don't understand."

"You never will my love," he gently removes her hands from his face, "I didn't understand when we were in Orlando why you couldn't be what you are now… Or at least what you seem to be."

"What is it that I seem to be baby?" she crosses her arms firmly in front of her. "*Perfect*," he whispers, "you appear to be so in love with me… *now*."

"I am," she swears, "Why do you keep saying seem? My love is real."

"Is it Cameron?" Carlos looks through her. "Yes…" she replies.

"You just called me Keldrick…" Carlos screams as he pushes her down to the cold hard floor.

"No, I didn't," she cries looking up at him, "When the hell did I ever call you his name?" "In your sleep Cameron," he kneels down over her, "you were dreaming about him. Keldrick Cole lives now and forever… deep inside the recesses of your silly heart and mind."

"Are you serious," she asks, "baby I'm so sorry."

"Don't be," he says standing up, "It's just who you are… and who *he* is to you."

Carlos heads towards the door. Before he walks out he turns around to look at her with a sick smile on his face. "I guess that's what gives me so much pleasure knowing you will ***never*** see him again." Carlos slams her door behind him and locks it from the outside.

(In the cave)

"Whitney." he whispers in the darkness.

She thinks she's dreaming. "Whitney." he says again.

"***Charlie***… Charlie is that you?" she moans.

"Perfection only shows you its face once in a lifetime." he says.

"How did you find me?" she asks.

"You're never alone." he tells her. "You were watching me?" Whit asks.

"You sound disappointed girl," Charlie steps closer to her, "you should be delighted that I'm always aware of you."

"And why is that?" she asks.

"Because," he frowns, "What is your next move Whitney? You ran away from Carlos' house, you know nothing about the island, and you have no means of transportation if you were planning on escaping."

She puts her head down. "It's okay," he promises, "you got me bae."

She looks up at him fighting her tears. "You're going to get me out of here?" she asks.

"I thought you'd never ask." he smiles.

"Umm…" she looks down at her feet.

"Umm what…" he wrinkles his forehead tightly. "I can't…"she mumbles.

"You can't what Whitney," he says, "You can't stay on this island that's for damn sure. I just left the mansion, Carlos plans on making this into some kind of sick game with the local islanders. He's going to place a price on your head and have them hunt you down like wild game. You have exactly forty-eight hours to get the hell off this island orelse."

56

"Oh my God, are you serious Charlie?" she asks.

"Does it look like I'm playing?" he stares back at her with sincere eyes. "Damn it... Well you have to get me out of here then Charlie." she cries. "But," she continues, "there is no... I mean I can't, well we can't..."

"What are you stuttering for," he asks, "we are both adults say what's on your mind Whitney Powell."

"I don't want you to help me..." she starts.

"You don't have a choice." he interjects.

"No, you didn't let me finish Charlie," she folds her arms tightly, "I don't want you to help, with the hope that me and you will end up together once I'm back safely in the states. My children and my fiancé need me."

"I'm sorry." he looks away from her.

"Sorry, what do you mean you're sorry," she whines, "So if I can't be with you, you're not going to help me get off the island?"

Charlie looks deeply in her eyes. "Whitney..." he says.

"Yes Charlie?" she replies. "I see straight through to your inner soul," he claims, "I know you have broken a lot of hearts, but never a heart like mine."

"What does that mean?" she positions a hand on each hip.

"Let me finish," Charlie says, "I know you've broken plenty hearts in your lifetime, and I know why. You look like wifey material but you're only a temporary girlfriend. You never matured passed the point of just being someone's momentary girlfriend."

"What?" She snaps her neck defiantly.

"Shut up Whitney," he demands, "I've watched you closely for years now and I can read you perfectly. It's easy for you to go from man to man, and place no value on a monogamous relationship because mentally you're not capable of being a good wife to me or anyone else for that matter."

"Charlie Breeze you don't know me, or a damn thing about me." she says as her entire face turns red with rage.

"Oh really," he smiles, "let's see; you were engaged to Keldrick

"Kool Hands" Cole, and you have two children with him. A little girl named Jazemene, and a little boy Keldrick Jr. You were almost killed years ago by your ex-lover, who happens to be your ex-fiancé's psychotic little brother Lance, because he wanted to get back at his brother for tormenting him as a child."

"Damn!" she says. "I know everything about you. Dr. Sanchez and I are closer than you think. Rescuing the woman, I love from this island, risking my job and my own life… just to get you back to another man, and your kids you have with him is way too much to ask of me." "Okay." she looks out towards the ocean.

"But… I do love you," he says, "I love you enough to allow your happiness to take precedence over mine."

(K.C.'s Mansion)

Hours later Kel and his girlfriend arrive in Miami. As they ride down the street to his home their hands are still locked together the exact way they were when they left the movies in Orlando hours ago.

"Home sweet home…" Keldrick smiles proudly. "This is your house?" she asks. "Yeah, do you like it Cam?" he asks.

"It's just like I dreamed it would be," she whispers with wide eyes, "just me and my gorgeous husband in our huge gorgeous mansion." "So, you're ready to be my wife now," Keldrick laughs, "and you mean just you, your gorgeous husband, and his two adorable kids in our huge gorgeous mansion."

"*Kids*…" she looks at him with her left brows raised slightly.

"Yes," K.C. says, "after you left Whit gave birth to my son Keldrick junior."

"Your son," she says, "And the other one?"

"Oh, your little princess is ten years old now." K.C. reports proudly.

"My princess…" her brows wrinkle again.

"Yeah Jazemene is ten now," he tells her, "It seems like just yesterday you were babysitting her for me while I was working. Do you remember?"

She hesitates. "Yeah... I um, yes of course I remember." K.C. parks the car, and then walks around to the passenger door to let her out.

"Aww you didn't have to do that." she blushes. "Get used to it," he says gazing at her intently, "you are *everything* to me."

She smiles bashfully. "This is important to you huh..." she asks.

"I will never lose you again," K.C. vows, "I was a very stupid man, who allowed insignificant people and situations to cloud my judgment. Trust and believe me when I tell you, you are my first and only priority."

"That sounds good," she grins, "what about your kids?"

"My what, oh yes, you and my kids are my only priorities. Are you ready?" K.C. holds out his arm to lead the way to the front door.

(PTA MEETING)

Parent Teacher Association meetings at Key Point Academy are always fun due to the fact that most of the kids, and parents all get along with each other very well. The atmosphere is almost like a family reunion. Everybody wears their green Key Point Academy PTA shirts, the school serves tasty refreshments, and spirited conversations always last hours after the meeting is already officially over.

Jazemene is especially excited tonight because usually her Mama Cole brings her to the PTA meetings, but tonight her daddy had time to bring her himself for once. All the other parents and students are excited as well to be up close and personal with Mr. *"Kool Hands" Cole.* Jaze made sure to show K.C. every art, and science project she did this school year. She even took him to show him the cafeteria and where she sits for lunch every day.

"It's getting late baby girl," Kel tells Jaze, "and you know Cam is back at the house we have to get back soon." "Not yet daddy," she pleads with her mother's eyes, "we can't be the first family to leave." Kel hesitates to respond.

"Ten more minutes then we're out of here little girl." he says with a warm smile.

"Yes!" Jaze exclaims. "Come on dad," she grabs his arm to lead him down the hall, "I wanna show you the picture Josiah drew for me the other day."

As they walk Keldrick finds himself lost in an indescribable daydream. The only thing in the vision that is clear is Cameron, everything else around her is too wondrous to even attempt to express. It's clear to see he's in love all over again, and much deeper this time than ever before.

Kel, still being led down the hall by his anxious daughter's tiny yellow hand, pulls his phone out to briefly check all of his social networking pages. He posted new pictures of him and his girlfriend earlier, so naturally he wants to see how his followers and friends are reacting to the breaking news of them reuniting after six long years. The caption beneath the last picture Kel posted of them kissing on Instagram reads, *"InstaLove… Love at first sight 3 times in a lifetime is a blessing. But being in this woman's world once again is the ultimate gift God could have ever given me…"*

The picture has over 450,000 likes after being posted just one hour. There are also plenty of happy, encouraging comments below the pictures from his various fans and friends wishing him and Cameron well in their future together. Most of the comments though are strictly about how beautiful Keldrick's new girlfriend is. At the very end, of one of the very long hallways Kel and Jaze find a collage of about fifty pictures obviously drawn by the students of Key Point Academy. Jaze can't stop smiling at one picture in particular.

She looks up at her tall father. "Well Daddy…" she says in adamant anticipation.

"What babe…" he looks down at her. After reading her eyes and face he looks back at the pictures.

"Oh," he says, "they are all wonderful and very artistic. Which one did you draw princess?"

"Daddy," she pouts, "I didn't draw one. You weren't listening to me at all, were you?" Jazemene folds her angry arms tightly turning her back to her father.

K.C. takes another look at the fifty very different pictures. He studies each one closely; he knows there has to be at least one that stands out in respect to his disappointed baby girl. After a moment, he spies one drawing towards the middle that definitely catches his eye.

The picture is of a little girl. Her skin color has been represented with yellow colored pencil, she has long curly hair, and she's wearing a jersey that says *Florida Fire*. She's also holding an orange circle. The signature in the bottom right hand corner of the picture reads *Josiah B.* The orange circle is obviously a basketball, and the little curly headed yellow girl is Jazemene. K.C. smiles down at his sulking daughter with her back still turned to him.

"Wow." K.C. breaks the uncomfortable silence. Jaze turns around slightly with her arms still folded tightly.

"Wow what?" she looks up at her father.

"Well this picture that Josiah drew," he smiles down at her, "the girl is so pretty… he must really like her. Do you know her Jaze?"

Jaze's eyes immediately light up, as her once angry arms melt to her sides.

"Daddy… you really think Josiah likes her?" she whispers.

"It's obvious princess." he tells her.

"How do you know Daddy?" she asks stepping back by his side.

61

"Well just look at how much detail and time he put into the picture itself." K.C. says. "Why, do you know her?" he asks playfully.

"It's me daddy." Jaze whispers in adorable confidence to her dad.

"Really," K.C. replies, "I never would have guessed it princess. It's a very nice picture though." Jaze smiles up at her new favorite picture in the whole world lost in a curious daze.

"It's about *that time* baby..." Kel tells her looking down at her with his head slightly tilted as he taps lightly on his rare Armani watch.

"Okay," Jaze pouts, "we can go now..."

"Keldrick," Cidra calls out from down the hallway, as they head towards the exit, "May I speak with you before you leave?"

"Sure Cid," he yells back, "looks like you have a couple more minutes, little girl…"

"Yes," Jaze says, "that's why I love Ms. Bell. You know daddy… sometimes I wish Ms. Bell was my mommy instead of Whitney."

K.C. hesitates as his hands begin to sweat. "Um," he starts, "baby go find Josiah and you two hang out while I speak to Ms. Bell for a second."

"Okay daddy." Jaze skips happily down the hall in search of her adorable buddy.

As Keldrick makes his way down the hallway he remembers just how attractive Cidra Denise Bell is. She stands about 5'7; she has a slim firm shape, strawberry blond hair, and bright green eyes.

"Yes ma'am Ms. Bell, what's going on my friend?"

"Don't you *Ms. Bell* me K.C.," she smiles and hits him gently, "it hasn't been that long Mr. Superstar, and I am still *Cid* to you."

"Yes ma'am Ms. Cid." he says with a mischievous grin on his dark chocolate face.

"How have you been K.C.?" she asks.

"Oh, I can't complain," he says, "some days are better than others." "I know," she agrees, "my number hasn't changed. You know

62

you can call me if you ever need to talk… or whatever else you might need." Cidra blushes instantly. K.C. smiles at her.

"Are you blushing Cid…" he teases.

"Wow," she nervously strokes her hair, "I'm sorry I can't believe I just said that."

"It's okay Cid," K.C. assures her, "It's no big deal. I know what you meant."

"No Keldrick," she looks deeply in his eyes, "I don't think you do." "What are you talking about then Cid?" he flashes an uneasy grin.

"Come on K.C.," she crosses her arms gently, "don't be as blind as my ten-year old son is when it comes to your beautiful ten-year old daughter. I've always wanted to be the woman in your life Keldrick." "Cid…" he starts. She cuts him off quickly.

"Did you think it was an accident when my boys and I just happened to pick up and move two hundred miles away to Miami," she interjects, "just a few months after you and Whit did?" she asks.

"I didn't know Cid," he claims with his brows furrowed, "but I was engaged when I moved here… And you were married in Orlando… how come you never told me this before?"

"I don't know," her pretty face reddens again, "I just figured you didn't like *white women*."

"What," Kel says, "I've never discriminated… in fact I love white women." "Really…" she replies. "Yeah, just never knew you were interested." K.C. says.

Cidra looks down towards the end of each hallway, and finds it completely deserted. Then she grabs K.C. gently by his penis and pulls him towards her. Up on the tips of her toes she kisses him for the first time outside of her constant fantasies and dreams about him. She can't seem to control her mental orgasms as she searches his hungry mouth with her skillful tongue.

She can feel his bulge growing in the palm of her hand as she strokes it. With her free hand, she reaches behind herself to open the door to her classroom. Then K.C. picks her up in his arms as she wraps her legs around him, and he carriers her inside closing and locking the door behind him.

They continue to devour each other's faces, while lustfully groping each other, as Kel makes his way to her desk. Cidra has a firm grip around his strong neck as she begins to grind up and down on him. With his free hand Kel knocks everything off her desk including her brand-new cell phone. But she doesn't care, she living in this moment. Her dream and ultimate fantasy for the past four years has become her reality in seconds, even if only for one night. Cidra Bell has decided to drown herself completely in this tasty instant gratification.

Once the desk is completely cleared Kel sits Cidra down in the middle of it. As he stands back to take off his shirt, she quickly kicks her sandals off, and unfastens her tight Wal-Mart khaki Capri pants. After removing them she quickly throws her pants on the floor a midst the other miscellaneous items that Kel knocked from her desktop. With her legs spread wide towards him, Kel approaches her as he desperately searches his pockets for a condom.

Her knees are tingling, and her body is quietly aching for him. He starts back kissing her to stall for time to locate his protection. He knows he only has maybe five minutes before their children are going to come looking for them, so he makes a quick decision. He's known Cidra for over five years and she was only with one man for that entire time as far as he knows.

No time to take her panties off, Kel slides them to the side and enters her as deeply as he can. She's even tighter than he thought she would be, and twice as wet. One stroke, two strokes, three strokes, four strokes... Cidra's loud moans and screams are uncontrollable now.

Keldrick picks her up in his strong arms, and walks her away from the desk kissing her softly. He slowly lets her down on her feet still kissing her. Cidra turns around bending over one of her student's empty desks, smiling back at him. Keldrick steps close to her and gladly slides inside her from the back. Cidra picks up her

64

left leg and then places her left foot comfortably on top of the desk. "Damn Cid…" Kel moans, "You're so wet girl…" "I've been wet all night daddy," she moans, "From the moment I saw you walk in the front door of the school."

"Damn…" he growls loudly as his body tenses up. "Damn," he repeats as his body begins to shake, "Cid I… I can't come out… yet." He fills her center with his seed, and then falls forward atop of her. "What if you get pregnant Cid?" Kel moans still tucked deep inside of her center. "No worries my love, I got fixed right after I had my son," she laughs gently, "I couldn't have your child if I wanted to."

Someone grabs the door handle, and tries to open the door. Kel jumps up to quickly fix his clothes. Cidra dives on the floor to hide behind her desk.

"Daddy," Jaze yells from outside the door, "are you in here? I'm ready to go home now." "Just a minute princess," he yells back, "I'm coming." After fixing his pants, and putting his shirt back on, he crawls behind the desk and kisses Cidra one last time before leaving her classroom to head home to his fiancé.

(OBT)

(Love)

My city, my city… In Orlando, you can find everything you want from International Dr. to Orange Blossom Trail, better known as "OBT". My city never sleeps and neither do I. I'm truly free of my past and all my old demons. No evil spirits can haunt me anymore, and the demons can't control me because I am the darkest demon that has ever walked this earth.

My insides are oozing pitch blackness; I have no room to love anyone or anything. I'm going to steal, kill, and destroy any damn thing I want to until the day I die. Of course, salvation is always a possibility I suppose, but I'll pass, this blood thirst is all I need to survive.

Love turns onto OBT, in a fire red Camaro at top speed. As he approaches **Club Purple Palace** he checks the rear-view mirror to make sure he looks okay. Love wishes he could see what so many women seem to see when they look at him. He has become very fluent at pretending he knows how handsome he is, but it's just a façade.

He parks around back as quickly as possible as not to be seen in his new car. Reaching in the passenger seat he grabs his black and red Chicago Bulls snap back hat, and puts it on just the way he likes to wear it.

Stepping out he kneels down to knock a small red string off his, black and red retro bred eleven Jordan shoes. His red leather sweat pants fit him perfectly, at the ankle he has the gold zippers open just slightly. He has his signature all black trench coat on buttoned tightly down the front.

Beneath his trench coat his black and red Givenchy shirt is

contoured to his body, as he has continued working out vigorously since his release from prison. Before he was released, he vowed he would never be one of those muscular dudes that get out of prison and then get lazy, and allow their muscle to turn to fat.

Standing at the front door of the club is a group of women. As Love approaches them their conversation pauses instantly.

"Damn." a short thick white lady whispers. Every step he takes towards them seems to be in perfect sensual slow motion.

"How you doing tonight lil daddy?" she says as Love finally reaches them.

"I'm blessed ladies." Love says with a charming smile.

"Yes, you are." three of the ladies say in unison. They all share a nice laugh together before; Love politely excuses himself from them to enter the club.

A cute brown skin girl showing off her perfect smile accented by twin dermal piercings in her dimples is manning the admission window, just inside the front door of the club. Love is almost certain this smile isn't displayed as broadly for every person who steps foot inside this club.

"How much is it to get in beautiful?" Love asks. "Twenty dollars handsome, but uh just throw me a ten... I like your vibe." she tells him. Love licks his tempting lips as he steps closer to her.

"Here you go." Love hands her a fifty-dollar bill. "You are the definition of gorgeous," she tells him, "and you are even more handsome the closer you get to me. Is this your first time here?"

He looks towards a stripper walking by counting money wearing only a thong.

"Um no ma'am," he says, "I used to come here a few years back. But um, keep the change though."

"Hey," he leans in close to the lady, "is Star working tonight?"

"Oh, you like light skin bitches huh?" she says showing her obvious disappointment. Love laughs in response to her sad facial expression.

"No ma'am," he smiles comfortingly, "I don't discriminate boo. I love all kinds of women. Starlita is an old friend of mine."

"Oh okay," she relaxes with a brand-new smile on her thin brown face, "wait here I'll go get her."

"No, that won't be necessary, but thank you." he tells her. "Are you sure?" she asks. "Yeah, it's uh kind of a surprise." he tells her.

As he steps into the main area of the club, Love is only interested in seeing one dancer tonight. Making his way to the back corner of the club he pulls the brim of his snap back down low on his head. It's Friday night and the club is packed as usual.

All around the club men and women are getting lap dances, and tipping the gorgeous dancers sporadically. "Can I get you something to drink handsome?" a young waitress asks Love.

"No, I'm fine. But thank you though." he replies. "Your blue eyes are gorgeous." she says. Love smiles at her. "Thank you, but they're green not blue baby girl…" She returns his smile. "My mistake, Mmmm mm Mmmm…" she moans.

As she walks away from Love she can barely take her eyes off of him.

"Who is he?" the waitress asks one of the dancers pointing back towards Love. "I don't know the light skinned dancer replies, "but, he does look kind of familiar. I'ma, go introduce myself."

As she approaches him he can tell it's her because she still walks exactly the same way she did years ago. "Hey do I know you?" Love chills her with his dangerous smile.

"We went to Dr. Phillips high school together," he tells her, "It's me, **Red**…"

"**Lance**… **Lance Cole**?" she asks. She screams loudly as she jumps in his lap. He smiles as he holds her close.

"You look good Starlita." he says.

"**No boy**," she says, "you look like a **light skinned god**… You really look good Lance. Where have you been all these years?"

"Around…" he says.

68

"Oh really…" she twists her cute mouth to the side. "So, what's going on with you boy," she continues, "what are you doing now? Are you in school?"

"No, I'm a thief and serial killer right now." he tells her. "Yeah whatever Lance," she bursts into hysterical laughter, "You are way to pretty to steal or kill anything or anybody."

"Yeah, you're right," Love laughs to himself, "but I'm not here to talk about me. Can I get a private dance or what boo?"

"Wow," she frowns up slightly, "Okay. Do you want me or one of the other girls?"

"How much…" he asks. "How much is what?" Starlita replies.

"How much for a private dance from my high school sweetheart…" he looks her up and down.

"Fifty dollars..." she tells him getting out of his comfortable lap. "Damn really?" Love asks.

"Yes Lance," she cocks her head sideways, "it's very nice to see you but this is my job and my bills do not pay themselves. Honestly, it's only ten bucks, but you don't look like you're hurting at all Lance..."

Love stares up at her without responding. "I mean if you want one of the other girls," she turns to point at the dancers on the other side of the club, "they may charge you a little less because I'm *sure* they're all sweatin' you real hard anyway…"

"Fine." he tells her.

"Fine what," she replies, "you want me or another girl?"

"You." he confirms through another damning smile. She takes him by the hand and leads him to a private room in the back of the club.

Once inside the room she sits him down in a large comfortable blue chair. With her hand held out Starlita licks her lips slowly. He hands her two fifty dollar bills.

She places both bills on the floor and then begins to dance slowly in front of him. After unfastening her bra, she makes her way towards Love. She continues to grind and shake in front of

69

him in flawless teasing fashion.

The music seems to be intoxicating them both. She's obviously feeling herself as her dancing has become very precise and hypnotic to him. As he looks at her she appears to be glowing. The colorful florescent lights in the smallish room reflect off of her yellow skin well. She looks like an untouchable alien goddess illuminated by her own perfection.

As she takes another step forward she's finally in his reach. With his left hand, he decides to test the waters. He reaches out and rubs her left thigh gently with the back of his hand. She smiles. Sitting forward in his soft blue chair, he reaches up with his right hand and squeezes her right breast.

She continues to dance as he gropes her. She kneels down to him and kisses him softly on the lips. Then she turns around and bends over with her hands on her knees. His passion and excitement are exceeding the level in which he can control them. With tremendous force Love grabs her, and then pulls her back towards him. On his lap, she can feel his excitement growing, as she continues to dance on him. With his hands on her hips he begins to pick her up and bounce her harshly on his lap.

"Calm down Lance." she begins to panic. "Shut the hell up Starlita!" he growls. She turns around to see his face. His smile has faded.

"I hate you." he tells her. "Then why didn't you choose another girl?" she asks. "Because I came for you…" he replies. "What the hell does that mean you came for me?" she asks. "I came here tonight just to find you." he clarifies.

"Wait, how did you even know I was here?" she asks. "Facebook," he growls, "I tracked you down like a filthy animal."

"But why…" she inquires. He laughs snidely still holding her down tightly on his hard body.

"Eight years ago," he starts, "our senior year…"

"Yeah what about it?" she asks.

70

"I proposed to you." he recollects.

"We were kids Lance!" she exclaims looking back at him. He quickly pushes her face back forward so she can't look at him. "So, what," he screams in her left ear, "I loved… well I **needed** you to make me okay… and you made a fool out of me."

"How did I make a fool out of you Lance?" she asks.

"Oh, you don't remember?" he smiles a deadly smile. "No, not really," she lies, "but I do remember I didn't tell you no."

"You didn't tell me no, and you **damn** sure didn't tell me yes," Love laughs again to himself, "In fact, after I proposed you never spoke to me ever again."

"What's funny…?" she asks. "The ring," he yells, "I spent every penny I had at the time to buy you that ring." "I didn't know that Lance," she cries, "and I honestly don't even remember what happened to it."

"Don't worry because I'll never forget," he promises in a dark tone, "you gave it to Gavin Thompson the brown skinned dude on the basketball team with the perfect waves in his head. Then he left you that next week for Shannon Treadwell."

Love squeezes the back of her neck as hard as he possibly can. "I'll make it up to you." she mumbles barely able to breathe. Love laughs. He leans forward and places his wet lips on her left ear. "Make it up to me," he whispers, "you can't make that up to me." "Yes, I can…" she cries.

"How bitch?" he screams. "I have money," she cries, "you know to replace the ring." "Replace… **Replace** the ring," he laughs harshly, "the damn ring was for you Starlita! If you did replace it who the hell would I give it to?"

"I don't know Lance," she swears, "but you're hurting me."

"You don't know who I would give the ring to…" he growls, "nobody Star! I have nobody to love or love me. After you, I spent the next few years of my life thinking I was… **something** I'm not."

"Well I'm sorry but you don't have to hurt me," she whimpers, "I can show you a good time Lance I promise."

He squeezes her neck harder, still holding her down on his lap with his other hand. "Lance please." she squeals. "A good time," he says, "I don't want your ass or your cash Starlita."

"Then tell me," she can taste her own tears as she opens her mouth to speak, "Tell me what you want Lance. Whatever you want you can have it…"

"I want you to feel *exactly* how I felt when you destroyed me years ago," he whispers in her ear in a demonic tone, "I was a walking dead man Starlita. The emotional and spiritual pain was *so damn* unbearable. What do I want from you? I want your blood, your soul, and your life!"

With her neck, firmly in the grip of his left hand he pulls his gun, out of the pocket of his long black trench coat. He carefully puts the gun to the back of her trembling head. She puts both of her hands in the air.

"Lance Orlandis Cole, please don't kill me." she begs. "And why not?" he asks.

"*Because damn it everything you're angry about happened over eight years ago*!" she yells. He doesn't respond.

Removing his left hand from her neck, he places her left hand in his lap. As if she can read his mind she unfastens his pants and pulls him out through the open slit in the front of his pants. She smiles with relief as she pulls her own panties to the side and he enters her warm wet body slowly. Grinding to the beat of the music Star leans forward in an attempt to please him more.

"I really did miss you Lance." she moans. Beyoncé's song "Drunk in Love" comes on. This is Starlita's favorite song. With her hands on her knees she waits for the beat to drop and then she begins bouncing rhythmically on his lap.

Love bites his lip and closes his eyes tightly. Opening his eyes momentarily he looks down at her perfect yellow behind and he drops his gun on the floor. With both hands now on her hips he almost forgets why he came looking for her.

"Damn Starlita…" he moans. "You like that daddy?" she asks. He doesn't respond. He reaches down to pick up his gun.

"Lance…" she moans still bouncing away lost in the moment.

With the gun only an inch away from the back of her head, Love closes his eyes tightly. She has no clue that her fate has not changed in the slightest bit. As she comes down on him hard, he holds her in place with his free hand. His body tenses up. Her thighs begin to vibrate.

"Oh Love…" she moans softly with her mouth open wide. After he feels the last drop enter her thirsty body he pulls the trigger twice, splattering the contents of her once pretty head all over the walls and himself.

He throws her limp headless body forward onto the bloody floor. Then he pulls out a small bottle from one of the deep pockets in his trench coat. He pours its blue contents all over her body. Then he lights two matches and throws them on her lifeless corpse. Staring down at her remains being consumed by the growing flames he smiles, as a huge burden has finally been lifted off of him.

He wipes the blood off his hands and face with her bra, and then throws it into the flames as well. Love knows by the time anybody notices Star is missing, or before they smell the smoke he'll be long gone. As he leaves the room and makes his way back to the main floor, he weaves through a crowd of horny regular club patrons on his way to the front door.

Several minutes later, Love inattentively speeds past an old light blue Camry, on his way out of the club's parking lot.

(In the cave on the Island)

Charlie Breeze is kissing Whitney's back softly as she lies in the dark sand. Her entire body is on edge with immense passion.

73

As he slides up her body the pressure from his weight atop her is shifting, and sending sporadic chills down her anxious spine. Charlie slowly bites the back of her soft neck. With his tongue, he gently caresses the lobe of her left ear.

"Do you want me?" he whispers.

"Yes…" she moans. "Yes what…" he says. "Yes, Charlie I want you." she replies. Of course, she wants him she's always the horniest when she's on her period.

"Charlie…" a small voice says from the mouth of the cave.

"What Senji?" Charlie inquires.

"The plane leave, now Mr. Breeze." he says in a thick island accent. "Alright," he replies, "are Ms. Powell's belongings already on board?"

"Yes sir," Senji replies, "Just like you asked me to do two days ago sir, now please hurry while Master Carlos is still sleeping."

Charlie stands up, and picks Whitney up as well. She stares down at him, as he carefully brushes the black sand off her knees and ankles.

"What does he mean, you told him two days ago," Whitney asks, "I just ran away yesterday?"

"What's your point?" he asks her.

"How could you know I was going to run away," she steps away from him, "And if you knew he was going to try to kill me… how did you know I would escape?"

"Whitney put your clothes back on and let's go please you're wasting time." he tells her. "Answer my question Charlie," she screams, "If you knew he was trying to *kill me* why didn't you save me?"

"I did," he yells picking up her clothing, "Who do you think sent that maid to the door to distract Carlos? Now put this on so I can get you out of here!"

She does as she told, and then follows Charlie hand in hand to the small plane that's waiting to carry her home to Florida.

Chapter 6
Breaking the Mold

Ty, Jay, and Osiana are bringing boxes into their new apartment in Orlando. Osiana, the pretty, thirty-one-year-old, white girl Ty met at the Starbuck's has been his lady ever since that day.

"This was a good move." Ty sighs. "Yeah you keep saying that." Jay replies. "Because it is…" Ty says. Osiana exhales loudly.

"Yeah, I don't know," Jay crosses his arms and looks at Ty, "I think you keep telling yourself this was a good move because deep down you know it wasn't."

"Really," Ty looks back at Jay, "that's not why I keep saying it Jay." "Then why?" Jay asks. "I don't know," Ty replies, "but I do know this move was for the best. I quit my job, and your career was going down the tubes."

"That is not true Ty and you know it." Osiana interjects. "Don't worry Osiana I can handle myself," Jay says, "my career is fine, but you didn't quit your job… Six Flags fired your crazy behind."

"Blood of Jesus," Ty shakes his head, "now why does a black man have to be crazy just because he refuses to continue to be a slave?"

"Slaves didn't get paid Tyrone." Osiana interjects again. "Yeah, and they damn sure couldn't just quit," Jay agrees, "If *Massa* fired they asses they either got shot or hung."

"Ya'll know what I mean," Ty says, "a black man will never

become successful working for white people." "Ty that's not true bruh…" Jay laughs to himself.

"Plenty of black men who work for predominantly white companies are very successful." Osiana throws her hands up in adamant protest.

"Osiana who's side are you on anyway," Ty asks, "tell me this how often, do those black employees reach the level of their white employers?" Osiana hesitates. "Not that often," Jay replies, "wait let me think for a second."

"Don't worry about it fam," Ty smiles to himself, "trust me that almost never happens. It's no mistake though." Jay looks at Ty with his brows wrinkled tightly.

"What you mean it's no mistake Ty?" Jay inquires. Ty takes a seat in a nearby chair across from Jay. Jay leans in close to hear his friend's next words clearly.

"It's all by careful design Jay," Ty tells him, "no matter who you are and where you work, you are not brought into that company with its intentions of promoting you to the highest level in the company."

"You know what Ty… I can't win this argument so I'ma let you have this one." Jay tells him. Osiana shakes her head trying not to smile, and then the three of them start back arranging their new home still lost in spirited conversation.

(Keldrick's mansion)

Jazemene is talking to herself quietly in her room with the door wide open. *"Daddy can't be this blind. I know it's been years, and we've all been through a lot but there's definitely something strange about Ms. Cam now.*

I still basically look the way I did the last time she saw me, I'm just taller now. But Cam looked at me as if it was her first time ever seeing me. She basically raised me for two years when I was a baby, how could she have ever felt that disconnected from me to react to me the way she just did? Nope I'm not buying it, something isn't right."

76

"Jaze…" K.J. enters her room.

"What…" she growls. He looks at her with his tiny head tilted to the side. "Who are you talking too nobody is in here?"

"I was talking to myself…" Jaze tells him.

"You're crazy." he replies shaking his curly little head.

"Nope I'm the only one around here who's not crazy little bro." she tells him.

(In the kitchen)

"Cameron…" Keldrick croons in his deep voice as he enters his large kitchen. "Yes baby…" she responds looking back at him invitingly. "What are you doing in here cooking bae," K.C. asks, "we have people I pay to do all that for us."

"I know babe but I sent them all home about an hour ago." she tells him. "You what?" he asks. "I sent them all home an hour ago, I don't need them." Keldrick walks towards the back door in the rear of his kitchen in search of his hired help.

"Um, babe they've already been paid, a very healthy amount of money to take care of what I hired them to do in *my house*." K.C. tells her.

"I understand that Keldrick," she hugs him tightly, "but I'm a woman and not just any woman… I'm your woman. Wifely duties are a part of my importance in my man's life, if I allow you to take that away from me… sooner or later my stock value will drop drastically and you'll begin to replace me in other ways as well."

"What," he says looking down in her amazing eyes, "that… will never happen Cameron. We have been through way too much for me to ever forget what you represent in *my* life."

"I get that too Keldrick," she smiles up at him, "but I'm perfectly capable of handling everything you want and need myself. I will never crowd your life but I will always be near when you need me."

"Girl," he looks down into her happy eyes silently, "I don't know what you've been up to for the past six years but I'm really digging the new you."

"Well I'm glad." she closes her eyes with her head resting on his broad chest and continues to smile.

(Several hours later)

"Come on Herman hurry up." she whispers in the darkness.

"Girl I'm coming," Herman replies, "but why am I sneaking in and out of your house aren't you well into your fifties Linda?"

"Oh, shut up, you old fool and come on." Mama Cole tells him.

Before opening the back door, she kisses the old man on his cheek, hands him a hundred-dollar bill, and ushers him out of the door without a word. Mama Cole checks her surroundings to make sure she hasn't been found out. She smiles mischievously to herself and then makes her way back upstairs to her room.

Once inside her personal bathroom she begins to undress so that she can shower before getting back into her large bed. Mama Cole starts the shower, turning the dial to the exact point in which the water temperature will be perfect for her.

As she looks in the mirror she doesn't recognize the woman she sees. The dark circles under her eyes tell it all. Years of sleepless nights and shady dealings that affect the ones she claims to love the most.

Mama Cole notices a foul odor coming from her toilet. Looking over at it she realizes one of the children must have had diarrhea earlier and decided to use her bathroom in her absence. After trying to flush it twice she realizes the toilet is not working properly. She solemnly makes her way back to the foggy mirror. The harsh steam from the shower is at her back like a large, beast breathing down her neck in anticipation of taking her pitiful meaningless life.

Mama Cole has grown tired of capitalizing off of her son and his children, her greed and lies are killing her slowly. She knows her end must be near because the shadows are always there. Her mother always told her that ***death is upon you, when your body begins to cast multiple shadows.*** Closing her eyes tightly she looks up to the ceiling.

"Lord I…" she hesitates as the pattern of the breathing on the back of her neck has changed drastically. It's smaller and more direct now. Her heart rate has reached a speed it never has before. Looking in the mirror she can see him standing behind her.

Even through the fog his face is unmistakable. A thousand scenarios run through her mind as to something, anything she could possibly say or do to change what she knows he has come to do. She soon realizes there's nothing.

He punches her hard in her lower back, with one of his gloved hands. Her painful scream is inaudible. With her hair wound tightly around his fist he slams her face down hard on the bathroom sink, spilling bright red blood everywhere from her eyes, nose, and mouth.

He allows the pain to register to her face, and then he slams her head down on the unforgiving sink face first again. "No…" she mumbles through her own blood, tears, and cracked teeth. He slams her head down again, even harder this time.

With a triumphant smile on his face he drags her to the toilet never loosening his grip on her thin graying hair. He kicks the back of her chubby yellow legs with his hard combat boots. She falls to her knees with her face resting on the soiled toilet seat.

"Why are you hurting me like this?" she mumbles. He doesn't respond. He lifts the toilet seat up and then roughly forces her head beneath the filthy, unusually high water in the toilet. Her arms begin to fling wildly in protest.

After ten seconds, he raises her grimy head. She gasps for air. She doesn't know which is worse, the stench of the filth in the toilet, or suffocating when her head is submerged beneath it.

"I love you son." she cries through the waste on her lips. Still ignoring his mother, he forces her head back beneath the waste again. Pushing her head deeper and deeper still into the bowl his smile never fades. He releases her head, as she gasps loudly. Then as she exhales she vomits harshly all over herself.

"Baby, please…" she begs.

He stands her up and walks her back to the mirror. He still has her hair wrapped around one hand and with the other he reaches up and wipes some of the mist off of the mirror.

"Look…" he commands. Both of her eyes are swollen considerably. "Damn it, look at yourself!" he growls. Only her left eye is capable of opening. Her vision is blurry from the tears and feces that are in and around both of her eyes.

"You see what you've done," he growls at her, "You see how… extremely ugly you are Mother? This is how you made me feel when I was a kid. I felt this ugly, and at least ten times the pain you think you feel right now!"

He waits for her to say something, anything to at least try to justify single handedly destroying his childhood. Mama Cole doesn't respond.

"Speak!" he demands.

"I only whooped you once in your life." she mumbles through the blood, and grime on her barely recognizable face.

"Yes… Yes, mother you did only whip me once," he tells her, "because you didn't love me enough to discipline me on a regular basis. You preferred verbally assaulting me and destroying whatever self-esteem I could have ever had. Yes, I was different. And no, I was not the average little boy, but I didn't deserve the way you all tortured me Mama."

He begins to cry. Love hugs his mother tightly from the back. "I love you Lance," she mumbles through the blood, "and I am so sorry…"

"Mama…" he cries. "Yes Lance." she replies.

"I loved you so much Mama," he confesses, "I didn't want much.

I didn't need the world, or even nice clothes and shoes, I just wanted you to look at me for once like I mattered to you. The way you're looking at me right now."

She doesn't respond. Mama Cole falls limp in Love's regretful arms. "Mama…" he whispers, "Mama, please don't leave me. No, Mama I love you don't leave me now Mama I need you." he begins to rock side to side with her as he hums an old lullaby he can't quite remember the words to. "I love you no matter what Mama." he tells her. Mama Cole never utters another word.

Love knows she's gone now. He lets her hair go. Then he calmly reaches around and closes her left eye that appears to be still staring at him in the mirror.

After scooping her up in his arms he carries her to her bed. In his pocket, he finds a small bottle containing a thick blue substance. He empties the contents on her body from head to toe. The concoction begins to seep inside her skin down to her bones. Then he pulls out a red lighter and sets her body aflame.

He takes off his soiled t-shirt and throws it into the fire as well. He watches the brilliant, controlled flame as it incinerates his shirt, and every inch of her body even her bones are melting away into nothing. Then he puts the small flame that remains out, and then retraces his steps to make sure no mistakes were made.

After cleaning himself adequately in her bathroom sink he opens all of her bedroom windows in an attempt to air the room out. After cleaning the sink properly, he exits her room to murder his next unsuspecting victim.

The pungent aroma of Mama Cole's burned flesh is especially strong in the hallway. He knows his next kill shouldn't be as messy, just a couple quick gun shots to the head.

Making his way down the long elaborate hallway he finds a door with the large letters K.J.C. on it. He opens it slowly and peeps inside. He finds his big brother sound asleep holding what appears to be Cameron Jiles. He reaches inside his trench coat pocket and grips his gun with the silencer already attached to it.

He's ready… he pushes the door open wider now. He pauses at the sound of tiny footsteps behind him. He turns around and finds a little light skinned boy with curly hair wiping his little eyes.

Then K.J. stares up at Love with those unmistakable green eyes.

Love's heart stops, as he falls to his knees before the boy. Every ounce of hatred in Love is gone. All the old pains are slowly bleeding away from him even if only for the moment.

They can't help but stare into each other eyes. K.J. has never met Love before but he feels so drawn to him. As Love stares into the boy's eyes, a mirror image of his own, he can barely catch his breath. K.J. reaches out to touch Love's dreads. He smiles at how soft they are. Love wipes a lone tear away from his own face.

"Wait Lance, the child can save you. You will love the child." Pastor White's words are echoing loudly in Love's head.

"What is your name little boy?" he asks. "Keldrick Jermaine Cole Jr." he tells him. "Son, are you…" he starts, "your eyes *are my eyes*. Your tiny face is *my face*… you are just… *you're me*." He hugs the little boy tightly.

"*Uncle L*…" a shaky voice whispers from a few feet away. "Jazemene… Come here baby give me a hug." Love smiles. She does as she's instructed.

After hugging him she steps back and lifts her pajama shirt to show him the scar he left her with when he shot her five years ago.

"I'm so sorry honey," he tells her, "I was sick back then, but soon I will make it up to you. Your father is going to go away, and I'm going to come take you both to Disney World and the three of us are going to live together in *Mickey's Magical Kingdom forever*."

He hugs them both again and kisses them both on the forehead, then like a ghost he vanishes just as quickly as he came.

(Back on the Island)

82

The night air on the island seems so much calmer and sweeter than the air back in the states. Life on the island for anyone in Master Sanchez's good graces should be wonderful. There are no worries beyond dressing yourself, and feeding yourself.

The calm waves that are forcing their way onto the beach are just as gorgeous as the water miles out in the middle of the ocean. The sand here is so soft that for Cameron late night walks on the beach have become a pure addiction.

But tonight, there's no walking, only drifting, as Carlos has invited her out on one of his smaller boats, for an evening out on the ocean.

Her longish dress is flowing in the calm, sweet ocean breeze. Her hair is pulled back into a tight ponytail, and her naturally stunning face is glowing in the moonlight. Carlos is dressed in a black V-neck polo shirt, red slacks, and black Polo boat shoes with the red polo logo on them.

Near the front of the boat he's standing all alone staring out into the water. Cam wants so badly to approach him, but she can't muster up the nerve to do so. She can hear him mumbling to himself about Whitney.

She walks closer to him. "Carlos... Are you okay honey?" she asks. "Aren't I always?" he replies still facing the water. "Uh, no not really..." she tells him.

"What's that supposed to mean?" he turns around slightly to look at her. "You have everything any man could ever dream of having," Cam tells him, "but it's not enough. I know you're not happy." "And how do you know that Cameron?" Carlos asks. "It's written all over your face," she says, "I don't even think you know what happiness is." He looks away from her.

"Have you ever been happy Carlos?" she asks him. He doesn't respond. Close enough now to touch him Cam begins massaging his tense lower back. "Carlos... do you know what happiness is?" she

83

asks again.

He turns around abruptly to face her again. "Do you," he replies, "why don't *you* tell me what happiness is Cameron. Have you ever been happy before?"

"Once…" she stares passed him into the dark waves.

"Keldrick right…" he roughly pushes her away from him.

"I don't understand it," he continues, "that man must make love with a passion fire that would shame a dragon. And his penis must be made of pure gold. I brought you and Whitney here and gave you both your own private fantasy world, but somehow, it's never enough. Nothing I could ever do will be enough to fade his memory from either one of your foolish warped minds."

"It's not that Carlos…" she walks back towards him.

"I will never understand." Carlos interjects. "How is it that a man with no education, no valuable skills, and no future could adequately captivate women the way he obviously does the two of you?" Carlos asks stepping further away from her.

"Carlos," she says, "you are a very loving… and compassionate man when you want to be. And you used to be the man of my dreams…"

"What do you mean used to be?" he asks. "Let me finish," she tells him, "when you first wanted me, years ago you were already the man of my dreams. But I was already heavily involved and in love with Keldrick."

"Oh, so now he's **Keldrick**." Carlos interjects. "Let me finish Carlos," she shakes her head in disbelief, "When you were ready for me… I wasn't ready for us. And so, in turn I destroyed your heart and your love for me. Now you're lost inside a moment, and the notion that you have to prove to me how much better my life could have been if I had chosen you, over him. But the truth is I didn't. I chose him, and then I left him for his best friend Ty. But after I found out Ty is K.C.'s half-brother, I just had to get away. So, I called you, and you flew me out here. That's the truth Carlos." He

84

looks away.

Moments later Carlos holds his head towards the boat's deck to shield his face from her. This new silence is deafening to Cameron. "You evil, conniving bitch." he mumbles.

"Excuse me Carlos," she steps towards him, "I don't think I heard you right." He looks up at her with his face covered in tears. "I said you're an evil conniving bi…"

She slaps him hard across his handsome face before he can finish his statement. Without hesitation Carlos slaps her back knocking her to the deck. Cameron screams loudly. Carlos kneels down and picks her up. With Cam held tightly above his head he walks towards the front of the boat.

"I hate you and everything about you," he vows, "*You evil Conniving bitch!*" With every inch of power in his body he tosses Cam as far as he can over the edge of the boat, into the pitch-black ocean.

The splash her body creates is magnificent. The cold water assaults her entire body instantly, but she quickly becomes numb to it. As she resurfaces she searches desperately for Carlos' boat. *"Carlos," she yells in obvious panic, "I can't swim! Baby I can't swim.*

Please come back and save me!"

Chapter 7
The Funeral

Outside the church, the parking lot is not very packed at all. In the very back row of the lot a fire red Camaro is backed in, in the very last parking space. Inside the church Jaze is sitting quietly on the front row of the magnificent church her father had built for Pastor White, as the old reverend eulogizes her late grandmother.

She's staring at the old man as he speaks but she can't hear a word he's saying. Her own thoughts are way too loud for her to be able to focus on anything else.

(Jaze)

It seems to me when something bad happens to someone who is not particularly liked, there's always an uncomfortable vibe during their funeral or whatever gathering is being held on their behalf. I had this same feeling at my Uncle Lance's sentencing five years ago. I love my uncle and I'm glad he's out. I know my father hates him and I understand why.

But my uncle explained to me before the funeral that he did everything he did because he was in love with my Mommy. I don't like the fact that he kidnapped me, shot me, and almost killed my mommy, and I don't like the fact that talking to him has to be a secret from my daddy but I still love my uncle no matter what. The worst thing of all, and I know I can never tell a soul but I'm angry I saw my uncle kill my Mama Cole.

After the service is over Jaze and her baby brother follow their father, Jay, Ty, and the other pallbearers as they carry Mama Cole's symbolic casket out of the church.

They really didn't need a casket because there wasn't much of Mama Cole left over to bury, but K.C. wouldn't have it any other way. The last person they pass as they exit is a hooded man with the tips of his dreads barely protruding out of his hood. Jaze smiles at him as they pass, he returns her smile.

The gravesite is just as quiet as the funeral service inside the church was. Jaze closes her eyes tightly, and puts her hands together like her Mama Cole taught her years ago.

Dear Jesus, if you're listening… and if you love me like my Mama Cole said you do please take her home with you Lord. My Mama Cole wasn't always nice, and a lot of times she wasn't even there for me at all. "But she was still my Mama Cole, and I don't want her to burn with the devil."

Her last sentence she says aloud unintentionally. Pastor White and everyone else turn to look at little Jazemene. Her face is covered in fresh tears.

"Come here baby." the pastor beckons to her. Jaze walks slowly to his side. "Jaze, do you have something you would like to say about Ms. Linda?"

"Yes," she wipes her eyes, "her name was Linda, but nobody ever called her that. She was Mama Cole to everybody who knew her. She wasn't perfect, but my Dad said nobody is perfect, so that's okay. She was and will always be *my* Mama Cole. I just… I just don't want her to go to Hell with the devil."

Jaze is crying in full force now. This surprises her more than anybody because she didn't expect to cry at all today. Pastor White

87

looks down at the child with a comforting smile. He kneels down close to her and begins wiping her tears away from her cute reddened face.

"You know Jaze," he hugs her tightly, "I think your love for Mama Cole alone should be enough to get her into God's Kingdom. He knows her heart and yours, so don't worry your pretty little head because our God is so gracious and merciful. Your father is right, none of us are perfect and that is perfectly okay... But God has a plan for all of us and it is perfect in every way. Always remember *love* covers up a multitude of sins."

He hugs her tightly, and then stands up to walk her back to her nearby father. The church choir begins to sing a medley of inspirational songs as the grave workers begin to lower Mama Cole's near empty casket into her lonely grave.

As K.C. pulls off from the church parking lot, the fire red Camaro is secretly following him a few cars back. Love knows what he has to do to get what he really wants. That little green-eyed boy is *his* legacy and he will stop at nothing to raise him himself.

The thought that pains him the most is the chance of someone taking advantage of his son the way Paul, and Dr. Granger did him. As he gets closer to his brother's mansion Love's palms begin to sweat. The moment has finally arrived for him to be face to face with the *black beast*.

He parks at the corner of the street, in almost the exact spot he parked the night he murdered his mother. His designer jeans are fashioned with large pockets on each side, large enough to conceal a weapon. As he walks down the quiet street he removes his hood, and freely shakes his strong golden tipped dreads.

As he gets closer to the house, he can feel himself losing concentration. All he can think about is the little green-eyed boy. In his mind these strategic murders, are what must happen in order for him to ensure the protection of his child.

He has a plan that could allow Keldrick to live if he decides to cooperate. After checking his surroundings, he makes his way to the left side of the mansion, and stealthily crosses the tall iron-gate.

Upstairs he can hear his brother talking on the phone loudly through an open upstairs window. Through the downstairs window he sees Jaze and K.J. watching cartoons. The backdoor is unlocked, as usual.

As he creeps in, he can see Cameron in the kitchen absorbedly scrolling through her cell phone, most likely on Instagram or Facebook.

Love swiftly makes his way to the stairs and takes them three at a time. At the top of the stairs he turns towards his brother's master bedroom. Step by step he nears Keldrick's room.

"Damn it!" K.C. screams out as he throws his cell phone behind him on his bed. He's rocking back and forth with his head down in his hands, if he could look up for just one second he would see his murderous baby brother standing in his door way.

Love begins to approach his unsuspecting brother. He's close enough to touch him now. He reaches down to his pocket double checking that he has his gun.

Keldrick looks down at the floor through his tears, and he sees Love's feet. He jumps up quickly to defend himself, but thinks better of his chances with his brother's quick gun now pressed hard against his stomach.

K.C. calmly sits back down on his luxurious bed. "What do you want Lance…" K.C. starts. "Shut the fuck up! And don't call me that!" Love yells. "Don't call you what," K.C. says, "it's your name. Your name is La…"

Love cocks his gun. "Call me that again… it will be your last word ever." "Why are you even here," K.C. asks, "And how the hell did you break out of jail?"

Love smiles. "First off big bro, I was in prison not jail. There is a huge difference in the two, trust me."

"And what is that?" K.C. inquires.

"You don't wanna know." Love replies. "You're right *I don't* wanna know. But what the hell are you doing in my house?" K.C. asks.

"I want the boy." Love admits. "What boy, my son…" K.C. asks.

"He is not yours," Love tells him, "Just because you named him Jr. does not make him your flesh and blood."

"What the hell is that supposed to mean?" K.C. asks.

"He is the spitting image of me bro, his face, his eyes, his entire being is me." Love contends. "Have you lost your damn mind?" K.C. asks.

"Where do his eyes come from Kel," Love says with his gun still ready, "hmm, from the contacts Whitney used to wear in high school? Be real with yourself man, that child is *my seed*. I'm not leaving here without him."

"If you leave with him," K.C. says, "I can't stop you because you have a weapon, but trust and believe after you're gone I will be calling the *folks* to have your ass arrested for kidnapping. And how can you even do this *right now*? Don't you know I just buried mom without you? I did that all by myself."

Love smiles his sadistic pretty smile. "What's funny?" his big brother asks.

"You didn't bury Linda alone Keldrick, I helped you more than you know." Love tells him.

"You have a real problem with names don't you," Kel asks, "You do not call my mother Linda. You refer to her as Mama, Mom, or Mama Cole…"

"I call that bitch Linda," Love growls, "always did always will!"

"You might as well go ahead and shoot me," Kel stands back up, "because she wasn't the best mother in the world, but she was the only one I ever had. I'm not gonna sit here and listen while you degrade her… When she just got brutally murdered and burned to death right down the hallway… while I was sleeping."

K.C. puts his hand over his mouth. "I didn't know," he continues,

"The police can't do shit, there's zero evidence. They don't even really know what happened that night. Damn it why didn't I wake up; I could have stopped it… I could have saved her." K.C. forces back his emotions.

"You couldn't stop it, and you shouldn't have Kel…" Love tells him. "What the hell do you mean by that?" K.C. asks. "She was a terrible person," Love explains, "that woman…"

"That woman was our mother!" Keldrick interjects. "Do not interrupt me again brother," Love growls with finality, "that woman was a snake, how do you think she was making all of that damn cash with no job, and no talent?"

Love pulls out a thumb drive from his front pants pocket. "I want you to put this in your laptop when you get a second." Love hands the thumb drive to his older brother.

K.C. throws the thumb drive down immediately. "What the hell is that Love?" K.C. asks.

"Your mother," Love explains, "had been exploiting your children for over a year. Every Saturday and Sunday while you're busy off being an irresponsible father, she took them down to the T.V. 5 television station and your children are the signature guests on a T.V. show called, *"When I grow up"*."

K.C. wrinkles his brows tightly. "What the hell does that have to do with anything?" Kel asks. Love smiles. "She made over $300,000 off their appearances," Love says, "and how much of that money has she given to you or the kids?"

K.C. hesitates and then he looks away. "I don't need any money," K.C. lies, "I didn't need my mother to take care of me I'm rich now." "I agree you were rich at first my brother," Love says, "I'm not denying that. What I'm telling you is your mother was richer than you until the second she died, because she was exploiting *you and your children*."

K.C. laughs snidely. "You're going to need way more ammo than that to prove to me that my mother was using me," K.C. tells his baby brother, "I mean how do you know she didn't set that money aside for the kid's college funds or cars when they become of age?"

"I have been following her around for two weeks I know everything that woman has been doing and what she planned to do next." Love takes out his phone and pulls up a recent picture he took with it. He tosses the phone to K.C. "Do you know who that man is, that Linda is meeting with in this picture?" Love asks.

"Yeah," K.C. responds, "that's Luke Clay he's a major Miami bookie." "Right," Love confirms, "and who do you think she's betting on... or against?" K.C. looks at Love.

"Mama was using me to gamble?" K.C. asks.

"Oh yes, she was pimping you out in impressive fashion big brother," Love smiles, "the woman knew when you were sick, she knew when you were well. Damn it the woman played you, like a PlayStation 3 bro. Just off you and the kids she had over two hundred and thirty million dollars in her bank account as of two weeks ago, until I hacked into her bank's most sensitive databases and stole every penny out of her account."

"You did what," Kel asks, "Bro are you trying to go back to prison?" "No sweat bro, the transfer is untraceable I was logged in with one of the bank manager's passwords all of the heat, if there ever is any will all fall on her."

"What did you do with the money?" Kel asks. "Well I bought a car, some clothes, paid rent at my condo for a year, oh and I also purchased a high-powered handgun as well." The last item was expressed with a slightly different tone.

"And what did you do with the other two hundred twenty-nine and a half million dollars' bro," Kel asks, "you haven't spent much at all?"

Love calmly reaches down into his pocket and pulls out a folded piece of paper. He then hands it to his big brother. Kel opens the paper hastily.

"You're giving all of it to me bro... Why?" he asks. "It's yours bro." Love says. "Damn, thanks bro." Kel replies emphatically.

"All I want in return is *my* son." Love reaches his hand out to shake his brother's.

Keldrick looks up at his baby brother, and then back down at the huge check.

"So, do we have a deal?" Love asks. Keldrick hesitates.

"Come on bro," Love prods, "I've seen *both* of your bank accounts I know you've spent more than you should have. We both know this money would be a fresh start for you." Kel quickly balls the check up and throws it at Love.

"Get the hell out of my house." he says. "Keldrick..." Love starts. "My name is K.C.," Kel replies, "I am *never* going to give you my son. Now, either you can shoot me and take him, or you can turn around and get the hell out of my house."

"I can't do that." Love aims his gun at his brother again. K.C. stands up boldly. Taking two strong steps forward he pulls Love's gun into his stomach.

"Shoot bro." he says. "You don't want me to do that bro." Love replies.

"Yeah, I do," Kel replies, "you already said it bro I have nothing, and what I have left is fading fast. Without my kids, I have nothing to live for. I finally got Cam back but she's gonna leave me too when she finds out we're broke."

"We're broke?" a soft voice says from the doorway. Kel looks passed his brother into the eyes, of the woman of his clouded dreams.

"Cameron..." K.C. looks at her through misty eyes.

"Yes, my love." she replies without hesitation. Walking towards him, and now

93

stepping around Love she sees the gun in K.C.'s stomach.

"What's going on here?" she asks. "I have no money baby," K.C. admits, "and my little brother wants to take K.J. away from me."

She looks deeply in Love's eyes for several seconds. From the calm look of understanding in his eyes, she now knows that she's in total control. She calmly pushes Love's gun back away from Kel's stomach and steps in front of the gun herself to protect him.

"I heard a little bit of what's going on, on my way from down the hall," she says, "I don't know the whole story, but I do know you don't want to kill your big brother. I can see in your eyes that you don't want to do this." Love holds his gun steady.

"Baby what are you doing?" Kel asks. She turns her back to the gun and throws her arms around K.C.'s waist.

"You saved me, so now it's my turn to save you." she tells him.

Love reaches his gun around her and points it at K.C.'s forehead. K.C. is sweating profusely now.

"For everything you ever did to me, or allowed me to go through I should kill yo ass right now," Love screams, "and the fact that you want to raise my son as if you really believe he's yours sickens me. After what I went through as a child how could you even think I'd allow anybody else to raise my own child? I know no one can protect my son the way I can, because I have absolutely nothing to lose except him. And I damn sure ain't leaving him in your care; you've never been good at protecting small children from danger."

"Love," K.C. starts, "look, man I didn't know…"

"No man, you didn't care!" Love interjects.

"I didn't know bruh… I swear I didn't know." K.C. cries falling to his strong knees, choking back the obvious emotion.

Love looks down at his big brother waving his deadly gun at him, and around the room recklessly. "You didn't know what Keldrick, oh perfect big brother? Tell me dude, what didn't you know?" Love yells at the top of his lungs.

"That he…" K.C. starts. "He," Love cuts him off quickly, "he who? Your father…" Kel can't hold back the tears any longer. "He's not my father," Kel cries, "He's a monster, a pervert…" Love kneels down near his sobbing brother.

"Then what does that make, you big bro," Love asks, "You are his seed." "I am nothing like him!" Kel exclaims. Noticing the gun is still aimed at him, Kel pushes his lady back onto the bed out of harm's way.

"Oh, but you are Keldrick…" Love contends. "What the hell are you talking about?" Kel asks. "I saw you…" Love tells him. "You saw me what?" Kel looks back at his lady with his face covered in sweat and tears.

"Twice," Love says, "I saw you pass my door when Paul was in my room destroying my innocence. You looked in and then walked away. The second time you even closed my door. You closed my door and left me in there with him all alone…"

"I was so young." Kel cries. Love smiles a deadly smile at K.C. "Not as young as I was *dear brother*." he reminds him.

"Lance Orlandis Cole," Kel whimpers, "Or whoever the hell you want to be, from the bottom of my heart bro I am so, so sorry for everything my father ever did to you. And I'm even sorrier that I never had your back when we were kids."

Kel looks up into his baby brother's eyes as he kneels over him. "I'm sorry man," K.C. says, "I swear to God I am so…"

"God has nothing to do with this!" Love interjects with an almost demonic tone.

"God has everything to do with this Love…" Kel replies. "Just give me my son…" Love says. "Love I can't just…" Kel starts.

"Just give me my damn son Keldrick," Love falls down on his knees near his big brother crying now himself, "please man I don't wanna have to kill you, but that little boy is my whole world, and he's the only thing that will help preserve whatever is left of my broken sanity. I need him so that I can be okay bro. Can't you understand man? I just wanna be okay. I wanna be… normal and liked. No, I wanna be loved *like you*. That's all I ever wanted was to be just like my perfect big brother, *"**The Black Beast**" the great **Keldrick K.C. Cole**.* I just wanted people to notice me. Me… not the way I walked, and talked. Or the way I dressed. I was a kid, a confused and abused kid. And I didn't understand at all… who or what I was supposed to be. I just didn't…"

Love is shaking and sobbing hysterically now. His powerful display of emotion is frightening even himself.

Keldrick stands his little brother up and hugs him tightly. With his left hand Keldrick calmly grabs the gun. Love tightens his grip on the dangerous weapon. "Let it go…" Kel, whispers to his baby brother.

"I can't." Love cries out. "Yes, you can Love," Kel tells him, "Let the gun go. You're okay now, and you have no enemies here. I love you little bro, I really do." Kel feels Love's grip on the gun loosen considerably. Once his grip fades completely K.C. safely takes the weapon away from Love and tosses it behind him on his huge bed.

"Lance," Kel says, "and your name is Lance little bro. You don't have to run anymore or ever be alone. You have family right here. I want to fix all the wrong that my father and mother ever inflicted on you. We are going to pray and fast, we are going to attend church together. You are no longer my little brother you are *my son, my friend, and my brother in Christ*."

"I just want to be okay…" Love explains. "And you will son." Kel assures him. From the doorway a tiny voice says, "Daddy…" Love wipes his face as he turns around to look at his tiny twin.

Then he slowly begins to walk towards him. K.J. looks up into Love's eyes with his head tilted to the side. "Why are you crying?" K.J. asks Love.

Lance kneels down in front of the boy, and then hugs him

tightly. Then he tranquilly picks the small child up in the air, and holds him back just far enough so he can really look at him.

Love turns to look at his big brother with tears in his eyes and a smile on his face. He can barely see K.C. through his watery eyes, but he can still tell his brother is smiling back at him. Love looks back at the baby.

"K.J.," Love wipes more tears away, "I want to introduce myself to you all over again. I'm your Uncle Love, and me and you are going to be very good friends. In fact, little man, you and I are going to be best friends forever. If you ever need anything you come find your Uncle Love, and I will fix whatever the problem is. I will never let anyone or anything hurt you, okay little man?"

"Okay." K.J. replies in his tiny adorable voice.

Jazemene rushes in the room frantically. She runs right passed Love and K.J. Standing just a few feet away from her teary-eyed father she says, "Daddy..." "Yes baby." Kel replies.

"Mommy is home." Jazemene is obviously trying to hide her true emotion. "What?" K.C. says standing up from his bed.

"I swear it Daddy," Jaze says, "Mommy is downstairs right now... she's so, *pretty* Daddy..." Jaze puts her head down in her hands, and begins to cry harder than she ever has before.

K.C. rushes forward and picks his baby girl up into his huge comforting arms. "No, baby, don't cry," he begs her, "please don't cry Jazzy..."

"She's so pretty Daddy," she whimpers, "I didn't remember Mama being so *damn* pretty. Why did she leave me Daddy, what did I do... what did I do that was *so* bad? I needed her to show me how to be a woman, but now it's..."

"Now it's what Jaze?" K.C. asks. Jaze chokes on her painful confused tears as she coughs several times. "I'm a grown woman now daddy it's way too late for her to teach me anything," Jaze replies wiping her tears away fiercely, "and I don't need her, *we* don't need her!"

"You don't mean that princess." an alluring voice says from the doorway. Everybody turns to look at the yellow goddess standing there built to perfection.

"Mommy…" K.J. screams as he jumps from Love's arms into his mother's arms, in one almost unbelievable leap. "Awe baby," Whitney kisses her handsome son, "Mommy missed you so much."

"Put me down Daddy." Jaze demands with her tiny yellow arms folded tightly. Kel kisses his daughter on the forehead and then does as she asks. Once on the floor Jaze runs as fast as she can, past her mother all the way to her room, and then slams the door hard behind her.

Her dramatic pain filled cries can still be heard from the other side of her door all the way down the hall in her father's room.

"You see what you did to her Whitney?" Love asks.

"Seriously dude," Whitney looks Love up and then back down, "the last time I saw you and my daughter together we were both being rushed to the hospital because you attempted to murder us both."

"Well you shouldn't have broken my heart, shit happens." Love replies shrugging his arrogant shoulders.

"Oh, shut the hell up Lance." Whit barks.

"How the hell did you even get out of jail?" she asks him.

"Good behavior." he lies with no emotion. "If my son wasn't in my arms I'd kill you right now." Whit swears. "The feeling is mutual… trust me. This time I won't fail." Love replies.

"Whitney…" Kel steps forward from his bed, "What the hell Whitney? Where have you been, why didn't you call, and what the hell are you doing here now?"

"Nice to see you as well Keldrick…" she replies, never taking her eyes off her handsome son. "Do not play with me Whitney," he demands, "you need to start talking, and I mean right *damn* now!"

"I, uh… took a hiatus." Whitney kisses K.J. again.

"This is a joke to you isn't it," Kel asks, "What the hell kind of woman leaves her fiancé' and two small children without any notice, or explanation?"

"I don't know Keldrick." she replies calmly.

"Oh, you know damn it!" he exclaims.

"Do, I…" she replies. "Yeah you know exactly what kind of woman you had to be to pull something as selfish as that!" he exclaims.

"You know what Kel," Whit frowns, "you're right I do know. The only kind of woman that acts in that kind of desperation is one who is undeniably unhappy. I wasn't happy Keldrick."

"Ok," he crosses his arms over his chest, "so why did you propose to me then?"

"Because Kel," she says glancing at a quiet blank faced Love, "damn it. Love was about to expose everything. I didn't know you were brothers, and I was sleeping with you both. I was embarrassed, nervous, and pregnant so I panicked and I proposed to you. End of story."

"So, you never intended on actually marrying me?" Kel asks.

"No," she says, "I mean yes. I don't know. I mean you are, and will always be my high school sweetheart; it's been my dream, to one day become Mrs. Keldrick Jermaine Cole, since I was sixteen years old. But life changes us all."

"So, you weren't happy anymore," he asks, "after everything that happened within the year leading up to our engagement we had been to hell and back. But we made it through, like we always do. I thought that was enough, what made you so unhappy that you left the way you did?"

"Everything," she claims, "we were finally living *our dream*, but to me it didn't feel or look anything like I imagined it. You became this perfect… well *imperfect* robot. Everything you were doing was so concise and thought out. Even in bed there was no passion, just precise movements and seemingly calculated grunts. I missed your old natural spontaneity. The boy I fell in love with back in

99

high school finally became the NFL star he always wanted to be, but in the process, he lost himself. K.C. was officially dead, and you killed him Keldrick. You, nobody else just you…"

"Why didn't you say something, anything baby… you didn't have to just disappear." Kel says.

"**Baby**…" the pretty dark-skinned girl says from behind Keldrick, "maybe I should leave." Kel turns around to look down at her perfect little wrinkled forehead.

"No this is your house Cam," he tells her, "You don't have to leave."

"Cam…" Whitney hands K.J. back to Love, and then proceeds towards the bed. As she approaches the bed Whitney begins to lose her breath as she takes in the site before her eyes.

"Cam," she says, "bitch how did you, I just left… Wait, because this doesn't make any damn se…" Before she can finish her statement, Whitney passes out cold on the floor.

(Later that Night)

Jaze has been tossing and turning all night. She just can't seem to shake the images in her tiny head. The blood, the screams, the tears… there was so much blood. The look in his eyes was unholy. She knows he has to be a living demon. But still she loves him.

Every time Jaze drifts off to sleep she can see her Uncle Love standing over her Mama Cole brutally punishing her for some obviously despicable unknown crime she must have committed against him.

She heard her Uncle say when he was little boy Mama Cole destroyed him. He said she was verbally abusive to him. And then he beat her head on the sink over, and over, and over. He even tried to drown Mama Cole in her own toilet filled with K.J.'s poop.

Jaze swears she heard Mama Cole's face and teeth as they were cracking from being repeatedly slammed on her own hard marble sink top. Everything is just playing back through her mind like a sick gory horror film. She can't make it stop.

She tries to stay up as long as she can every single night, so she doesn't have to battle the demons her nightmares never fail to summon every time she finally dozes off. Staying up is just as bad though because she's always trapped all alone in her large bedroom with no one to protect her.

She wants so badly to tell her daddy what's wrong but she fears her Uncle Love a lot more than the nightmares he created for her. Jaze believes if she tells her father what Love did now, he will try to avenge Mama Cole, and probably get killed by her Uncle in the process.

Tonight, Jaze decided to sneak over to her baby brother's room and sleep next to him so she wouldn't be alone. Lost in the worst nightmare she has had thus far; her entire body is covered in sweat. Finally, Jaze is awakened by a strange warmness beneath the covers growing further and further down her small legs.

The feeling is foreign to her, so in turn she's afraid to move. She looks over at her baby brother. He's sleeping peacefully. The warm feeling on her legs and thighs is now growing cold and she can tell it's liquid.

"Oh no." she whispers. "K.J. must have peed on me." she tells herself as she climbs out of his twin bed. As she reaches under his covers to check him she finds him to be completely dry. "Oh no," she cries again, "it was me. When did I start wetting the bed?"

With no other options left Jaze rushes from her baby brother's room all the way down the hallway to wake her father up. It's time she had a long-detailed talk with him about his little brother, her dangerous Uncle Love.

(Back to School)

K.C. called Cidra the day after his mother passed and told her the news. He called her again early this morning to let her know that Jaze would be returning to school today. Kel requested that Cidra instruct her students to be extra nice to Jaze as she mourns the loss of her beloved grandmother, and begins to cope with her mother's mysterious return. Cidra promised him she would speak to the class beforehand, on Jaze's behalf.

"Good morning class." Cidra smiles out at her twenty bright eyed students. "Good morning Ms. Bell!" they shout back.

"Listen children," she starts, "as you all know Jazemene Cole's grandmother passed away last week. So, when she returns to school today I want everybody to be extra nice and considerate of her feelings please… and thank you."

"Yes ma'am Ms. Bell!" most of the students shout back.

The door opens, and Jazemene walks in with her father close behind her. K.C. walks her to her desk, takes her back pack off, and hangs it on the back of her desk for her.

"I got it Mr. Cole," Josiah approaches them, "Jaze will be okay, I got her back." Josiah then opens her back pack and pulls out her history book and puts it on her desk and turns it to the right page for today's lesson.

"Thank you, Josiah," Kel pats him on the back gently, "you're a good boy." His mother smiles at him as he sits back down in his own desk, right behind Jaze's desk.

"Okay baby girl daddy has to go but if you need me you have Ms. Cidra call me and I'll come running." he tells his beautiful daughter. "Okay daddy." Jaze replies. Kel kisses her on the forehead twice and then leaves the classroom quietly.

"Okay class… today we're going to learn about the *Emancipation Proclamation*. Can anybody tell me what that is?" Hands shoot up across the room.

Chapter 8
Sole Survivor

I no longer have a clue how long I've been trapped in this never ending ocean. My senses escaped me long ago. I have become one with the waves, and they are now my only hope. The methodical pattern of their flow is the only thing that can possibly carry me to the shore.

I know there is a God now. I should have drowned hours ago. Maybe I did drown hours ago… and now I'm just a lost lingering spirit, forever trapped in these never-ending waves, reliving my last earthly moments.

I made myself believe I was a gorgeous mermaid just drifting through the waters without a care in the world. That's kind of the way I've grown to look at my life in general. Like I'm not supposed to genuinely enjoy it, it's just something I have to endure… like prison.

God where is Keldrick? I miss that tall, strong, dark chocolate man so much Lord. Damn it, when he proposed to me all I had to do was say yes. Forget all the things in our past, and just finally become his one and only heart.

But, I was so lost. My mind was heavily clouded with doubts, and countless unanswered questions. I should have never gotten that abortion. If I had his baby, maybe we would have been okay.

No, what am I saying? Having a man's unwanted child never makes a relationship any better, it just further complicates things.

And what about Whitney, I'm still in love with her as well, but I know she doesn't feel the same way about me. Who could blame her? I ruined a love she had known ever since she was a child.

Wait, I think I can see land. I do, I can almost see the shore, and there's a man standing on the beach. I'm so close.

My dress is gone, I'm completely naked now. And what are my arms doing? They're moving, like flapping... or straining.

Oh my God, I'm swimming, where is this strength coming from? I can see the man clearly now. It's Carlos, kneeling down at the edge of the beach waiting for me.

God, I don't have the strength to fight this man. Please make him, disappear Lord. I can't survive any longer in this water, but if I go ashore I'm sure he will kill me.

As she gets within a few feet of him, Carlos pulls Cameron Jiles on to shore and snatches her up into his arms passionately. After searching her tired eyes, he kisses her as fiercely as he did the very first time.

Down on his knees in front of her, Carlos looks up at the gorgeous girl that stole his heart away over five years ago. Carlos grips her waist, and then her firm behind, as he presses his strong face into her perfect stomach. He holds her like he needs her.

All around Cam, in her peripheral vision all she can see is pure beauty. So many indescribable colors and shapes, pure abstract ecstasy. The fatigue has sent Cam's brain into a state of hyper hallucination. This island should be any woman's dream home, but it has now become her *deepest darkest nightmare ever*. She falls down on her knees in front of him. Carlos holds his hands up in front of her; instinctually
Cam uses the rest of her strength to put her hands up to his.

Once their hands are palm to palm he begins to move his hands around slowly, challenging her to keep up with his pace and pattern, and ultimately mirror exactly what his hands are doing.

Their eyes are locked inside of each other's. Their minds; become one as he mentally and physically guides her moist wrinkled palm's through the air as they match his to absolute perfection.

(Cam)

Lord why have you given this man so much power over my life. He owns my whole world, my entire being rests in the palms of his large powerful hands. I used to think that was an amazing thing, now I know much better. What does he want from me, he has spent countless dollars turning me into his dream girl, but somehow, I still don't measure up to his unreachable standards? I am as close to physically perfect as I have ever been in my life. I am submissive to a fault.

My emotions were destroyed, and then recreated by him. I feel as if I am only capable of loving him and his world. Outside of this man I no longer exist. So, since in essence I am only an extension of him, why does he still not love me or respect me?

I want freedom, and true love but I no longer know how to exist without him. He simultaneously murdered me and gave birth to me about four years ago.

The intellect that you have blessed this man with Lord… would have been much better served to a potential world leader. His mental prowess should be possessed by somebody, anybody else who would use this talent of literal mind control for good not evil.

I am not questioning you God, but if you hear my prayer I'm asking you now to kill me instantly. Let me die right now in this man's arms who loved me, and hated me just enough to kill everything inside of me that made me who I was. Take me Lord… take me now because I'm already dead.

(Orlando)

Jay is in the kitchen boiling a couple of old hotdogs, and listening to the radio, when Tyrone and Osiana walk in.

"Wassup Osiana," Jay speaks, "hey any luck on the job search

Ty?"

"Yeah man, I got a couple things lined up," he replies, "but I told you I'm not looking for a job Jay."

"Oh, that's right I forgot," Jay lies in mock surprise, "you're about to open your theme park, right?"

"Stop being an asshole Jay!" Osiana yells.

"Damn," Ty shakes his head a few times, "with a friend like you Jay, who needs…"

"Damn it Ty," Jay interjects, "I am not your enemy. But I'm not a dreamer like you man, I need tangible things in my life. I need things to be real, and in the physical realm."

"So, because you don't believe in my dreams," Ty scoffs, "I'm not allowed to dream around you?"

"Man, I can't stop you from dreaming bro," Jay says, "but we are about to be living solely off my parent's money. And they're not gonna let that happen for too long."

"And what the hell job are you looking for Jay?" Ty asks. "I have a bunch of shows lined up, um like next week, and the week after that." Jay mumbles.

"Nigga paying a strip club DJ to play a couple songs off your unofficial mix tape is not a show," Ty yells, "and no matter how many times you do it, it will *never ever* be a real show bro! And it sounds to me like *you* are a dreamer just like me, your dream just seems more real to you than mine. Kel has a lot of money now, from what I hear… Why don't you ask him to push your career for you? You have the talent no doubt, but you need the right brand and financial backing."

"That's the question I should be asking you Tyrone *Cole*…" Jay smiles a wicked smile. "Don't call me that." Ty tells him. "Why not," Jay asks, "he's your brother. K.C. is your half-brother. I'm sure he wouldn't mind pulling a few strings for you to help speed the process along for your theme park."

Ty sits down at the kitchen table, and presses his hands

106

together tightly as if he plans to pray. "Man," Ty says, "I haven't spoken to him since Cam turned his proposal down, and then briefly at the famous bloody family reunion. I'm sure he's still angry."

"Well," Jay sighs, "If my second-best friend in the world stole my fiancé to be, away from me, I'd be angry too."

"Exactly," Ty agrees, "wait, what you mean second best friend? K.C. and I were always tighter than you and him."

Jay laughs gently, and then Ty joins in with him.

"I'm just kidding with you, bro," Jay tells him, "but I'm sure K.C. isn't mad anymore."

"Wait," Ty says, "Did you speak to him, what did he say?"

"I haven't actually talked to him, talked to him." Jay Claims. "I'm sure he's still angry though," he continues, "I mean hell we didn't even really say anything to him at his mother's funeral." Jay looks down at his phone in his hand, "But I saw on Facebook yesterday that he's in a happy relationship." Jay tells Ty.

"With who…" Ty asks. "You'll never guess." Jay walks into the next room. Ty quickly follows his friend into the den area. "Who is it Jay?" Ty asks.

"Gimme a second for my phone to refresh and I'll just show you," Jay hands Ty his phone, "If I didn't see it, I wouldn't have believed it myself."

Ty's eyes begin to bulge immediately.

"*Cam*…" Ty says. "In the flesh bro…" Jay replies as he takes his phone back. "Where the hell did he find her?" Ty asks. The status said he found her working at a local movie theater here in Orlando. Then he made her quit her job on the spot, and then took her home with him all the way to Miami. *Romantic right*…" Jay says through a crooked smile.

"Go to hell Jacody." Ty mumbles.

"I gotta call her… I mean him." Ty continues. "Yeah you better get that straight," Jay shakes his head, "because if you disrupt his relationship again brother or not K.C. is going to kill you this time."

(Jaze)

Lying alone in her perfect, princess, pink bedroom, Jaze is trying to pray. Just outside her window the sun is just beginning to rise. It'll be time for her to get up for school soon. The only way she can sleep peacefully is in her father's bed. But since he has a woman living with him now, she doesn't have the privilege of resting safely at the foot of Daddy's bed anymore. So, she sleeps in her own bed with her head completely under the covers.

Her nightmares don't occur as often anymore. So, at night with nothing to distract her mind, except total darkness she finally falls asleep. Her young spirit is still troubled though of course, and normally she would speak to Mama Cole about how she feels, but she no longer possesses that luxury. So now she often prays alone, not quite sure if God hears her or cares about her thoughts, and troubles.

"Lord, it's me Jazemene... How are you Jesus? I hope you're doing very well. Is my Mama Cole up there with you? Are you taking good care of her? She likes warm tea in the morning and cold Tequila at night. Jesus... my mommy came back yesterday, and I don't know what to do. I miss her but she left me when I was just a baby. I wasn't bad at all. Well not all the time. If she loved me and my daddy, and my kid brother K.J. then why would she just leave us all behind without a single word?"

"Because." a voice says from Jaze's bedside. Jaze slowly peaks from under the cover. After confirming that the voice was from her mom, she recovers her head with her fluffy pink blanket, after rolling her eyes fiercely.

"Because what lady?" Jaze rolls her eyes beneath her covers.

"My name is Mommy, Jazemene. Do not call me lady again." Whitney tells her daughter.

"What makes you my mother," Jaze agitatedly throws the blanket off of her head, "because you gave birth to me?"

"I also carried you in my stomach for nine months, little girl." Whit tells her. "So that's about it huh?" Jaze rolls her eyes again.

"No, baby…" Whitney starts. "I'm not your baby," Jaze exclaims, "and why are you on your knees?"

"I was praying with you…" Whit tells her. "I don't need you to pray for me or with me," Jaze exclaims, "I am already a grown lady Whitney." Whit shakes her head at herself. Then she looks back at her child. "Baby," she starts, "you are only ten years old. You are not an adult, nowhere near it."

"Yes I am." Jaze insists.

"No, you're not," Whit shakes her head, "you are still a child, you are still *my child*. And I know it had to be very hard for you without mommy here with you, but I'm here now baby and I will never, *ever* leave you again."

There's a knock at the door. K.C. sticks his head in the door. "Rise and shine princess…" he says. "Good morning Keldrick." Whitney smiles a wide smile.

"Whitney," he replies coldly, "get up for school munchkin, don't worry about catching the bus, I'm driving you today."

"I can take her." Whit says. "In what car…" Kel and Jaze ask in unison. Whitney looks at K.C. as if he should already know.

"Oh, hell no," Kel shakes his head, "You must be out of your light skinned mind."

"Fine," Whitney stands up and leans over to kiss Jaze on her cheek, "Have a good day at school baby. I don't know if I'll still be here when you get home."

"She'll be here," Kel promises, "I'm not throwing you out Whitney. I'm taking you to find an apartment."

(Ms. Bell's classroom)

"Okay class you know what today is…" Ms. Bells yells to her anxious class. "***My Future report day!***" the students eagerly yell back.

"That's right," she says, "today everybody is gonna get the chance to report to the class what they want their future job to be, who they want their future spouse to be, and what city and state they want   to live in. Now who wants to go first?" Hands shoot up across the classroom.

"Okay Brian you go first." Ms. Bell points to him. Brian, a short white ten-year-old boy, with a mustache and snotty nose stands up and proudly holds out his report so he can read it to the class.

"When I grow up," he starts, "I wanna be an astronaut, I want to live in Queens New York, and I'm going to marry *you* Ms. Bell." Brian then turns around and gives one of his classmates a high five before sitting back down. Ms. Bell blushes and shakes her head. The class bursts into jubilant laughter.

"Alright, alright class calm down," Ms. Bell holds one finger to her lips, "good job Brian, now whose next?"

"Me, me, me…" they yell simultaneously.

"Ok Maria your turn…" the teacher says. Maria, also ten years old is the tallest girl in the class. She's a homely, brown skinned, bully with a terrible attitude to say the least. She stands up and holds her report out in front of her.

"When I grow up I'm going to be a super model," she claims, "I'm going to marry Chris Brown, Tyga, and August Alsina, and all of us are gonna live together in Barbados."

"Maria them niggaz don't want you." Wally, a curly headed Puerto Rican kid tells her. "Whatever Wally, don't get beat up," Maria replies, "you're a hater."

"Okay who wants to go next, how about you Jazemene Cole?"

110

Ms. Bell asks her. Jaze hesitates, still sitting down staring at her report with shaky hands.

She finally stands up but still doesn't speak. "Go ahead Jaze if you're ready…" the teacher tells her. Jaze clears her dry throat twice. She has gone back and forth in her mind about exposing herself to the class and Josiah as to her true feelings for him.

She could read it and change it as she goes, nobody's ever going to actually read her report except Ms. Bell, and she would never tell a soul. But if Jaze doesn't take this opportunity to express her love for Josiah, then when will she get another one as perfect as this?

She clears her throat once more. "Okay," Jaze begins, "When I grow up I'm going to be a star point guard in the WNBA, I'm going to live back home in Orlando during my off seasons, and I'm going to marry… my best friend Josiah Bell." The entire class gasps, and then starts laughing at Jazemene.

The bell rings, thank God class is over. Jaze starts packing her bag trying not to make eye contact with anybody. Her palms and neck are sweating badly.

"Hey…" Josiah says from behind Jazemene. "Hey…" she replies. "You okay," he asks, "forget those other kids I don't think what you said was funny at all Jaze. I mean, it's cool you know…"

"You don't have to be nice to me all the time Josiah," Jaze turns towards her best friend, "It's okay to tell me the truth too sometimes." Jaze stalks out of the classroom without looking back once.

As soon as Jaze exits the classroom Maria the bully is right there waiting on her. She knocks Jaze's books out of her hands onto the floor. All the kids begin to crowd around them laughing menacingly.

Jaze's palms are sweating more now, her vision isn't clear, and her heart is racing faster than she can bear. "Well aren't you gonna say something stupid…" Maria teases.

Maria slaps Jaze hard across the face. Jaze looks around for Ms. Bell, but she's gone. Warm liquid begins to run down both of her legs. She can't stop shaking.

"Do something, bitch!" Maria taunts. Jaze just holds her head down as the tears begin to fall. All the kids continue to taunt Jaze and laugh at her as she cries. She wants to die right now. That would show them all if she could just fall down in front of them and die right now they would all regret torturing her. Maria pushes Jaze down to the floor hard.

A second later Josiah bursts from the class and tackles the 5'9, ten-year-old tyrant Maria to the ground. She easily pushes him off of her and stalks back towards Jaze who's still lying on the floor in a puddle of her own urine.

"Josiah would never marry you Jaze," Maria says, "you're black and he's white. You're not good enough for him." "Leave her alone Maria!" Josiah demands. Maria ignores him and kicks Jaze's in her back twice.

Josiah swings at Maria and misses. She pushes him to the ground hard, and then climbs on top of him punching him in the head repeatedly. The class begins to laugh and point at Josiah.

As Jaze looks on she can feel her temperature rising dangerously. She can focus now, her composure has returned, she feels powerful. She remembers all the boxing combos her daddy taught her, the same ones he taught her mommy years ago to win her fight at Dr. Phillips High school back in Orlando.

Jaze stands up and rushes over to Josiah's rescue. She pulls Mariah off of him and swiftly hits her with a two-piece combo, left hook right jab. Maria's eyes instantly roll into the back of her head, as she falls hard to the floor.

All the kids rush over to Maria's limp body and point and laugh as she begins to urinate on herself. "Jaze I think you killed her." one kid says.

"Yeah, she ain't moving." another kid agrees. Jaze grabs Josiah by the hand and helps him up. "She ain't dead," Jaze looks down at the limp bully, "but if she ever touches my future husband again she will be." All the kids begin happily screaming and shouting Jaze's name. Maria didn't die but she did have a mild concussion. After that day Jaze almost never had another problem with anybody at Key Point Academy.

(Five hours later at K.C.'s mansion)

As Whitney enters the kitchen, she finds Kel's fiancé bending over looking in the refrigerator, while listening to R. Kelly's "Black Panties" album.

Whit takes a second to admire her luscious dark shape. Whitney licks her soft pink lips, as she walks towards her. With her body now pressed behind Kel's fiancé Whit whispers, "Damn I miss you…"

"What the hell is going on in here?" Kel enters the kitchen with his forehead wrinkled tightly. "Whitney, keep your damn hands off my fiancé." he demands.

"She's my baby too." Whit says slapping Cam on her butt. "Ain't that right Cam?" Whit continues.

K.C. looks at his fiancé with his brows still wrinkled tightly. "Am I missing something Cam?" he asks.

"No baby," she replies, "I don't' have a clue what she's talking about." K.C. looks at Whitney.

"Seriously Cam," Whitney quickly puts her hands on her hips, "so you gone pretend like you're not in love with me? You know what it doesn't even matter. The question is when did you leave the island and how did you get to Florida before me?"

"What island," she replies, "once again I don't have a clue what you're talking about lady."

"Who the hell are you," Whit asks stepping back, "Keldrick who the hell is this? Because, she definitely ain't Cam…"

113

"Oh," she interjects, "you mean *that* island?" She steps close to Whitney and kisses her passionately on the lips.

"Now that's more like it," Whit says through a relieved smile, "I knew you wasn't gone just play me like that."

"Cam," K.C. frowns, "What the hell is going on?"

"We were both living together on an island with Dr. Carlos Sanchez…" Whit explains. "Doing what?" Kel asks folding his huge arms tightly. Whitney hesitates, taking joy in Kel's obvious jealousy. "Baby," Whit looks deep in his eyes, "Cam and I did any, and *everything* Carlos wanted us to do. And we loved it, didn't we Cam?" "I have to use the bathroom." the sexy dark-skinned woman rushes out of the kitchen.

"Wait baby, the pot on the stove is boiling over." K.C. yells out behind her.

"I got it," Whit walks towards the stove, "there's nothing in it yet.
It's just water."

(Inside the Bathroom)

Inside the bathroom, the dark-skinned woman looks at herself in the mirror intently. ***"Wise up… and get it together or you are going to lose the best thing, and the best man that have ever happened into your***
miserable mediocre life. No one knows who you are, but they all think you're Cam. So, Megan, damn it just be Cam. That's all you have to do. The woman was never that complex a person. She was emotionally detached, jealous to a fault, a prude, borderline crazy, but in all still not hard to imitate at all. All I have to do is make everybody believe I'm her until I can adequately train Keldrick to love Megan, instead of Cameron. Fake it till I make it.

If I know Cam she's coming back for him at some point, so I have to work hard and fast. Everybody here is so stupid, and they talk so much,

114

they'lljustcontinuetogivemetheinfoIneedtopulltheimpersonation off perfectly."

"I knew it." a tiny voice says from the other side of the bathroom door. Megan quickly opens the door to find a tiny Whitney staring up at her with her arms folded tightly and her brows wrinkled fiercely.

Megan immediately snatches the little girl into the bathroom by her taught ponytail. "Listen you little bitch," Megan growls, "if you even think about telling your dad I'm not who he thinks I am, I'm going to personally cut every last one of your tiny toes and fingers off and feed them to your *retarded* little brother."

"My brother *is not* retarded." Jaze crosses her arms. "He will be after he eats your fingers and toes," Megan says, "Mark my words you little slut, I will kill you if you mess this up for me."

Jaze continues to rub the top of her head in silence, trying to soothe the pain from being yanked by her hair like a raggedy old Barbie doll.

"Do you understand me," Megan asks, "Or should I just hide your little body now?" "Yes ma'am." Jaze replies.

"Good." Megan smiles an uneasy smile at her. Then she kneels down, fixes Jaze's ponytail, kisses her on the forehead, and then opens the door for her to leave out of the bathroom.

As soon as the child steps into the hallway she tries to scream. Before much sound can leave her mouth, Megan snatches her back

into the bathroom and hits her hard in the top of her head with a closed fist. Jaze quickly falls to the ground completely limp.

(Back in the Kitchen)

Whitney has on an old t-shirt, and a pair of pink boy short panties, that are easily visible beneath her short shirt. Every move she makes causes her round behind to jiggle just enough to make Kel's blood begin to boil again and again.

He grabs himself as he watches her in silence. Whit reaches over to the kitchen sink to grab a dish rag to clean the stove top. As she bends forward to clean the very back of the stove, Kel feels himself growing larger, and harder. Whit is talking but K.C. can't understand a word she's saying, he can only focus on her pretty yellow body.

Whitney finishes with the stove and then begins to straighten up the area around the sink. On his hands and knees almost in a trance now, K.C. crawls to her as she continues to clean. Once close enough he grips her waist with his powerful hands, lifting her onto the tips of her toes.

She moans joyfully, as she covers her own mouth. Keldrick buries his strong face deep in to her soft upper thighs, and behind. His tongue hungrily begins to taste her through her underwear. As his mouth massages the core of her intimacy, his hands continue gripping, and massaging her lower back and waist methodically.

With all of her strength Whit holds onto the edge of the sink as "*Kool Hands*" lifts her up higher into the air. Pulling her wet panties to the side with his tongue and teeth, K.C. sends Whitney to a level of ecstasy she hasn't known since before she went missing.

With her knees resting on his broad shoulders, Whit tries hard to stop squirming for fear of falling hard on the gorgeous tile floor as Kel eats her body and spins her around in the air simultaneously. "Don't worry *Suga Mama*, I got you." he moans sensing her fear.

He knows no fear and no fatigue when he's near her like this. He feels as if they are connected again mind, body, and spirit. After prompting her to straighten her legs as he supports her weight, he carefully removes her passion soaked panties.

With her hands now secure on his shoulders, he allows the small woman to slide down his firm body into his ready and capable arms. Pressing her soft body back against his he forces her to bend over on the sink. With two eager fingers, he enters her slowly from the back. "Mhmm…" he mumbles.

"What baby?" she moans. "Still feels the same," he grins,

"guess Doc wasn't really putting in any work huh…"

She smiles back at him, with a crooked smile. "Oh, would you shut up and just do me already…" she demands playfully.

"Cam is in the bathroom," he replies, "what the hell am I doing?" "Hopefully me…" Whit says almost whining now. "No," Kel hesitates, "I can't do this."

He removes his large fingers and backs away from her quickly.

"Come here baby," Whit moans, "I know, you miss mama's goodies. They still belong to you, and always will." Whitney sets herself up on the nearby kitchen counter, with her yellow thighs spread wide open for him.

"I can't Whitney," he says, "so just stop it and put your clothes back on."

"Hell no," she snatches her shirt off and throws it at him, "I'm not putting anything back on until you finish what you started."

"I'm engaged Whitney." he whispers.

"Hell no, don't start whispering now," she yells, "and I agree you are engaged… to me. I still have my ring, and it's not too late for us."

"Oh, but it is," Kel's fiancé reenters the kitchen, "he's mine and you lost him, when you left him. So, stop acting all desperate, and get your old thirsty miserable ass the hell out of my house Whitney." She picks up Whitney's shirt and panties and throws them both at her. "Kel honey," she continues, "you are not taking her to find an apartment, give her some money, and call her a cab she can find her own damn apartment." Without another word Megan leaves the kitchen striding like a confident queen.

Chapter 9
Black Don't Crack

(Cameron)

Staring at her reflection in her third story bedroom window, Cam realizes even though she can obviously look beyond her reflection to the world outside of her window, there is no point in doing so. Nothing outside her window, or this house, or beyond Carlos' world will ever matter in her life ever again. This is just a cold hard fact she's finally come to grips with.

I want to leave this island. I want to go back to Orlando, and spend every night until I die searching for K.C. the only real man I have ever known. I wish I had just let everything be as it was. I should have accepted his mistakes, as he accepted mine and became his wife for forever and a day. I have to leave this place, but it's just not possible.

I don't want to die… Lord knows I do not want to die. But death may be my only way out of this life, and off of this island. How did I end up like this? When I was younger I never thought a man like Carlos would even speak to my black ass, but for him to fall in love with me, and then eventually hate me enough to imprison me blows my mind. I blame myself…

Cameron's door flies open wildly, as Carlos rushes in. Obviously frantic, he stares at Cam in confusion before collapsing on her bed completely out of breath. Cam rushes to him. "Carlos," she gasps, "Baby, are you okay?"

He tries to respond, but is still having trouble breathing. Two maids rush in. "Doc, are you okay?" one of them asks. "We saw you race in through the front door, like somebody was chasing you." the second maid reflects.

Doc, still lying there gasping for air doesn't respond to them. "I'll take care of him ladies." Cam tells the panic-stricken maids as she walks them out to the hallway and then closes the door behind them.

"Cameron…" he mumbles as she sits down on the bed next to him. "Yes, my love," she replies, "What's wrong?" She notices all the sweat on his forehead, and around his eyes. "Baby what is wrong with you? Talk to me…" she tells him.

"Get me a cold wet towel please." he says.

She hurries to her private bathroom, and then returns moments later with the towel as requested. Cam gently kisses his forehead and face, as she slowly wipes his sweat away.

"I thought, you were gone…" he mumbles. "You thought who was gone?" she asks through a sarcastic smile.

"You, I saw a picture of you," Carlos explains, "with… with him. And I thought…" "Wait," Cam says, "you saw a picture of me with whom?"

"Who else Cameron?" he asks.

"Who Keldrick?" she asks. "Yes, I saw a recent picture of you and him on Instagram together." he tells her. "Boy," she holds back a laugh, "I haven't seen that man in over six years." "Then what the hell is this?" Carlos asks, as he tosses his expensive phone in her lap. Cameron gasps, as her eyes bulge wildly. "Oh… my… God!" she screams. The two maids burst back in the room. "What's wrong?" the first one asks. "Yeah, Doc, are you okay?" the second one asks.

"Both of you bitches get the hell out of my room right damn now!" Cameron exclaims. "Oh no… No, no, no, no!" Cam continues.

With his composure back intact, Carlos rolls over on his stomach to face Cam. "So, you tell me Cameron," he says in his thick accent, "If you are here with me, and have never left my island in over five years… how is it possible that *he* was able to post a brand-new picture with you just two days ago in Brazil?"

"He's never been on the island if that's what you're insinuating." she tells him. "Of course not," Carlos laughs a harsh, wicked laugh, "If he were ever here on my island, I would kill him."

"When I was young," Cam starts, "I was never close to my mother. She was always working or with some good for nothing guy."

"Do you have a point here Cameron?" Carlos asks.

"I'm trying to get to my point," she tells him, "my trust issues stem from my childhood. My mother looked at me and saw everything she wanted to be at my age, and she hated me for that. I did well in school, I was respectful, and I was a virgin. So, in turn she resented me, and treated me like dirt. I didn't begin to understand it all until I was grown. My mother wanted all of her children to be rotten, over-sexed, scum bags just like her. She found herself in my sister. My sister slept with every boy I ever liked, and had four different STD's before she ever reached the tenth grade."

"I never knew you had a sister Cam," Carlos says, "but why did she do that?"

"Because it was easy…" Cam says. "What do you mean?" Carlos asks.

"Megan Nicole Jiles," Cam scratches the top of her head, "Is not just my sister… she's my identical twin sister, as you should be able to tell from the picture you *thought* was me."

"Unbelievable." he shakes his head.

120

"She's the one in the picture with Keldrick," Cam mumbles, "She's the one back in Florida stealing *my* life."

"What did you just say?" he asks. "I said Megan is in Florida pretending to be me." she replies. "You sound as if you're jealous." Carlos tells her. "Not at all," she replies, "I'm just stating the obvious."

"But is it obvious," Carlos asks, "how do we know he didn't meet her, and just fall for her just like he fell for you, Whitney, and God knows who else? What makes you think, you're so special, that he would only love your twin if he believes she is you?"

"I just think…" Cam starts. "It doesn't matter what you think," he tells her, "you have no clue why he's with her. He may genuinely love her."

Carlos stands up, and dusts himself off. "In any event," he says, making his way towards the door, "I'm very tired so I'll see you in the morning."

"Of course," Cam mumbles, "so do you plan on having sex with me in my sleep, or have you made other arrangements for your nightly pleasure this evening."

"Wow," Carlos smiles at her, "you almost sounded like me, *almost* elegant. But, to answer your question though I won't be creeping back in here this evening to disturb your sleep."

"Too bad…" she sighs. "And why is that…" he asks. "I've grown to like it my love." she tells him. "Hmm, I'll keep that in mind." he says.

"So, tell me," she says, "which one of your whore maids will you be slaying tonight in your California king bed?"

"Good night Cameron." he leaves the room without another word.

As Carlos makes his way down the hallway he sees Charlie Breeze in the kitchen talking on the phone. "What are you doing up so late Charlie?" Carlos asks. "Hold on baby…" he whispers to the person on the phone, before looking behind him nervously.

121

"Doc," Charlie smiles, "I'm just up talking to my sister back in the states, checking on her and the kids." Carlos shakes his hand, as he studies his face intently.

"Charlie," he says, "you're sweating. Are you quite alright?"
"I'm fine," he replies, "it's just a little warm in the house tonight." "I guess you're right," Carlos agrees, "Jessica, and Twyla, would you both come with me to my room and help me make my bed please?" The two maids obediently head towards Dr. Sanchez's master bedroom, knowing full well what the "international play boy" has in mind for them.

"Charlie..." Carlos whispers to his confidant as the ladies exit the kitchen. "Yes Doc?" he replies. "It's okay if you're banging the women in the house they're for you too, my friend." Carlos tells him. "Any one of them..." Charlie asks.

Carlos leans close to whisper in his ear, and then he pats the handsome dread head on the back. Charlie listens closely to what Master Sanchez has to say, and then he nods in acknowledgement. Carlos shakes his hand again and smiles genuinely at him, before heading towards his room behind two of his most beautiful maids.

Carlos had his master bedroom in this particular house remodeled the day after Whitney went missing. He said it was just time for a change. Deep down he knows the way the room was before would have continued to haunt him and remind him of the yellow goddess he lost forever. He still has his Nubian queen Cameron, but in his mind, she still has to be broken a little bit more, her love for K.C. is still very much intact.

Everything from his enormous bed to the paint on the walls is completely new. Carlos even had his veranda balcony redone in illuminating gold. The good doctor feels like King Midas himself whenever he's standing out on his exquisite balcony enjoying the breathtaking island view.

His bedroom floors have been redone in blood red marble, with cream speckles throughout it. His bed is made from deep mahogany wood. The headboard has the Virgin Mary carved in it, holding the baby Jesus carefully in her arms. The ceiling is adorned with attractive modern light fixtures emitting lights that can set whatever mood he prefers, with the flip of a switch.

"What is your desire this evening Dr. Sanchez?" one of his maids asks, unbuttoning her tight shirt. Carlos smiles at her, but doesn't respond. Out of his back pocket he pulls two pair of handcuffs. After cuffing one girl with her arms and legs spread to each post at the head of the bed, he cuffs the other girl to the foot of the bed and tells her to bend over.

(2:00 AM)

Cam is sound asleep, nestled in her expensive Afghan sheets. She pretended to be sleep for as long as she could, in hopes that Carlos would come surprise her with some midnight lust. Cam's entire room is dark except for the still moonlight shinning in through the window directly on her large bed.

If the great painter Leonardo da Vinci was to paint this slumbering angel just as she is at this very moment, the famed Mona Lisa would pale far in comparison to Cameron's quiet perfection. Her breathing pattern is so sweet it could put anyone's mind at ease, to watch her sleep you would think her life was complete euphoria.

A key enters the lock on her thick bedroom door. The lock is off; the knob begins to turn. Once he steps inside her bed chamber he closes and locks the door behind him. He steps close to her bed, and then pauses for a moment.

His spirit is conflicted. He wants Cameron so badly right now, but lately Whitney has been the only thing on his mind. He takes another step closer to the black china doll. He thinks to himself, he can make love to Cam, and just imagine she's Whitney. He reaches out, and touches her lower back softly.

She doesn't move. He rubs her firm behind for several moments, heightening his own arousal. Her bedroom window isn't quite shut, as a soft breeze, wafts in slowly.

The soft wind is calming to his nerves, even in the midst of all the tiny chill bumps its creating on his strong arms. As the breeze grows stronger, it just barely raises her soft sheets off of her body momentarily, giving him a better glimpse of her.

He kneels down on his knees and begins kissing and massaging her smooth chocolate lower back. Then he makes his way to the foot of her bed and gently pulls her covers down off of her body.

Cam is lying on her side ever so comfortably. He gently pulls her knees down to straighten her body out and lay her down on her stomach. She exhales loudly one time as she tries to get comfortable in her new position.

He crawls up on her bed and makes his way up to the back of her thighs, he begins kissing them deeply. She stirs, but she's still not quite awake. He gently spreads her legs from the back, moving his hands in a swift forward motion. Her short silk nightgown is just barely covering her bottom.

With his teeth, he pulls the gown up to her lower back. Cam has on nothing underneath her gown. This fact turns him on more than anything else, as he dives in face first devouring her wet center.

Cam begins to moan softly in her sleep, as his tongue drives deeper inside of her. He eats her body for twenty minutes nonstop. Now with her bottom gripped firmly in his two hungry hands, he bites her upper thighs several times trying to regain feeling in his now numb jaw and lips. As he bites down hard on her left cheek Cam opens her eyes and smiles to herself.

(Cam)

I knew he would come. He's not the best man in the world, but just before I lose what little sanity I have left, he always comes through in a big way. He must have taken one of those pills, because he seems overly eager tonight.

Honestly, I hope he remains this way for hours. My body is so wet and my spot is throbbing fiercely. I wonder... how much I've missed. Did we already have sex, is this post sex head?

I have to stay as still as possible because I know Carlos likes to believe I'm asleep when he sneaks in late at night to have his way with me. He is the most sexually explicit man I have ever known, in that respect not even Keldrick can compare to him.

The way his lust-filled mind works is sheer genius. My God the things Whitney and I have done for, and to this man. I wouldn't change one second of the heated situations, and journeys we've experienced together on this gorgeous island.

Ooooh I love when he slaps my ass like this, well he's never quite done it this hard before, but I still like it. Now more biting, oh lord do your tongue just like that. Yes, yes, I love when he rubs it on my butt before he actually enters my body.

Yeah... he is definitely on some kind of pill because now that he's slapping my bottom with it, I can tell he's longer and more full than usual. Then again, the word usual doesn't exist on this island.

He enters her with his fingers first. Then without warning he enters her completely with his penis. She gasps for air several times, but she can't seem to find any. He continues to stroke masterfully.

"Oh, Carlos I love you..." she moans as he strokes harder, and deeper.

"Carlos... Carlos baby, say my name." she tells him. He remains silent. "Carlos..." she repeats. He quickly grabs one of her soft satin

125

pillows, and pushes it down hard on her head. Her arms begin to flail wildly. She can breathe but, the fact that he put a pillow over her head caught her by surprise.

With her lower back in the grip of his left hand, he continues to hide her face with the pillow held tightly in his right hand. With the pillow, still in his right hand, he puts his left hand down firmly on the bed and rises up in pushup position.

Then he begins jumping inside of her again at a completely different angle. In pushup position herself now, Cam arches her back upward to invite him to go deeper. Noticing the tight lavender garter on her leg, he takes a break to pull it down off of her leg.

Reaching under the pillow he puts the garter over her eyes, and blindfolds her with it. After making his way to the head of her bed he pulls her on top of him, and puts himself in her mouth. She chokes several times, but never stops.

With his hand on the back of her head he guides her quickly up and down. She knocks his hand out of the way and begins taking control of her own head, and mouth.

She gently bites the tip before engulfing it completely again. She strokes it perfectly, as she licks and kisses his chiseled stomach. He growls sensually as she bites the side of it while licking it simultaneously.

Unable to take another second of this mind-blowing pleasure, he grabs her head again and puts himself in her mouth completely as she catches and swallows all of his juices. After the last drop is gone he puts her back on her stomach and enters her from the back again.

The sexual chemistry has to be all but phenomenal for a man to finish as explosively as he just did, and still be able to keep going strong like this. He pulls her up on her knees as he continues to pound her from the back. Scratching, biting, and licking her back, he feels like he can go on like this forever.

"Carlos, I love you baby, forever and always." Cam swears. After the ten most powerful strokes of his entire life he falls forward on top of her, both of their bodies completely drenched in sweat.

As his head falls slowly on top of hers, his soft dreads fall all over her blindfolded face one after another. Cam reaches up and grabs a few of his strong locks. She pulls the garter up just high enough to see the bright red tips of his long dark dreads. She smiles, and then blindfolds herself again. They lay their together for hours just breathing in harmonious tandem.

Another key enters her door. Charlie and Cam jump up hastily, but it's too late. Carlos is standing right there staring at them both, with one of his guns in his hand already cocked. "Et tu Brute…" Carlos says, obviously drunk out of his mind.

"Doc, it's not what…" Charlie starts. "Shut up Charlie," Carlos aims the gun at him, "It's not *what,* you lazy bum? It's not what it looks like right? Well my nigga neither are you. *My nigga,* that is what you people call each other right?"

"What the hell do you mean, you people Carlos," Cam asks, "this must be a joke." "Bitch," Carlos starts, "don't *speak to me, you* will never address me again ever in your life!"

He quickly shoots at her left leg. Cam falls to the floor screaming in pain as the warm bullet grazed the side of her left calf.

Charlie knows the next shot will hit him, so he doesn't even look in Cam's direction. "Yes," Carlos continues, "you people, I said exactly what I meant to say. You people are a thousand years behind every other race, and most of you are either to blind or way too stupid to see or realize the fact."

"Carlos, you're drunk, please calm down…" Charlie pleads with him. "Call me Dr. Sanchez, boy," Carlos interjects, "we are not friends, and so don't you ever refer to me as the name my dear old mother gave to me. You don't know my mother."

"You're right Doc," Charlie agrees, "I don't know your mother but I'm sure she's a wonderful woman." Carlos laughs loudly, almost drowning out the sound of Cam's constant cries.

"Are you sure mate," he replies, "you're sure my mother is a wonderful woman? Well my mother is dead, is what she is, and she was a *ghastly* woman. Never nice to anyone, and she wasn't very pretty to look at either. My mother was a whore. She worked at a brothel back home in my country. My father, God rest his soul got my slut of a mother pregnant by mistake. He was a good man so he took her in, at least until she gave birth to me."

"Then what happened?" Charlie asks. Carlos shrugs. "He raped her in front of me when I was nine years old and then he killed her."

"I'm sorry bro…" Charlie starts. "We are not brothers," Carlos spits at him, "and no need for apologies. I was the old man's sole heir to his fortune, so after I killed him and hid his body, I only had to wait until my eighteenth birthday to reap the full benefits of my trust. I've literally been wealthy since the second I was born. But you people will all live and die with the mentality of a slave. Where is the entrepreneurial spirit in you people? Did you know that only seven percent of the business owners in America this year are black? That's sad and sick."

"If this country is so bad Doc, why did you come here?" Charlie asks.

"It's not the country's fault, you idiot," he replies, "It's you people. No one is holding any of you back from working for yourselves, but you all choose to run around working meaningless jobs, living off government assistance, and stabbing each other in the back metaphorically and literally."

"Carlos my leg is getting cold…" Cam whimpers. "Good," he replies, "If I allow you to live, hopefully they end up having to amputate it." She screams out louder than before. "Carlos…" Charlie speaks.

"Boy," he interjects, "Do not call me Carlos again. And you… after I gave you everything turned your back on me. I told you, you could all but impregnate any of the other wenches on my island, anybody except Cam! I just told you *three hours ago*! She's *my* whore!"

"I couldn't help it." Charlie admits. "What the hell does that mean?" Carlos asks.

"Carlos, you stalk in here at 4am," Cam interjects, "wearing nothing but boxers, smelling like everybody's pussy... how dare you, even pretend to be mad!" He ignores her.

"Why Charlie..." Carlos aims the gun at him once again. "Honestly," Charlie says, "I did it because I miss Whitney. She's the one I'm in love with, not Cameron."

"Damn," Carlos lowers his gun, "and you're serious aren't you Charlie?"

"I love her Doc." Charlie reaffirms.

"Who am I to stand in the way of true love," Carlos replies in his drunken accent, "it's real my boy I see it in your eyes. I was once just like you before these black whores ruined me. I'm not going to kill you tonight my friend."

"Thank you, Doc, I really appreciate that." he replies.

"What about me Carlos?" Cam asks. He ignores her again.

"Charlie," Carlos says blankly, "you have one hour to get you and this bitch off my island or you will both sleep beneath the ocean tonight."

Chapter 10
I Can Cry if I Want To

K.C. and his fiancé are riding down the street headed to their mansion. "This is so exciting," she gushes, "I've never done anything like this before in my life." "Well, there's a first time for everything baby doll." K.C. tells her.

"You're right," she agrees, "and I plan on making a lifetime out of feeling like I feel right now, being a part of things like we're doing right now, right by your gorgeous side every step of the way Mr. Cole."

(Uncle Love)

"I hate wearing puffy dresses like this Uncle Love." Jaze pouts. K.J. giggles happily from his comfortable car seat in the back seat of the car. "You look beautiful sweetie," Love tells her, "and your step mom went through a lot of trouble to pick out that dress out for you."

"Yeah, I'm sure," Jaze scoffs, "she probably had to carry the dress all the way to the counter, and then hand the cashier *my dad's* Black Card all by herself to pay for it. Ooh so much trouble…"

Love shakes his head with an amused smile on his face. "Well either way honey you look beautiful, just like your m…" "Don't say it Uncle Love," she interjects adamantly, "do not say I look like Whitney."

"But, you do look just like mommy Jazemene." K.J. agrees from the back seat. "Shut up smurf," Jaze yells at him, "I do not look like that woman." she tells him.

"Wow," Love laughs, "you remind me so much of how I used to be with my mom." her uncle tells her. Jaze can feel her entire body growing cold now. "No, I don't hate my mom *that much...* at least I hope not." she whispers to herself.

"You have to wear the dress baby girl," Love says, "besides I know you don't want to hurt your step mom's feelings." Love insists. "Oh, I wanna hurt way more than just her feelings." Jaze mumbles. "Speak up Jaze I can't hear you honey..." Love leans closer to hear what his niece is trying to say.

"Nothing Uncle Love," she pouts, "where are we going now? I got my hair done, nails done, and a new pair of heels that I don't know how to walk in. I've had enough for one day Unc."

"Can we go to *Chuck E. Cheese* Uncle Love," K.J. asks, "that's where I always go for *my birthday."* he tells him.

"Well it's not your birthday today is it *munchkin*," Jaze says to her little brother. "Uncle Love," she whines, "please tell me where we're going next, I really hate surprises."

"We are headed back to the castle now big girl so no worries just sit back and enjoy the ride with your extra cool handsome Uncle Love." They exchange pleasant smiles.

As the fire red Camaro pulls in through the gate at K.C.'s mansion Love is trying his hardest to see inside the house to make sure everything is okay, and going according to plan.

Then he parks in his normal parking space near a tall beautiful palm tree right next to the Olympic sized swimming pool Kel recently had built in the yard. Once he turns the car off, he hops out and walks around the car to get the kids out. He opens Jaze's door first, and then opens the back door to release the adorable Keldrick Jr.

Jaze doesn't wait for the two of them. Trying not to fall in her heels, she hurriedly makes her way to the back door with her key already in hand. She finds the back door unlocked and slightly ajar. This is very strange since there are no cars home.

She pushes the door open and finds the house dark, quiet, and completely still. She walks into the kitchen trying to listen carefully for any strange sounds. She knows no fear right now because she knows exactly what kind of killer she has on her side right outside the back door. She leaves the kitchen and takes a step into the living room.

"Surprise!!!" everybody yells. The lights flash on. People are screaming happily, as they hug Jaze from all directions. Random color balloons with the number eleven on them are falling from the ceiling as well. Her beautiful smiling step mom is holding her cake standing next to her proud father.

"Happy Birthday princess…" K.C. picks his pretty daughter way up high in the air and hugging her tightly. "*Oh my gosh…*" Jaze gushes, "Dad how did you do all this? I had no clue." she admits.

"Well I did have a little help from somebody…" he says. "Happy birthday sweetheart…" Jaze's teacher Ms. Bell steps forward to hug her. "Thank you, Ms. Cid," Jaze smiles, "where's Jojo?" she asks looking behind Ms. Bell.

Cidra looks up at K.C. "What," Jaze asks, "What happened? Where is Josiah? Did something happen to him? If something happened to him, I'll…"

"Jaze baby," Kel interjects, "calm down princess Jojo is probably fine. He's just not here." "What… Why not…" Jaze inquires.

Her father doesn't respond.

"Come with me Jazzy…" Cidra takes the birthday girl by the hand.

Jaze snatches her hand back. "No," she barks, "tell me right here

132

and now why my best friend… my only friend is not at my surprise birthday party." "It's okay darling, half the school is here." Megan tells her.

"Don't you talk to me," Jaze barks at her, "I would rather have had nobody show up at all and it just been me and Jojo. These kids don't really like me they just tolerate me because I'm *Kool Hand's* daughter."

A crowd is starting to form around them now. Kel steps forward. "Baby…" he says.

"No, damn it daddy." Jaze says. "It's true nobody at that school likes me," she continues, "They all hate my guts. Why…? I don't have a damn clue but I would give up every dime you have daddy just to be liked by somebody… anybody. I had Josiah, now I don't even have him anymore. I knew one day he would wake up and realize how lame I am. I knew one day he would start ignoring me too." Jaze looks down.

Jaze notices that everybody at the party is staring at her now. The tears finally begin to fall as she takes a couple of shaky painful steps back away from everybody. The warm liquid running down her legs let's her know she's ruined the party for sure now.

"To every last student from Key Point Academy," Jaze stutters now standing in a bright yellow puddle of her own urine, "I know you all hate me, and you wonder exactly what it's like to be the daughter of a rich super famous athlete. It's wonderful, is that what you want to hear? I have every single thing any of you ever dreamed of owning and I live inside of a dream every damn day… but I am the loneliest person you will ever see on this *God forsaken planet*. I have no mom, a part time dad who's spends every second with his superficial fiancé, and my grandmother is dead! Like forever… she's never coming back. So, who wins? The rich heiress to the *Kool Hands* thrown, or all of you who have friends and family who actually pay attention to you and talk to you… and not just on your… *damn* birthday." she cries.

133

As fast as her little yellow legs will carry her Jaze races up the stairs all the way to her room. Once inside she strips off the dress and heels that she never wanted to wear in the first place. She rushes to her large bedroom window overlooking the front lawn. Then she hastily opens her window.

Staring out of it she contemplates how bad diving out of her window head first is going to hurt, if she makes the mistake of not dying in the process. Instead she throws the expensive urine stained dress and heels out of her window down to the perfectly trimmed lawn.

Then she snatches the rest of her clothing off before running to her bathroom to jump in the shower. For twenty minutes, she allows the warm water to wipe her never ending tears away. Everything around her is so dark and blindingly loud. She can't seem to focus on anything and nothing matters. Nothing will ever matter again. Josiah Bell was her only hope, her only piece of normalcy.

With the soap clutched tightly in her hands she ties to reach up and grab her wash cloth off the top of the shower rod. Her entire body is sore, and it feels immensely weak.

After the most difficult shower of her entire life Jazemene Cole lays down in her bed all alone, waiting for the voices. She feels herself understanding more and more just how her crazy uncle became the way he is.

"Jazemene…" She hears the voice. She ignores it. "Jazemene..." There it is again. She doesn't react.

"Open the door big head…" the voice says. "Jojo…" she gasps. Rolling out of her princess pink bed Jaze clumsily falls to the floor trying to make it to the door.

Now standing face to face with her bedroom door covered with Chris Brown posters, she weighs her options. If she opens the door and no one is on the other side, then she's officially crazy now.

But if *he* is on the other side of the door then maybe everything will be okay.

"Jazemene Argelle' Cole if you don't open this door right now…" the voice says. She snatches the door open, and hugs him tightly. "Jojo," she cries, "What are you doing here?" she asks.

"It's your birthday big head," he smiles, "of course I came. Here this is for you." he hands her a nice sized box wrapped in shiny red paper topped with a gold bow. Jaze walks the box to her bed. After sitting it down she opens it, careful not to tear the wrapping paper too much. Inside she finds a brand-new basketball, her favorite sour skittles, and a new videogame.

"Thanks, Jojo." she hugs him.

"No sweat Jaze." he replies hugging her back. "Now come on let's go enjoy your party," he tells her, "the Donaldson twins were just about to fight over Rebecca again." he laughs.

"No," she sits on her bed with her arms folded, "nobody wants me down there."

"Look big head," Josiah looks deep in his best friend's eyes, "this is your house, your birthday, and your party. I don't care what anybody says you and me are going to go down here and eat some cake, drink some punch, and play some PlayStation 4." he tells her. She doesn't respond.

"Jaze…" he reaches out to gently grab her shoulder. "You promise you'll stay by my side the whole time?" she asks. "Of course, big head," he smiles, "we gotta be side by side so I can beat you to sleep on the PS4."

"In your dreams, white boy." she teases. They both laugh.

Jaze and Jojo have been playing video games in the den for an hour now while the party continues to go on all around them.

"Five seconds left and I got the ball what you gone do *big head*?" Jojo teases Jaze. "So, you won one game out of five, you feel good about yourself punk?" she replies with a smile.

"Hey Josiah…" a short chubby white girl approaches them.

135

"What up?" he replies in a cool tone without even looking at her.

"Nothing," she replies. Her chubby freckled cheeks begin to redden as she looks behind her towards a group of girls standing close to the punch bowl.

"Hey… Mya was looking for you," the chubby girl continues to blush; "she said to tell you… hey. And… she thinks you're hot."

Jojo looks up at the girl, and then past her at the girls standing near the punch bowl. He smiles and then waves at them.

"Oh my God…" the chubby red-faced girl squeals as she rushes back to her friends so they can all continue to stare at him from beside the near empty punch bowl.

Jaze fixes her hair silently beside him, and then straightens her clothes just a little bit. "Who was that?" Jaze asks nonchalantly.

"When…" Jojo replies. "The girl…" Jaze says. "What girl?" Josiah asks.

Jaze crosses her arms tightly. "The girl that was just standing right there Jojo…" she tells him. "Oh, I don't know her name," he tells her, "She's Lacy Bryant's cousin. Lacy Bryant is Sara Reed's best friend. And Sara Reed is Mya Reed's little sister."

Jaze hesitates. "And so, who are they?" she asks. "That's them standing over there by the table." he tells her. "No, I know that," she reaches down to cut the video game off, "but who are they… like who is Mya to you?"

"Are you being weird again Jazzy," he asks, "please tell me you *are not* being weird again." "No," she smiles nervously, "I was just asking Jojo. I mean you don't have to tell me if you don't want to, because I really don't care." she lies.

"Good," he replies, "but to be honest Mya Reed is so *hot,* but I can't let her know I *really* like her… until I'm sure I know she *really* likes me. You know what I mean right?" he asks Jaze.

"Let's go play some basketball outside." she says. "Cool," he replies, "I already beat you on the video game, now it's time for me to beat you in real life *big head*."

As they head outside walking side by side Jojo continues to talk to Jaze about how beautiful Mya Reed is with her soft blonde hair, pretty clear skin, and big blue eyes. He's talking but Jazzy can't hear a word, she's way too far gone now lost deeply inside her own paranoid thoughts.

She knows one day soon when she and her best friend start middle school she will most likely lose him forever to the nature of the puberty beast. And she just realized from the way Jojo is talking his idea of beauty isn't anything close to a little black girl. Jaze shakes her head solemnly as she picks up her good ole basketball from behind her regulation basketball goal.

She and Jojo are only going to play one game of one on one this evening, because she's not in the mood for any extra games. Jazzy knows in her heart and mind that his game will be the best ass whooping Jojo may ever receive on a basketball court in his life.

Mya Reed and her gang decide to walk outside and watch the game as well. Jaze has been known to let Josiah beat her at one on one a time or two, just so she wouldn't seem like a total butch tomboy to him. But this afternoon, with these girls watching, Jaze has every intention to destroying her best friend quickly and decisively.

The game is the first one to ten points wins. Jaze goes up early 7 to 1. Jojo is tired already and he can barely breathe. Mya Reed walks out on the court in the middle of Jaze checking the ball to Josiah, and hands him a full cup of punch. He begins drinking it as he stares back into her big blue eyes. Jaze looks on with her entire heart in flames. She swears this is the absolute slowest anybody has ever drunk a cup of juice… *ever in life*.

Jojo throws Jaze the ball with one hand. Then he gives Mya the empty cup, thanks her as she exits the court, and then jumps into his defensive stance to try to stop Jaze from scoring for once this afternoon. No luck, Jaze fakes left and then crosses the ball back overto her right leaving Jojo where he stands as she dribbles straight to the hoop and finishes with a beautiful reverse layup.

"8 to 1." she exhales deeply. Jaze grabs the ball as it comes through the hoop and throws it to Josiah.

"Come on Josiah," Mya says, "don't let this dyke beat you!" she yells from the side of the court. Jojo looks at Jaze. Jaze puts a hand on each hip with her head tilted to the side staring back at him in anticipation.

"Let's just finish the game." he throws the ball back to her. Jaze looks at Mya. "What you looking at *LeBron James*?" Mya taunts, then all of her friends being to laugh at Jaze and call her LeBron.

Jaze looks down at the ground, and then finally back up at Mya.

"You're at my house," Jaze steps towards Mya, "at my birthday party, talking crap to me."

"So, what baby Jordan?" Mya replies as she and her friends all start laughing again. Jaze steps up in Mya's face with the ball still on her side. Jojo rushes in between them.

"Jaze can we just finish the game please," he asks, "and Mya you guys just leave her alone seriously."

"No Josiah," Mya screams, "she likes you. Everybody knows it… except you." Mya tells him.

Jojo looks at Jaze. Jaze looks at Jojo, and then back at Mya.

"What is wrong with you Mya?" Jaze asks.

"You," Mya steps back closer to Jaze, "you think you're perfect because your dad is rich and famous, and you live in this big ass house. But it doesn't matter how much money your daddy makes, he still can't change your face."

"My face," Jaze says, "What's wrong with my face?" Mya bursts into cynical laughter, and then her friends soon follow suit like perfect puppets. "It's hideous." Mya tells Jaze.

Jaze looks up at Jojo. Jojo turns towards Mya with a menacing glare on his young handsome face. "You know what Mya," he shakes his head, "I thought I *really* liked you, and I thought you were

138

pretty… but now that I see the real you, I don't like you at all. And just *F.Y.I.* Jazemene is way prettier than you on her worst day."

Mya covers her mouth with both hands as her eyes triple in size. "And I think you and your giggling friends should leave so my best friend and I can finish enjoying her birthday. Come on Jazzy." he says.

Then Jojo grabs the basketball from Jaze's side and heads back to the court. *"Best friend ever…"* Jaze whispers to herself as she follows closely behind him smiling like never before. The two of them play one on one all afternoon until the sun fades away into the moon.

(That night)

After the party, the birthday girl's demons never left. Jaze is all alone in her bathroom. In the mirror, she carefully tries to look at herself without seeing her mother. She finds it virtually impossible. Even with the two huge hot pink ribbons tied on each one of her cute pigtails, dressed in her acid wash cut off overall shorts, and hot pink tube socks, she still looks exactly like an eleven-year-old Whitney.

"I hate my life. I'm young, pretty, and rich but I am the most, unhappy person I know. I just wanna go back to before everything changed. I would give up everything this new life has to offer just to be back safe at home with my mom and dad cramped up in our tiny little apartment in Orlando. Our place wasn't a palace but so what it was home. And our life wasn't perfect, but then whose life is? My dad can buy me anything, I can travel to all four corners of the earth if I want, hell my dad could probably buy me a first-class ticket to Heaven if he wanted to, but all that still doesn't equal reality. I just wanna feel something that's real. And I know I'm only eleven, but I feel like I've seen and experienced so much in my life to the point I have the right to speak my mind. Problem is… I'm always alone when I do. There's

139

so much I wanna tell my dad, but I can't. I just can't, and the last thing I wanna do is stress him out. So, I just keep it all bottled up inside of me. One thing I do know is in seven years when I turn eight-teen I'm not taking any of my dad's money with me when I leave. I'm gonna struggle at first and then stand on my own two feet. And right now... damn it I'm gonna go tell him everything that's on my mind."

Jaze takes one bold step outside of her bathroom into the hallway. With every step, she makes towards his door her nerves seem to be growing stronger. As she enters her father's room everything seems to be moving in slow motion.

"Don't you know how to knock little girl!" Megan barks at her, peeping her own head out from under the covers. K.C. looks up at his daughter and then quickly scoots back away from his wife but makes sure to keep himself completely covered.

Megan jumps up with a scowl on her face and stalks past Jazemene into their bathroom. Once inside she makes her way to the toilet and spits inside of it before flushing it twice. Then she grabs her tooth brush, puts a generous amount of toothpaste on it, and then begins scrubbing her mouth vigorously with it. All the while she's staring at Jaze through venomous eyes.

Jaze can't move. She's just standing there in the doorway unsure what to say or do. Her father is having an equally as awkward moment. "Damn," Megan says, "One of ya'll say something it's getting weirder and weirder in here by the second."

"What's wrong baby?" Kel asks his daughter. "Nothing," she turns around to leave, "I'll tell you later..."

"No," Kel says putting on some pants, "come here princess and tell daddy what's wrong."

"I'll tell you what's wrong," Megan interjects with a hand on each hip, "you're more worried about your little emo princess than your queen!" "Cameron shut the hell up," he demands, "come here to me Jaze."

140

Jaze reluctantly obeys. "Are you still upset about the party," he asks, "Josiah showed up, and what his mother thought couldn't have been further from the truth."

"What is it exactly that she thought?" Jaze asks trying to sound mature in an adorable tone.

"Well…" her father starts. "Josiah told his mom," Megan interjects, "that he wasn't going to come to your party."

"What? But why…" Jaze asks. She can feel her heart beginning to race instantly. "Because," she continues with a smile on her dark face, "he said soon you and him couldn't be friends anymore."

"What he said was," Kel starts, "you are both going to middle school next year. And that the two of you should have friends… that you may have more in common with." "What does that mean Daddy?" Jaze asks.

"Baby it just means that you should make some female friends, and he can hang out with some guys from time to time." K.C. tells her.

"But Josiah is my only friend." she admits. "Well after what I saw today," he kisses her on her forehead, "I don't think he's gonna stop being your best friend anytime soon baby. But what was really on your mind when you came in here?"

Jaze looks at Megan and considers outing her to her father. She could tell him right now that this woman he's sleeping with every night; the woman he claims he loves is just the evil twin of the woman who he's actually in love with. But with her own personal troubles feeling like they're multiplying by the second, she decides to leave that story untold, at least for tonight.

"Nothing daddy," Jaze fakes a smile, "I just wanted to give you a kiss goodnight."

"Good girl." Megan smiles at her. Jaze hugs her father tightly, rolls her eyes at the phony Cameron, and then heads back to her own bedroom to rest lightly amongst the demons.

(Brazilian Vacation)

If you're ever lucky enough to be on location for the most popular Brazilian two-week holiday of the year, you have to start in the unforgettably vivacious ***Rio de Janeiro*** where you can sightsee and relax on the famed ***Copacabana Beach***. Copacabana is a neighborhood located in the South Zone of the city of Rio de Janeiro, Brazil. It is best known for its four Kilometer ***Balneario beach***, which is one of the most famous in the world.

"Bae this beach is unbelievable." Megan sighs. K.C. smiles down at her through his dark gold encrusted Versace sunglasses. "Believe it Cameron," he tells her, "welcome to the rest of your life. My mission is to make sure you wake up every morning inside of your own lucid dreams." "Damn," she smiles, "sounds good to me Mr. Cole."

As they walk along the beach hand in hand, they're both pleasantly lost deep inside of the rich, local, Brazilian beauty. From the scenery to the people everything seems effortlessly flawless. What is this wondrous land in the pure eyes of God that He blessed it so abundantly?

"Has this place always been this gorgeous?" Megan asks. "Always," he replies, "if we traveled to a different exotic location every day for the rest of our natural lives we could never see all the beauty this planet has to offer babe." he tells her.

"That's crazy." she says. "I know." he agrees.

"I read somewhere," K.C. starts, "that, this district was originally called ***Sacopenapã***, until the mid-18th century."

"So, what happened?" Megan asks bending down to pick up an exotic blue rock. "Apparently it got renamed after they built an enormous new chapel here. It houses a replica of the ***Virgin de Copacabana***."

"The, what kind of virgin…" Megan asks, happily placing the

exotic rock in her beige Michael Kors crossover bag. *"The Virgin de Copacabana,"* he tells her, *"the patron saint of Bolivia."*

Megan smiles up at her man. "You are way too smart to just be a football player babe." she tells him. Kel laughs. "Wait, what the hell does that mean baby? Not every athlete is a dumb jock." he protests. "I know but from the outside looking in who would ever think
you would be the man you truly are?" she gushes.

"Well thank you Cam," he smiles, "but honestly I owe a lot of it to you." "Me," Megan asks, "What did I do?"

"You know how Whitney used to try to handicap me?" he asks. "Um, yeah…" Megan pretends to remember. "Well Cameron you changed my life when you encouraged me and helped me get my G.E.D. Then you gave me your second car, and even helped me get a real job. I owe you the world, and that's why I'm giving it to you now."

"Wow," Megan sighs, "Cam did… I mean I did do all that huh?" "Yes, you did my gorgeous fiancé!" K.C. exclaims picking her up in his massive arms.

Holding her up in the air in front of him, and now close to his body he begins kissing her, never caring who or if anybody is watching them." He knows there is no better experience than to be lost inside of and drowning in an everlasting love that will never break or fold.

Megan cares less, and less every second about the fact that she is living and ultimately stealing a perfect life that rightfully belongs to her twin sister. She finds herself helplessly drunk in this moment, as her legs hang down, with both of her pretty dark chocolate feet dangling carelessly far above the pure white sand.

As her feet touch the ground again Megan is careful not to lose his eye contact, or to leave his grasp too soon. She knows she's fighting against the inevitable; she must build these moments and unforgettable experiences with this man so that if the time ever comes for her to battle her sister for his heart she will have just as many mental weapons as the real Cameron if not more. After the moment passes Megan surveys her surroundings trying to regain her calm.

"So where are we now babe, is this the third or the fourth beach so far?" she asks. K.C. looks around in search of a sign, or a landmark.

"Um," he pauses, "Copacabana begins at Princesa Isabel Avenue and ends at *Posto Seis*, which means lifeguard watchtower Six." he rambles trying to buy time. "So, where are we now exactly?" she asks again.

"Towards the end of Copacabana, I believe," he guesses, "on the other side of it there are supposed to be two much smaller beaches. One, inside of *Fort Copacabana* and the other, right after it is called *Diabo Beach*."

Megan pulls her phone out to utilize her GPS system. "We don't need that Cam." Kel smiles as he notices what his fiancé is doing.

"Come on the hotel is this way." he walks in the direction he's pointing towards. "Okay, I trust you babe." she says putting her phone back in her bag, as she follows closely behind him.

"This is our last night here in Brazil Cameron." he sighs. "I know," Megan replies, "let's stay another couple of days." "We can't babe." he tells her. "Why can't we…" she asks.

"The kids." he reminds her. Megan ignores the comment and continues to follow closely behind him. "Tonight, I'm taking you to *Iguazu Falls*," Kel says, "and we're going to get butt naked and make love underneath the waterfalls'."

"Where have you been all my life Keldrick Cole?" Megan smiles and grabs hold of his huge black hand. "Waiting on you *my life…*" he replies blissfully.

"You mean my *love*…" Megan corrects him.

"No," he shakes his head looking at her, "baby you're much more than just the love of my life, you *personify* it. Every single thing I am... *is you*."

(Six Hours Later)

Staring out their expensive hotel room window K.C. can see that because of the massive amount of rainfall he won't be able to keep good on his sexy plans for the evening with his gorgeous fiancé.

"So now what?" she asks walking up behind him. He sighs unable to find words to respond. "Hey," she steps around in front of him to see his eyes, "it's okay babe. We already had more than enough fun this weekend."

"Yeah, I guess you're right." he agrees. "I am right," she tells him, "and before we wake up early in the morning and catch our flight back home, we have this huge, beautiful hotel room all to ourselves."

Kel begins to run his fingers through her hair vigorously. "And so, what is your point Ms. Jiles?" he teases. "First of all," she smiles, "my name is Mrs. Keldrick *"Kool Hands"* Cole, and my point is for the next seven or eight hours you can do whatever you want to me. I wanna be your ultimate fantasy."

"You already are." he scoops his queen up into his arms in route to their huge grandiose hotel bed. On top of her in complete lustful control he puts one strong hand on either side of her head so he can stare down into her pretty brown eyes.

"Don't look at me like that bae." she pleads. "And why not?" he inquires. "Because..." She grins, "you know how I get, you're making me mess up my panties baby at least take em' off for me first."

"Or what..." he growls playfully. "It's your world," she tells him, "What would you like me to do for you first Mr. Cole?" she asks before slowly licking her full lips.

K.C. kisses her on the lips softly twice. Then he jumps up out of the bed impulsively, and walks towards the closet. "What are you doing now?" she asks still laying submissively in the middle of the enormous bed. "Getting ready." he tells her. "For…" she asks.

"Our date, come get dressed. Put on that tight white Alexander McQueen dress I bought you in New York last week." he tells her.

"Where are we going," she asks, "It's raining cats and dogs outside babe. And I'm having a hell of a private storm my damnself right between my legs, and I need daddy to come see can he **stand the rain** like Boyz 2 Men." Megan continues to watch him as she rubs herself just the right way. "Get up baby." he says.

"Fine." she groans.

Downstairs in the hotel dressed in some of their finest clothing the couple finds a near empty bar and some soft American music wafting through the calm sweet air. Keldrick orders a large bottle of champagne. "I'll be back," Megan touches his left shoulder, "I have to use the little girl's room."

"Okay." he replies.

As Megan walks out of the bathroom she sees two ladies whispering excitedly and pointing. "Hey is that K.C. Cole sitting over there." one of the ladies asks Megan before she can walk past them. "Yea he's my fiancé." Megan replies. "You are the luckiest girl

in the Universe." the second lady tells her. Megan looks over at KC solemnly.

"No actually my sister is the luckiest girl in the universe," she tells the ladies, "I just lucked up and put her shoes on one day, and never took em' off."

After Megan returns to the table, she and K.C. sit together for hours talking about nothing until they finish the entire bottle of champagne.

Hours later they stumble happily back into their room. "Let's play a game." Megan says. "Sure Cameron," he slurs, "What position do you wanna play?"

She laughs heartily. "No, not football silly," she tells him, "like a question game."

"Like **truth or dare**?" he mumbles with both eyes closed.

"No," she says, "I got it. I'm gonna name a movie, and then you name your favorite character from the movie, and tell me why you picked them."

"Okay you go first Cam." he slurs.

"Damn I'm drunk." she laughs. "I've never seen that movie babe, who was in it?" Kel asks in complete confusion.

"That ain't a movie boy," she giggles, "with yo drunk ass. Okay let's see your movie is… **The Best Man**." she says.

"Part one or two?" he asks "The first one." she confirms. "Aw man," he slurs, "that was a classic."

"Stop stalling boy," she tells him playfully, "you only have ten seconds to answer the question."

"So, you just making up the rules as we go huh?" he asks with one eye open. "Yep…" she replies. He laughs. "Let's see," he hesitates, "**The Best Man**, my favorite character was Harper. He reminds me of who I really wanna be in life."

Megan bursts into jubilant laughter. "Wait babe," she mumbles, "Harper though bae?" "Yeah…" he says.

"The writer K.C.?" she asks. "So now you De'Lure you write books and shit, right?" she continues barely able to control her amusement.

"Hell no," he laughs, "What was Morris Chestnut's character's name?" he asks. "Lance bae." she tells him.

"Yea, that's his name, *Lance*," he corrects himself, "you know who the hell I meant heifer." They both laugh.

"Anyways it's my turn," he says, "**Brown Sugar**." "**Brown Sugar babe**…" Megan sings soulfully. "That's an easy one boo," she continues, "I love Sanaa Lathan's character my girl Sydney, hell I use to be just like her. But my favorite was Taye Diggs old fine ass.

Yeah, he brought his character Dre to life for me. It was one of his best rolls ever for sure." she recollects. Kel smiles at his fiancés contagious excitement.

"My turn," she mumbles, feeling even drunker than before, "What about... **The Wood**." she says.

"The Wood," he smiles, "all the main women in that movie were gorgeous. But I gotta go with the whole clique as my favorite for **The Wood**. Mike, Slim, and Rowland, reminded me so much of Jay, Ty, and me when we were growing up."

"Are you kidding me," Megan asks, "you cannot pick all three of them. Pick one." she tells him. "I can't bae that's too hard." he tells her.

"Do it." she demands trying not to fall off the bed.

"Fine," he agrees, "Big Mike from **North Carolina.**"

"Ugh," she laughs, "you gotta say it **just** like him though?"

"Hell yea," K.C. mumbles, "that's my dude. **Big Mike**..." K.C. lies back on the bed to rest his eyes.

Megan lies on his hard stomach. "Last movie babe." she says.

"*The* **Titanic**... by Mr. Tyler Perry." he slurs.

"Tyler Perry **did not** write the Titanic," she giggles, "and it is not your turn, but nice try sir. **Anyways**... who is your favorite character from **Miami Dreams**?" she asks.

K.C. hesitates before responding. "I never saw it or heard of it baby." he admits. "Well, that's because it's our unique love story," she tells him, "I just haven't written it yet."

"Oh, in that case," he says, "my favorite character will **always** be the beautiful perfect Cameron Jiles." He leans forward and kisses her softly on the lips.

After he lies back down peacefully, Megan is left staring out of the dark distant window gloomily.

"That's what I'm afraid of." she whispers to herself.

Chapter 11
Unfinished Business

(LOVE)

I can't just continue to kill everybody who I have a problem with. It's going to get out of hand very soon. I can't lose, or die now because I have a son. My own child... to mentor and raise the way I want to raise him. I can stop killing people, the question is, do I really want to? The core of who I am is so evil now.

I'm so angry at people. They talked about me for years and made me feel like a terrible blotch on the perfectly knit fabric of their world. To be outcast by no fault of your own, that is the worst thing any human with a heart or soul could ever experience. And so, then your heart grows cold, and you lose whatever soul you thought you had before, because it doesn't matter how much good you are doing now, someone will try to hold you to the past because their present pales in
comparison to yours.

If I could speak to the youth all around the world I would say, never give anybody the power to hold you to your past. The only thing that matters is your present and your future. I can and will stop killing... for my son I will do that. But first, Dr. Granger, my brother's father Paul, and Whitney all have to be taken care of.
Dressed in all black pants, a dark hoodie, and black gloves, Love

pulls up near the house his GPS has guided him to. It's almost 1am, and the dark streets are deathly quiet. He parks his car two houses down from the victim's residence.

He checks his weapon to make sure it's ready to do his will. He places four tiny homemade explosives and their remote control inside his hoodie pocket. It's time. Love drove all the way from Miami to Orlando for this long-awaited mission. Just before opening his door he pulls his hoodie down far over his face.

As he exits his vehicle he notices a mysterious, but familiar light blue Camry parked just down the street. He doesn't mind though, if the person in the car wants to join the bloodbath, Love welcomes all willing participants. Love purposely leaves his car unlocked with the keys resting on the passenger seat.

He begins to walk normally, paying attention to every step he takes down the calm street. Just before he reaches the right house, he takes a sharp turn and quickly runs behind the house. He wanted to just be patient, and at least try to be normal, but he can't the intrigue and anxiety, are shooting his adrenaline to its maximum building point. He wants so badly to scream and shout for sadistic joy. He contains the strong urge because he can't afford to make a mistake, this kill is far too important to him.

The back door is locked. As Love tries to pick the lock to the back door, he notices the kitchen window at the back of the house is just barely ajar. He pushes it open wider, careful not to make any noise.

He can hear a television on nearby, but he doesn't panic. Why should he panic, he's the one with the gun and no conscious? He reaches through the window to move a couple of chairs back out of his way, so he can climb in through the window.

Once inside he crouches down to survey his surroundings. In the den, he can see three small children, who all appear to be up watching TV. Love doesn't care if the children see him but he doesn't want them to scream and alert their parents, so he makes his way near them as stealthily as possible.

On the kitchen counter, he sees scissors and duct tape. He places them both in his large pockets. Now that he's closer he can see two of the kids are awake but the third is sound asleep. Standing right behind the oldest child a girl, Love puts his gun to her head. Her little brother looks at her and covers his mouth, in pure fear.

"If either of you scream, I'm going to kill you all." he tells them.

In the corner of the room he sees some old rope. He uses it to tie both of their arms behind their backs. Then he takes the duct tape and securely covers their mouths with it.

On the small table, next to the sofa he sees car keys with the initials P.J. on them. He grabs the keys, and then makes both children walk through the kitchen towards the garage.

Inside the garage he finds a brand-new pearl blue Cadillac. Love has always hated the color blue. He steps forward and disarms the car by pressing a button on the remote part of the keychain. Then he begins carving his name in the side of the gorgeous car.

The scraping sound irritates the children's ears as they begin to wince. After finishing his art work on the side of the car Love opens the front door, and places the young girl in the driver's seat. Next, he puts the key in the ignition, cranks the car, and closes her door. Then he walks her little brother around and puts him in the passenger seat and closes his door. Then he disappears back inside the house.

Moments later he returns carrying the third child still sleeping calmly in his arms. With his free hand, he opens the back door and lays the child across the back seat, and then softly closes the door. Love then walks to the front of the car to admire his hard work through the front windshield.

The girl in the driver's seat is about fourteen years old, the child in the back seat can't be older than four, and the boy on the passenger side is ten.

He's definitely ten, Love can tell, and he can tell something else as well. The look, in his eyes is different from his sister's. He wants help, but not the same help she wants. Love feels drawn to the boy. He knows exactly what the look in the child's eyes represents. His soul is crying, and dying. Love slams his hands down on the hood. He can't in good taste leave these three innocent children to die in this garage, they've done nothing wrong. He walks around and opens the passenger side door.

He kneels down and looks closely in the boy's eyes. "Did he touch you?" Love asks the boy. The look of shock is all the confirmation Love needs.

"Don't be ashamed," Love tells him holding back old tears, "when I was younger than you he messed with me too. But… but he will never hurt another child ever again after tonight. Because tonight, Love is going to pull his number and send him straight to Hell. You did nothing wrong, and you will be fine in the future just love yourself and never look back."

Love closes his door and walks around to the driver's side door. He opens it. "Do you know how to drive?" he asks the young teen. She nods her head slowly. Love pulls the sharp scissors out of his pocket.

The young girl tries hard to scream but can't. Love takes the scissors and unties her hands. "Look," he explains, "you're going to drive down the street and around the corner to the McDonald's on Sandlake Road, and wait for your mother to call you. Do you have your cell phone?" the teen nods again.

"Okay, now go." he tells her. Love stands back and opens the garage door, by pressing the button by the top of the door that leads back to the kitchen.

They drive off, and then Love lets the garage door back down. Stepping back inside the house he pulls his gloves back firmly on his hands as he steadies himself for his next task.

Let's see what we can find. If I was a prick like Paul where would I hide anything of value? All the obvious prick places probably... like the freezer, rarely used closets, and under his mattress.

I really just want to end his life as gruesome as possible, but this asshole took so much from me and my childhood, I have to steal some of it back. I hated him, and lived a lie for years and years because I didn't understand that he was created by God, to alter my existence and elevate me to the creature I have become.

I will never know love again; Whit was my only chance but she's so far gone mentally now to the point I wouldn't even consider traveling back down that dim path again. And in turn she must die, and I have to be the cause of her death just so I can be okay.

So far in the garage, the freezer, and the broom closet I've found about five hundred cash, and assorted fine jewelry that I can probably pawn. This man stole so much money from my late mother, Satan rest her dark soul before you destroy it.

Paul to this day still sells thousands of illegal pills a week to minors. That's where the majority of his cash comes from. He is a monster in every sense of the word. Because of him I never even had decent clothes and shoes to wear to school. He used to pay me sometimes for what he did to me, but he would always get mad and take everything back from me.

This womanizing punk stole so much money over the years from countless insecure women, who were so weak they allowed him to come into their homes, and destroy everything he came in contact with. They supported all of his disgusting habits. The cocaine and alcohol would have been fine, but why did he have to touch... I'm done. I've dealt with this pain way too long it ends tonight, it ends now.

After several back and forth trips, Love has now stashed all of

153

the cash, jewelry, and assorted electronics in the trunk of his fiery red Camaro. As he walks back towards the house for the last time, everything around him seems to be moving in slow motion. He is no longer in control.

The little demon inside of him is taking over again. His alter ego Lance is in his mind teasing him, and simultaneously prodding him to commit each crime with flawless evil intent. Love used to fear Lance but now he embraces him and his careless thought process.

Once back inside the house, Love falls down to his knees to pray for Paul's sins, his own sins, and the sin he is about to commit. Lance laughs as Love finishes his sincere prayer. Back up on his feet Love heads towards the Promised Land.

Paul is only about twenty feet away from him now. Love can already smell the blood he will shed tonight.

Love slowly opens the door to Paul's master bedroom. The large man is sound asleep snoring something awful. The room is huge. Out of the window on the far wall he can see the calm street from which he just came. He knows when Paul laid down hours ago he expected to wake up the next morning and continue to live his sick lie of a life. Not this time.

The bathroom door is wide open, and Love can hear the shower head leaking methodically. There are assorted clothes thrown all over the bed and floor. The walls are covered with loads of seemingly happy family pictures. It's easy to see everything in the room because it's lit by a bright red-light bulb.

Paul no doubt used the light last night in one of his sick fantasies with his current whore. Poor woman, the horror she's going to experience tonight is going to be a bit much but one day she'll understand. "Enough!" Lance whispers to Love.

Love takes two more bold steps and now he's standing over the monster. He seems so much weaker and smaller now, completely vulnerable. This monster is mortal. Love can't help but revel in the power he feels in this moment.

He firmly presses his loaded weapon to Paul's head. His snoring stops and his eyes open immediately. Love has one finger to his lips with a sick gleam in his eyes.

Paul knows exactly what the one finger pressed against the young man's lips means. Scared for his worthless life he doesn't make a sound.

Love motions for him to get out his bed. He follows instructions very well with a powerful handgun to his head. Love walks him down the hall to the little boy's bedroom.

After walking Paul inside the small room, Love closes the door behind him. The child's bedroom is eerily reminiscent of Love's old childhood bedroom. There's an old football, an almost flat basketball, and countless other supposedly masculine childish toys strewn all over the place.

Love drops a couple of coldhearted tears, as he relives his past in his mind once again. He imagines what the little boy goes through nightly with this sick old monster, in this very room. Love thinks back. He remembers sometimes when Paul would finish him off he would stash his bloody underwear under his mattress.

Love swiftly lifts the little boy's small mattress up. Underneath it he sees five small pair of underwear, some stained with blood, others are ripped. He angrily grabs two pair and then slams the mattress back down. At this Paul flinches in real fear. Love no longer cares how much noise he makes, his new whore is never going to wake up, no matter how much racket he makes.

On the table, next to their bed Love saw a bottle of the same high-powered prescription sleeping pills, Paul used to make his mother take every night. His mother was dead to the world from 8pm to 8am almost every day.

"Sit down!" Love tells the monster. "Look man," Paul pleads, "I

155

don't know who you are…" "You know me very well," Love interjects, "Now sit your old ass down before I kill you prematurely."

"Son, you don't want to do this." Paul cries. "Never call me son again," Love tells him, "just shut the hell up and sit your sick ass down now!" Love exclaims.

"Sit where?" he responds nervously. "On the bed, you fucking retard!" Love yells. As soon as the large man sits down Love shoves the child's bloody underwear in his face.

"Inhale," he screams, "inhale the blood, pain, and innocence you stole and caused mother fucker!" Paul begins to choke at the harsh odor of the soiled underwear, being forced in his face. Love pulls the underwear back, and   then
slaps him hard in the face twice with them.

"Who the hell are you?" Paul asks in confused agony. Love snatches his hood off. Paul stares into his terrifying eyes, still completely lost. Love kneels down just a few feet in front of him and hesitates.

"Paul," he starts, "you, old miserable pervert, I am Lance Orlandis Vinson, but you knew me as Lance Cole, or "Red"."

"Red…" Paul whispers with his hands held tightly over his mouth. Love slaps Paul's hands away from his mouth. "Don't cover that evil mother fucker now," he says, "I want to hear you talk. Talk nigga! You been talking and running, ***and ruining people*** your entire life. ***Do not*** get quiet now. Tell me, I want to know why, you despicable cunt. Why do you do the sick things you do?"

Paul looks away, as his tears begin to fall down his hard face. "Answer my question Paul," Love screams, "and why did you pick me? I was a hideous little kid to say the least. Why me…"

"I um," Paul starts, "I have a problem…"

"Yeah, nigga I know," Love laughs harshly, "no worries though I'ma solve it tonight. Stand up!"

"No Lance, don't…" Paul starts. "Lance is not here you bastard," Love pauses, "you know what? Lance is here."

Lance smiles manically to himself. "You raped and molested Love," he continues, "but now you fuckin' with Lance the sick angry demon that lives inside of Love. I have always had what it takes to destroy you."

"What the hell…" Paul cries.

"Stand up and turn around now," he yells, "I will not ask you again."

Paul stands up hesitantly and turns his back to Lance. Lance pushes his head as hard as he can to make him bend over.

"Pull your pants down." Lance commands. "What…" Paul replies. *BANG!* Lance shoots him in his left Achilles tendon. Paul screams out in throbbing pain. He quickly pulls his pajama pants down to his ankles.

"Boxers too, you idiot…" Lance screams louder. Paul obeys. Lance grabs two pencils off a nearby dresser and sticks them both inside of Paul.

"Oh God!!!" Paul screams out. "No," Lance pushes both pencils in deeper, "Don't call on God now. Besides he won't answer your worthless prayers anyway."

Once the pencils are almost deep enough that he can barely see them he snatches one back out, and leaves the other in place. The soiled pencil in his hand is covered in feces and fresh blood.

"Just kill me damn it!" Paul screams out. "Oh, I plan to." Lance replies laughing happily.

"No please don't kill me," Paul begs, "I have a wife and kids. Your brother is my son as well. Where… where is Kevin, I mean Kendal?" "The best thing you ever did in life was create that man," Lance shakes his head, "and you can't even remember his damn name. My big brother's name is Keldrick."

"Justine!!" Paul yells out. Lance laughs loudly, as he turns

157

around towards the door. "Wait let me help you." Lance opens the bedroom door.

"Justine," Paul yells again, "Justine baby please come save me!" Lance kicks Paul swiftly in his behind pushing the other pencil completely inside of him.

"So, you went from calling on God, to calling on that worthless bitch?" Lance asks. "If God won't save you," he continues, "nobody will. And we both know Justine isn't coming. She's dead to the world. Those same pills you have her taking, kept my mother asleep for most of my childhood." The blood from Paul's rectum is running down the back of his old hairy legs.

Now Lance steps forward and forces his gun inside of him. In and out, in and out, he continues to penetrate the monster with his gun as he cries out in silent dismay.

"Cry you evil bitch," Lance screams at the top of his lungs, "Cry, I want you to cry. You could cry for a year straight nonstop and your tears still wouldn't add up to all the tears you caused me."

Paul lays his face flat on the bed.

"Say you're sorry!" Lance yells. "I am…" Paul mumbles. "Say it!" Lance screams. "I am," Paul cries, "I'm sorry Lance." "When Love calls, you answer motherfucker…" Lance whispers to him.

BANG, BANG, BANG!! Lance pulls the trigger three times with the gun stuck deep inside of Paul. Now that Lance has killed Paul, Love then snatches his gun away, and steps back to admire the beauty.

In his mind Paul's brain splattered all over the closet door and on the wall in front of him, is the most beautiful abstract art piece he has ever seen.

After putting Justine in his car still sound asleep, Love reenters the house. In the bathroom, he quickly washes his sweaty grimy face. Then he places the small explosives from his pocket, in four strategic places inside the house. Love sets Paul's limp body and the entire house on fire and then runs as fast as he can back to his car. As he drives off with Justine safely in his passenger seat he detonates all four explosives with the tiny remote in his pocket. The house shakes feverishly, and then implodes as it continues to burn.

"God, I feel so much better now that I sent that bastard to hell... and blowing the house up was extreme but I really don't give a shit." Love mumbles to himself as he drives off. Seconds later the mysterious light blue Camry, from down the street pulls up in front of the burning house. Then the driver of the Camry hops out and runs towards the house.

When Love finally pulls up to the McDonald's on Sandlake Road, he finds the three children all sound asleep in the car. He puts their mother in the back seat next to the youngest child. In their trunk, he puts twenty-five hundred dollars cash, and in her lap, he leaves a short note explaining about the money, where to find it, and most importantly who and what Paul was. In the note, he also advises Justine to pray without ceasing, never look back, and simply move forward with her life for herself and for her children.

Chapter 12
Familiar Pain

(Kel)

K el notices his baby girl hasn't been around lately. He begins to search the house for her, but he can't find her anywhere. He calls several of his neighbors who also have children to see if maybe she went to one of their houses without asking. None of the other kid's parents or the children themselves have heard from or seen Jaze either. Kel lays back frantically on his huge bed, growling in pure agony.

Megan walks in. "Did you check her room babe?" she asks calmly. "No," he replies, "it's way too early for her to be in bed, she's missing again."

"I'm sure she's just somewhere hiding in this huge castle of yours my love." she says.

"Where is my brother?" he asks. "Tyrone or Lance…" Megan asks.

"Don't play with me right now Cam," he shouts, "where is Lance? Last time Jaze went missing he had kidnapped her, and held her for ransom!"

"Oh wow," Megan replies trying to act like Cam, "well I'll go call his cell and see if he picks up."

After she's gone K.C. crawls out of bed, and makes his way to

Jaze's room. He hesitates briefly outside her door to pray. When he opens the door, his eyes begin to water as he races to his baby girl hanging limp out of the side of her bed.

"Jaze!"he screams. No response. "Jaze...Jaze baby what's wrong," he continues, "Are you okay?" He can feel her pulse. He picks her limp body up in his arms and carries her to his bathroom, shutting the door behind him.

The door slam wakes Jaze up. "Daddy..." she mumbles. "Yes baby," he replies, "Jaze you scared daddy. Are you okay princess?" "No Daddy." she replies. "What's wrong princess?" he asks.

"Cam..." she mumbles. "Cam what," he asks, "Did she do something to you Jazemene? Do not lie to me." "No Daddy," she replies, "I love Cam." K.C. smiles at his daughter's polite words.

"Then what's wrong baby?" he asks again. "She's not Cam," Jaze starts, "I had a nightmare Daddy. I was fighting with Cam's twin sister. Then I think I fell down and bumped my head, I really don't know what happened everything just went black Daddy."

"Awe baby," K.C. says, "I'm sorry you had a bad dream, but Cam doesn't have a sister. And never say nightmare, we do not have nightmares. Sometimes we just have bad dreams. Okay baby?"

"Okay Daddy." she replies obediently. "But Daddy," Jaze starts, "Why do you love her more than me and K.J.?" "I don't..." Kel says. "Yes, you do Daddy..." Jaze cuts him off quickly, "you never spend any time with us at all."

"You are absolutely right baby," he agrees, "first I was always too busy with football, now I'm spending every second with Cameron. But Jaze Daddy needs you to understand that I missed Cam very much, and I want to spend time with her too."

"I know Daddy," she says, "but why can't we spend time together as a family?" "Is that what you want baby?" he asks. "Yes daddy." she replies.

"Then you got it kiddo," K.C kisses his princess on the forehead, "after the wedding, I'm going to take everybody to some foreign country we've never been to before, and we're gonna stay gone for at least a week."

"Cool," she smiles, "you promise Daddy?"

"Pinky promise…" he offers her his right pinky. They shake pinkies, and then they hug before K.C. carries Jaze back to her room.

(Detective O. Blue)

I have never experienced a killer like this. This man is no everyday criminal mastermind, he is something extraordinary. No one on this planet would ever catch him without my help; they wouldn't even get close without getting murdered and burned alive themselves. But I've embraced the nature of the beast and the criminal element in general. To catch a killer as talented as Lance Orlandis Cole, one would have to research fiercely and then mentally become the man himself. The problem is once you know the tragedy that is his past, you no longer want to catch him or stop him. You find yourself rooting for him to make the bastards from his past life pay for every last injustice they
ever placed upon his young life.

I have never actually spoken to Lance, but I plan to. The beautifully insane havoc that he's reaping on the streets of Miami and Orlando has to stop, but he must be stopped the right way. He has to finish his unfinished business or it will continue to haunt and torment him, and so I want him to finish off the last legit hit on his list… Dr. Bruce Granger.

Just a block up the road and around the corner, Lance was waiting, hiding behind Granger's private practice facility almost twenty minutes ago. I'm sure he's done by now. I'm about to pass by the front of the office now.

162

The front looks calm, wait its deserted. I see a car, probably Granger's but I don't see anybody else. I'll just park my car right here at the corner. No need to lock it. There's nothing of any real value in here. Let's go, the office is about fifty feet up ahead.

The front door is unlocked. Okay I'm in now. Damn this place is eerily quiet. Dr. Granger has to already be dead.

"Daddy!" a child shouts. Detective Blue crouches down quickly and begins to crawl in the direction of the now continuous screams of the child.

When Blue reaches the area where the screams originated from, the detective carefully stands up to peek inside the window of what appears to be Granger's main office.

Close to the wall in the back of the office, Lance has Granger's wife and son tied down in office chairs. The child a young boy is screaming his head off as he watches Lance beat his father to a bloody pulp.

His mother, who's sitting right next to him, must have passed out minutes ago. Her restrained body is completely still, her eyes are closed, and the side of her lifeless face is covered in drool."

Love pulls his gun out of his pocket and walks towards the screaming little boy. "Shut the hell up little boy!" Love demands.

"Do not cry for you father," he continues, "your father does not deserve your tears. He is a sick bastard pedophile, who deserves every bit of what he's finally getting today."

Without another word Love cocks his faithful handgun and stalks back to Dr. Granger. Love then roughly grabs the aging psychiatrist by what little hair he has left on top of his head to hold him up strait.

"You set me free from a physical prison," Brucie, "but you also helped force me inside of an emotional and spiritual prison with an eternal life sentence. So, for that you don't deserve to exist in my world."

"You deserved everything…" Dr. Bruce Granger mumbles

through the blood. "What did you say?" Love asks. "Everything that ever happened to you," Bruce mumbles, "you deserved it. *You... little... ugly...faggot!*"

"I'm glad you feel that way Brucie," Love shoves his beautiful gun into Granger's fat hideous mouth, "*When Love calls bitch...*" Love empties the entire clip in his head and throat.

The young boy resumes screaming, now much louder than before. Love spins around with the second gun from his pocket and fires two shots in the direction of the boy. The boy immediately falls limp in a posture that is almost identical to the one his mother is in. Love didn't shoot him, but the bullets were enough to cause the child to faint. Detective Blue heads back to the car, after watching Love's display of pure glorious revenge.

(Later that night in Miami)

Kel is sound asleep in his bed lying on his back next to his gorgeous fiancé who is also asleep. He begins to stir. His lower body is tingling, and his blood is flowing rather feverishly now. He can feel himself squirming to a strange rhythm.

He's not quite alert, so his body just continues to go with the flow. He can feel a hand on his stomach. His boxers are soaking wet, and he can hear a familiar sound just barely now. He opens his eyes, and down below he can see a head beneath the sheets going up and down quickly.

He quickly looks to his left, and sees his fiancé is completely unaware of what's transpiring less than a foot away from her. Kel tries to push the head away from him, but the sensation is almost too much to resist.

He slowly lifts the blanket to find Whitney hard at work. She stops for a second to smile up at him. She puts one finger up to her wet lips.

"Shhh..." she whispers. As she pulls the blanket back over her

164

own head, he covers his mouth with both hands and tries not to move, or moan. Whitney has always had a special technique; she is very talented to say the least. This woman could cause a saint to sin something awful.

Kel can feel all ten of his toes curling upward involuntarily. His eyes are stuck rolling in the back of his handsome head. She begins to bite the tip gently, just the way he likes.

As she kisses and licks his perfect stomach she reaches up and grabs his right hand, and then places it on the back of her head, so that he can guide her like he used to.

He grabs her tight ponytail on the back of her head and puts her mouth back in place perfectly. With a force, she had not expected he begins to push her head down, filling her mouth and throat to capacity.

He holds her down until he's sure she can't breathe, then he lets her up just long enough to regroup and then he does it again. Her eyes are watering and her jaws are sore now, but she would never protest the pain, or allow herself to end the session too soon by making noise and wakening K.C.'s sleeping beauty.

Kel looks at his wife to be once more to assure she is still asleep. He looks at the clock sitting on the table next to his bed, its 2:45 AM.

Now with both of his hand firmly gripping the back of her head he pushes her head up and down slowly and then quickly again. After several minutes of this, his arms and legs grow tense, and Whitney knows exactly what this means. She braces herself, as he pushes her head down deep one last time.

Seconds later he fills her mouth and throat with the explosion she worked so hard for. She catches every bit, and swallows it gladly. After licking his stomach, penis, and thighs clean, she crawls out of the bed and disappears into the darkness.

(The next morning)

It's another gorgeous sunny day in Miami. The problems from the night and day before don't seem to matter anymore today. Keldrick "Kool Hands" Cole is up early this morning, with a full list of things to do. He hasn't actually gotten out of bed just yet, but he is alert and ready to get his day started.

Lying completely still on his back, he's simply staring up at the ceiling. The ceiling in his room rises up in an abstract spiral. A young genius fashion designer by the name of Charles Andrews designed the entire mansion.

Mr. Andrews usually designs clothing only, but as a favor to his good friend K.C., he put his designing expertise into the construction of this gorgeous house, inside and out.

K.C.'s fiancé is sound asleep beside him, breathing calmly. He rolls over and kisses her softly on her forehead. He finally musters up the strength to get out of bed.

With his feet now on the floor he begins to feel around and try to find his house shoes. Once both feet are comfortably in his bright orange and green custom Miami Dolphin house shoes he makes his way to the bathroom.

His bathroom is adorned with cream tile, walls, and sinks, all with rose gold flakes throughout them. This bathroom is Keldrick's favorite room in the entire house. The way the elaborate flakes of gold reflect and glisten in every direction in his peripheral vision, motivates K.C. in a way no one else could ever understand.

(Megan lying in bed thinking)

It's time for action. I've been procrastinating for way too long. I know more about men than most women and more than any man probably knows about himself. It's a natural gift I've always had. I just haven't been lucky enough yet to meet the Adam to my Eve.

So instead of waiting I'm going to mold and marry my twin sister's hand-me-down Adam. An engineered love that may have spawned from a dirty lie is better than no love at all. As an aging lonely woman, I became quite skilled at the art of wanting a man, while pretending I don't.

The truth is every man can be molded into a much better man it just takes the right woman to do so. For every man, there is one woman with the capacity to mold him into her perfect mate.

My sister is that woman for Keldrick Jermaine Cole, but luckily, I am her identical twin so I can make him feel and live inside of every emotion he ever felt for her. I get to live inside of the tragic but beautiful love they had without any true emotional attachment to the pain they caused each other. Now it's time I solidify my place in his heart forever, not just as Cam, but as Megan.

Megan steadies herself, before sliding her firm body out of bed, and letting her tiny feet hit the soft floor. She knows exactly what to say, and do to become what she wants to be in this man's life, for a very long time. With every step, she makes towards the bathroom she feels more and more confident.

Megan Jiles, peeps her head in the bathroom, looking exactly like her twin Cameron Jiles. K.C. smiles at her. She watches him as he takes his time to trim his mustache perfectly.

"You think you cute huh?" Megan says through a childlike smile. "No…" K.C. starts. "Cuz you're not," she interjects stepping towards him, "you're absolutely gorgeous."

She takes his mustache trimmer, and finishes trimming it for him. As she wipes his mouth with a damp face towel, he stares into the large mirror behind her. He can't feel or hear a thing.

(K.C.)

Is this what true love really feels like? I would definitely die for this woman without hesitation. Lord, you gave me Cameron Candace

167

Jiles for a reason. Please never allow me to lose her ever again. I will continue to grow as a man, and a man of God…

"Are you listening to me baby?" Megan asks. "Yes, love I'm listening," he replies, "I was just daydreaming about our wedding."

She stands up on her toes to kiss him gently. "Listen to me Keldrick," she says in a serious tone, "you are more… important to me than any man I have ever known. I am the luckiest girl on earth, because I have you. You make me feel like the princess my dad should have told me I was years ago. I feel protected every second that I'm in your presence, and I hate being away from you. Nothing you could ever say or do could discount my love for you. You look at me… I mean you *really* look at *me*. You see passed my imperfect exterior, and into my soul that was crafted by God as a gift just for you. No matter what happens, let me always be your loyal, loving queen. Never let another woman take you away from me."

"You are the one I chose, that was no mistake. I don't regret a single second I've ever spent connected to you and your unconditional love." he replies with genuine sincerity in his voice, and on his face. "So, as for me leaving you," he continues, "that's never gonna happen Cam."

"No," she screams, "forget Cam!"

"Wait babe, what do you mean forget Cam?" K.C. asks with his strong brows wrinkled tightly.

Megan hesitates. "I just mean forget me as a person and fall in love with my heart and soul," she tells him, "love me deeper than just on a physical level. Know that no one in our past matters. Nothing that happened between us and other people in the past will ever matter again. The only thing that matters is you and I."

Megan begins to cry. "Baby," K.C. hugs her, "Why are you crying? Is there something you're not telling me? Look, if this is about Whitney, trust me she will be gone this week. I just can't put her on the street because she's still the mother of my kids."

168

"It's not Whitney I'm worried about," she cries softly, "I never want to lose you, or this beautiful potential life we can have together." "What do you mean potential?" K.C. asks. "It's not real to me," she cries, "until we walk down that isle and get everything in writing. Until that moment everything just hangs in the balance forever waiting on us."

Keldrick pulls his fiancé into his hard chest and holds her tightly.

"Listen," Kel starts, "I'm going to take Whit to find an apartment right now, and after we're done I'm taking you to the mall to do some shopping at the Louis Vuitton store. How does that sound?"

Megan stares down at the bathroom floor, trying not to smile.

K.C. picks her chin up gently and says, "No worries my love, I will always belong to only you."

(5 Hours later)

As Cameron and Charlie Breeze get closer to the Aventura mall on Biscayne Boulevard in Miami, the parking lot is exploding with people as usual. "Where are we going to park?" Cam asks. Charlie smiles at her. "You're so cute," he smiles, "We will have a valet park for us of course."

"How much money did you steal from Carlos before we left the island?" she asks. "Steal," he laughs, "I never steal boo. I had money before I ever met Dr. Sanchez." "What kind of money," Cam asks, "because all money is not good money."

"That's where you're wrong Cam," he tells her, "and that is the *dumbest* saying on the planet. *All* money is good money. The trick is doing the *right thing* with your money, even if the money was obtained in the *wrong way.*"

"Wow," Cam gushes, "you are smarter than you look." Charlie

laughs again. "What the hell does that even mean?" he asks through an unsure smile. "Now don't get me wrong," Cam starts, "you are a gorgeous man, I just didn't take you as the intelligent type. You know with all the muscles, tats, and the dreads and what not. I guess I got caught judging a book by its cover."

"Yeah I guess you did." he replies. "Don't judge me," she hits him playfully, "I apologize. Also, what you said about money makes a lot of sense. Your view of the world is nowhere near conventional, and I like that Charlie."

"Thanks boo," he steps out of his brand new 2015 Phantom, "this is where we get out."

A valet opens Cam's door for her. By the time she steps out Charlie is almost at the entrance of the mall. "Charlie…" she calls out. "Come on girl," he calls back, "I gotta find my Whitney."

Cam shakes her head. She's from Orlando, born and raised. This is her very first time in Miami, so she knows she has to try to keep up with Charlie as not to get lost. "Charlie," she yells, "Charlie slow down."

Seconds later she catches up to the love-sick dread head. "So, I have a question." Cam says. "Shoot…" Charlie replies. "Where did all your money come from?" Cam asks.

"Honestly?" he asks. "Yes honestly…" she replies. "I um," he starts, "I come from a long line of wealthy, successful, self-employed men." "Okay," she replies, "and what kind of service did this long line of successful men provide for people?"

Charlie hesitates. "They kept the streets in check." he replies. "So, you were born into some kind of South Miami Mafia type situation?" she asks. "You could say that." he replies. "Wow," she says, "Um, but you don't like kill people, right?" "No." Charlie replies.

"Oh good…" Cam puts a hand on her heart.

"*I* don't," he says, "That's not my line of work." "And what is your line of work Charlie, inquiring minds want to know?" Cam grins.

170

"Well right now," he says through a coy smile, "I'm your tour guide and best friend."

Cam crosses her arms tightly as they walk. "That's cute Mr. Breeze," Cam replies, "but what makes you think you and I are friends?"

"Right now, I'm pretty sure I'm the only friend you have." Charlie says. "And what makes you think that?" Cam asks, with an obvious change in demeanor.

"Cam," he starts, "everybody who knew you here in Florida six years ago, probably thought you were dead *four years* ago, and then probably stopped missing you a year after that."

Cam hangs her head. "I guess you're right." she tells him. "And besides," Charlie continues, "I know you **biblically** now, so we connected for life boo!"

They both share a good laugh. "Boy you snuck me," she pokes him gently in his chest, "otherwise you would have never experienced all of this." They laugh together again. "Hmm mm, so are you mad?" he asks. "No, I didn't say I was mad." she replies.

"Who's better?" Charlie asks. "What…" she replies. "You know what I'm asking you," he says, "between me and the good doctor. Which one of us is better in bed?"

"I'm tired of walking can we go sit down in the food court?" Cam asks. "Of course…" Charlie says.

They make their way to the only empty table in sight next to an oriental family, enjoying a large pizza. Charlie pulls out Cam's chair for her. She thanks him as she sits down.

"So, lemme find out you're a thug with manors." Cam says with a sexy smirk on her face. "First of all, I'm not a thug," he tells her, "I'm a grown ass man."

"Hold that thought." Cam says looking past him. "What do you see Cam?" he asks.

"Do not move," she stands up, "I'll be back, I'm bout to drag this bitch around this entire mall by her cheap ass sew in." Without another word Cam stalks off into the distance. Charlie stays put, but continues to watch Cam's every step.

"Baby, do you like this dress?" Megan asks, sporting a beautiful tight white dress. "Yeah that's the one babe." K.C. replies.

"You really think so?" she asks. "Yes Cameron, I love it," he smiles at her, "You can wear this dress to the wedding reception at the club." "Its $1,200 Keldrick..." Megan says. "Tell em' ring it up," he replies without hesitation, "you only get married, once right? Let's go
all out baby."

"Perfect," she says, "well let me try one more on." Megan walks back towards the dressing room. As she makes it back close to the ladies dressing rooms, another lady rudely bumps into her.

"Excuse me bitch!" Megan says. "No, bitch excuse me!" Cameron screams. "Cam…" Megan gasps. "Hell, yea trick," Cam says, "I'm about to whoop your ass all through this damn store."

"Wait," Megan holds her tiny hands up in defense, "it's not like that." "Oh really," Cam asks, "It's not like that? Then bitch by all means please tell me what it is like."

"What's going on Cameron?" K.C. approaches both women from around the corner. "That's right Keldrick I am Cameron," Cam says, "but this worthless bitch is…"

"Your fiancé…" Megan interjects wrapping her arms around K.C., "I'm the one you proposed to baby."

"Oh really," Cam says, "So you're the real Cam, right?" Megan looks at Cam. "Yes I am." "What the hell," K.C. exclaims, "am I tripping? There's two Cam's?"

"Hell no," Cam yells, "There's only one me!" "So, Megan," Cam says, "If you're the real Cam, "tell me K.C.'s birthday, favorite color, and his favorite food?" Megan hesitates. "Or how about this," Cam continues, "When Kel had amnesia what fell and hit him in the head and triggered his memory to return? I'm sure you remember that. No? Okay where did he propose to you the first time? Nothing... Keldrick I am the real Cam, this bitch, my identical twin sister Megan is a liar, and an imposter."

Megan begins to cry. "Damn Cam." K.C. shakes his head.

"Don't tell me you don't believe me," Cam says, "not after I just exposed this hoe right in front of your face." "No," he grins, "I know you're the real Cameron."

"Good." Cam replies finally able to smile. "Is it good Cam," he asks, "your sister is pregnant with my child, and we are engaged to be married next week."

"What..." Cam gasps. "Yeah," he replies, "and of course I knew you were the real Cam, I could recognize your loud mouth and evil scowl anywhere."

Megan smiles through her tears. "Kel," Cam starts, "it's me. How can you do *me* like this baby?"

K.C. laughs loudly. "Are you serious Cam," he asks, "you left me in the middle of the mall next to my daughter on one knee, forever frozen in the minds of thousands of people as your fool? You refused my proposal, and ran off with my best friend Tyrone, who ended up being my half-brother. Cam, you may have exposed your sister, but she still wins today, because tonight she's going to be the only woman in my bed."

Kel laughs again, as Cam begins to cry. "In fact," he continues, "your twin sister is the only woman I will ever love or touch again, for *the rest* of my life."

Cam wipes some of her tears away. Then she lunges forward as she slaps Megan hard across the face, and punches her hard in the stomach several times. Kel pushes Cam to the floor hard.

"Cam, you better get yo trifling, thirsty ass out of this store, before I call the police, and tell them how you just assaulted my pregnant fiancé."

Cam stands up slowly. "Baby... Keldrick I'm sorry, please take me back..." Cam cries. "Never," he replies, "see Cameron, the most beautiful thing about being with Megan is I get *you,* without actually having to be *with* you. I don't have to live with all the passed hurts, and baggage from our *real* past."

"You're sure this is what you want?" Cam asks. "Oh yeah," he replies, "And you know what the hardest thing is I have to deal with in this entire situation?"

"No, what is that K.C.?" she asks. K.C. laughs again snidely. "The hardest thing I have to do is change the name on all of the wedding invitations from Mrs. Cameron Jiles Cole, to Mrs. Megan Jiles Cole."

Cam's sobs are becoming uncontrollable. "Really Cam," Kel leans towards her to see her eyes clearly, "all this though? For whom, these tears and emotions can't be for me... Not the man you left hanging. You know what I don't even care, cry me a river bitch."

Cam rushes out of the store unable to withstand another second of the mental abuse. As Cam runs out of the store Kel kisses Megan... as Megan for the very first time.

"That wasn't right son." a deep voice says from behind K.C. and Megan. They turn around quickly. "Pastor White," Kel says, "I'm sorry you had to witness that, but that woman..."

"It doesn't matter what she did son," he explains, "I already know the story. But you as a man of God cannot continue to act as if you are just another one of Satan's worldly pawns."

"I'm sorry Pastor, you're absolutely right." Kel agrees. "Come to my office in the morning," Pastor White instructs him, "Congrats on the baby, but I'm not so sure I'm ready to bless and preside over this marriage."

"Yes sir, I'll be there in the morning." Kel promises, as he hugs the old man. Pastor White leaves the store with the world on his shoulders.

Cameron runs full speed all the way to the food court into Charlie's arms. Her heart is racing rapidly. As she ran through the crowded mall Cam never once cared who saw her.

"Oh my God Cam," Charlie walks towards her, "girl what's

wrong? Stop crying please, and tell me what's wrong."

"Just get me out of here please…" she whimpers. Charlie swiftly sweeps the tiny woman up into his perfect arms, and proceeds to carry her through the mall towards the exit.

As he carries her, several men pat him on the back as women stare in awe and whisper random nothings about how they wish they had a man like Charlie. Charlie is used to getting attention for his good looks, but this attention is totally different, and somehow feels better to him. He leans forward and kisses the sobbing Cam on her forehead. "Charlie," she whispers, "thank you." "No problem beautiful." he replies.

Chapter 13
The Hotel

Just minutes after leaving the crowded mall Charlie and Cameron pull up to the Trump International Beach Resort hotel at 18001 Collins Avenue, Sunny Isles Beach, FL.

Charlie leaves Cam in the car to go pay for a hotel suite for a few nights. All alone in the luxurious car, Cam closes her eyes tightly trying to help her mind escape all the pain she experienced today.

"You ready?" Charlie gets back in the car. "I um… I don't know what I am." Cam replies. Charlie laughs lightly. "That's okay, you don't have to know anything tonight," he says, "I just want you to get some rest."

"There's no way, I'm gonna be able to sleep tonight." she says. Charlie smiles at her as he places a comforting hand on her right knee. "No worries boo," he tells her, "I know exactly how to put you to sleep."

"Oh really?" she says through a sleepy smile. Charlie pulls around the hotel parking lot to find a good parking space.

Inside the room Cam can feel herself falling head first into a deep depression. Nothing seems to matter in her world without him. Without the man, she left stranded in life with a broken heart she has no purpose.

She doesn't have any idea how painful and embarrassing it had to be for K.C. to propose to her in front of thousands of people, and then be left all alone looking stupid, but she's sure it had to feel something like the way she feels right now.

"Cam…" Charlie steps out of the bathroom. "Yeah…" she

replies. "I ran you a bath," he beckons to her, "come here so I can take your clothes off for you."

Cam kicks her heels off, and obediently heads to the bathroom as the tears begin to fall again. As she reaches the bathroom Charlie puts his hands on her shoulders.

"No tears in my bathroom Cameron." he says. Then he smiles and kisses her tears away gently.

Looking deeply into her eyes, Charlie pulls the straps of Cam's dress over shoulders and lets her dress falls to the floor. In nothing but her panties in front of this true stranger Cam has never felt so comfortable.

Charlie kneels down and gently pulls Cam's panties off, just before kissing her sexy stomach three times. Next, he picks her up off her feet and carries her to the tub.

"Wait, wait Charlie," she panics, "Make sure it's not too hot." "Girl let me do this." he says through a placating smile.

As her toes enter the water she can feel her entire body begin to tingle. Once her entire body is beneath the water, all the pain seems to be gone and nothing matters but this moment. Charlie begins massaging her shoulders softly and then firmly. Slowly the unforgivable mental pain begins to leak back into Cam's mind.

"Charlie." she whispers. "Yes Cameron." he replies. "This all feels so good," she says, "but if you don't mind I'd like to be alone for a while."

"No problem," he stands up, "I understand. Take your time I'll be in the bed, wake me if you need me." "Okay…" she whispers to him. As he exits the bathroom, Cam is left to her own devices. She feels, and wants to feel helplessly alone. Because without Keldrick that's exactly what she is. She knows she never, ever stopped loving him, but once she ran away to be with Carlos on the island, from that point she was never afforded an opportunity to leave.

She always believed that if by chance she ever did make it back into his presence, he would immediately stop whatever he was doing in life and accept her back with open loving arms.

Cam wanted to be connected to Keldrick in every way. The moment that scarred her forever was when he made her feel unworthy, and ultimately less than Whitney Powell. The moment he basically told her she wasn't good enough to have his child. He didn't want a dark-skinned baby.

How does a clearly dark-skinned man come to a point in his existence where he fears having a child that will carry on his own skin tone? Black is so bold, and undeniably beautiful. Why didn't he know that? Why did he hate himself so much that the idea of having a child in his own likeness was so obviously devastating to him?

Our child would have been gorgeous; there is not a shadow of doubt in my mind. But to please him, and save myself from eighteen years of loneliness, and embarrassment I did as he asked me to do. I lost my child. I purposely lost and destroyed what would have been my very own first child. Just to find out months later that Whitney's Light skinned ass was pregnant with his child again.

This was yet another slap in the face to me. I was good enough to suck him, fuck him, and take care of his black ass when nobody wanted him and he didn't have a dime or a prayer... but never was I good enough even for a moment to give birth to a child for him.

I wanted so badly to give birth to a child for us. In my mind, our child would have made our relationship so much stronger. Our son or daughter could have... would have been a beautiful extension, and a symbol of our pure love for each other. But instead he forced me to lose my child. Because baring his children, is reserved only for his perfect light skinned queen Whitney Powell.

The tears are tormenting her contorted black face now. Her hands are bald up in tight fists that she can't relinquish alone. Her numb body is shaking from head to toe, she's filled with unearthly rage, and the point of no return to the little sanity she had left has been reached fully now. Her tense body is completely locked up and excruciatingly vulnerable.

Losing a child is the most unnerving thing a woman could ever do. When a man tells you, he doesn't want your child... then in turn he is forcing your hand to get rid of it. Because if you have that child regardless of the fact that he told you he didn't want it your ultimate outcome in the situation won't be pretty.

He may even seem to love the child at first and even desire to see it and spend minimal time with it. But the time will come when he regrets you, the child, and himself because in reality your child is and will forever remain a mistake in his life. So, if you know a man does not want you to have his child, do not force a child on him. It's not good for anybody involved.

Keldrick actually told me once, that he believes it should be a law that if any woman has a man's child against a man's wishes, he should not be required to support that child. Years later sadly I am inclined to agree with his sentiments.

Keldrick said that according to his hypothetical law, if a man finds out that a woman is pregnant with his child within the first trimester of the woman's pregnancy he would be able to go to the police and tell them he doesn't want a child with the woman.

The police would create a case file and notify the woman of the man's decision. Keldrick's theory is that this would give her ample time to make whatever arrangements she desires.

If she agreed to have the child aborted, the father would have to agree to pay for half of the procedure. If she elected to have the child anyway the man would be permanently exempted from any child support order.

This he said would be much better than continuing to bring a record number of unwanted, unloved, and unsupported children into the world, thereby saving the government billions of dollars on social welfare programs in the United States of America.

He sounded like he was an actual politician who was speaking passionately to a large crowd of potential supporters. But in reality, he was only speaking to me, and thereby breaking my heart into tiny pieces that would put even dust to shame.

It hurt badly, but I guess in the grand scheme of things he was right, because so many woman force children on men who openly don't want them. I know women who have poked holes in condoms, purposely stopped taking birth control pills, and even women who have lied to men telling them they were incapable of having children.

They all tricked men into getting them pregnant, and then those same deceitful women turn around and bash those men when they don't take care of the children they never wanted in the first place. This is obviously not always the case, but for the women who do terrible things like that even I believe that Keldrick's law would be justified.

I am not a philosopher, nor am I a law maker but I know if a man doesn't want me to have his child I'll do whatever it takes to not be a fool. "My Lord... I really need to pray right now." Cameron cries out. *"Lord it's me Cam. I know we've been here before a time or two. I promise it was not my intention to love that man again. And I don't love this pain I feel now... But I also don't regret seeing Keldrick today. The torture I endured today is only a drop in the bucket compared to what I put him through. I'm not angry at him. My sister on the other hand, I have plans for her. Amen."*

Cam walks out of the bathroom an hour later in nothing but a towel. The room is completely dark. "Charlie." she whispers. "I'm right here, just walk straight." the dread head growls.

"Hey Charlie..." Cam steps towards the bed.

"Hey..." he replies. "Can you..." she starts.

"Can, I what?" he asks.

"Just make love to me with your mouth all night long until I fall asleep." she blushes in the darkness.

"I thought you'd never ask." he replies as he pulls her into his hard chest from the foot of the bed. He lays her down quickly, tossing her wet towel to the floor.

Charlie starts from her dainty toes and begins to work his way up, all lips and tongue. He pays close attention to every inch of her sweet dark-skinned body.

His mouth waters more and more with each new part of her, that his lips come in contact with. With his tongue, he licks off every bead of water he encounters on her skin.

As he finally reaches her soft center, he devours her hungrily. Her entire body locks up in ecstasy. Her moans and screams are music to Charlie's ears.

"Charlie..." Cam moans. "Yes..." he growls between licks.

"I don't love you," she moans, "but I promise I want to. I know Whitney has your heart, but if she doesn't treat you right, I'll show you how a woman should treat a good man like you."

Charlie proceeds to feed her body with his talents for another half hour. By the time he makes it up to her lips to kiss her, he finds Cam sound asleep. He smiles to himself, and then he snuggles up close to her with his chiseled chocolate arms wrapped around her tightly.

Chapter 14
Suga Mama

P astor White has a brand new beautiful church in Miami, thanks to a young man he helped raise years ago. One of Keldrick's very first big NFL endorsement checks went towards the construction of a building to house Pastor White's growing congregation.

Tax troubles actually caused him to lose his church in Orlando, but K.C. told him as soon as he was able he would help Pastor White get and build a new church home. He only had one condition in this, he wanted his pastor to move to Miami and preside over a church there.

The pastor agreed to this, and said it was time he moved on to a new battleground anyway. Pastor White's words and personality are of such that he possesses a God given ability to touch anybody. He can change your entire life with just a few words and some loving guidance from his faith in the Lord.

This Sunday morning Keldrick has more of his family in church with him than usual. Megan, K.J., Love, Jaze, and Whitney are all in attendance with the NFL star. The pastor is very pleased with what he sees on the front row of his church.

As he surveys their six faces, there doesn't seem to be any malice or confusion between them. This is a blessing in his wise old eyes, because Pastor White is fully aware of all of the circumstances that surround this group of individuals on the front pew of his church. There is very little that transpires in Keldrick's life now that he doesn't share with the good reverend.

"Good morning church!" Pastor White shouts. The congregation responds to him. "Today church is a very special day," he starts, "you see today is my forty second wedding anniversary."

The congregation stands and applauds the pastor and his wife. Pastor White beckons gently to his wife, to come up and join him on stage in the pulpit. Debra White, the pastor's wife, is one of those people that would lie down her life for a person she has only just met. She has a heart of gold. Once she reaches the pastor he kisses her softly, hugs her, and then has a couple of deacons escort her back to her seat.

"Yes, marriage is," pastor continues, "a beautiful thing. But it is not an easy thing. Let the church say Amen."

"Amen." the congregation replies. "Marriage," pastor says again, "is a beautiful thing... but it is not an easy thing. The union between a man and a woman is meant to be a lifelong bond. Marriage is a long, long journey. And just like any long journey, you have to be conditioned to withstand the trials on the trail of this *trying... expedition*. The definition of a *journey*... is an act of traveling from one place to another. You see People of God, before we enter a marriage... before most of us enter this *allegedly* holy union we are not yet ready to stop living the way we are living in that moment. We are happy living in, and amongst sin, and there for we do not want to commit to just one person. We have not yet grasped the concept of monogamy, and most of us live with a fear of commitment. *We*... have a *fear* of commitment. And if you are still at that point in which you fear commitment, do not rush into committing to someone else... when *you* have not *first* committed to yourself. Listen to me now People of God. If you, a man or a woman rush into a serious commitment, like marriage and you are not yet ready… You will *soon resent* your own choice to commit. You have to be ready to take that step, in order for your marriage to last longer than statistics say it will."

"Amen!" the congregation yells to Pastor White.

After church K.C. drives Megan and Whitney back to the house, as Love follows them with the children riding safely in his car. After receiving Megan's blessing Keldrick takes Whitney out to celebrate finding her a new house in Miami.

Giraffas Brazilian Kitchen & Grill at 1821 NE 123rd St., in North Miami serves the most delicious grilled burgers, steaks, and fries. They boast a casual modern atmosphere at over 6 locations in Florida. *Giraffas* has easily become one of "*Kool hands*" favorite dining spots, since his big move to the "305".

As they leave his mansion headed to the restaurant, K.C. feels chill bumps on his arms, but he doesn't know if this is a good thing, or a bad thing.

"Keldrick…" Whit says happily. "Yes ma'am Ms. Powell." he replies. "Can we make one stop before we go to *Giraffas*?" she asks. "A stop where?" K.C. inquires.

"The *Graffiti Shack* on Biscayne…" she tells him. "You want a piercing right now?" he asks. "Hell, no boy," she laughs, "I want a tattoo, like right now. I'm in the mood for some pain."

"Mhmm," he moans, "I used to be your source of pain."

"Operative word Keldrick," she says, "*used* to be. You belong to another bitch now, oh well."

"Whatever," he replies, "do you want the tat or are you just talking out the side of your neck?" "Yeah baby, I want a tat right now. If you're gonna take me." she says.

As they pull up they're both relieved that the parking lot isn't crowded. The *Graffiti Shack* is home to some of the most talented tattoo artist in the Miami area period. The prices are competitive, and the service is well above average, especially for a tattoo joint. Kel

184

had all of his recent tattoos done here.

"Okay so are you going in or what Suga Mama?" he asks. "Yeah wait here." she tells him. As she runs inside the shop Kel can't help but watch the movement of her round behind in her thin sundress.

The inside of the *Graffiti Shack* smells like cigarettes and rainbows. It's that kind of funky sweet smell that you don't love, but you could get used to. The walls are covered in Japanese and Chinese art. Also on the walls are about twenty random nude pictures of women who are covered in tats from head to toe.

The manager of the *Graffiti Shack* is an old white guy name Kyle Kissel. Kyle was a really awesome tattoo artist years ago, but now that he has arthritis, Parkinson's disease, and cataracts he was forced to put the tattoo gun down and step into management.

One lawsuit was enough to end old Kyle's career as a tattooist for life. All of the new young artists still look up to him and go to him for advice after all he is a living legend in the Miami tattoo world.

Whit is quietly searching the large books on the walls to find the perfect style for her new tat. "How can we help you today beautiful?" Kyle says from behind Whit, trying not to stare at her ass.

"Um I want a tattoo," she tells him, "but I don't know which letters I want."

"Okay," Kyle replies, "Maybe I can help you. What exactly do you have in mind?" "It's a surprise for an old friend." she claims.

After Whit describes what she wants, Kyle tells her it won't take more than thirty minutes, and seventy-five dollars would take care of it. Whitney walks back to the car.

"Gimme a hundred dollars K.C." she says.

"Girl, hurry up." he hands her four twenties.

"You said you wanted to come get a tat," he continues, "You never said you needed me to pay for it too."

"Oh, shut up Keldrick." Whit says over her shoulder on her way back inside.

185

(Whit)

I should not be getting this tattoo. Love, nor K.C., will ever be in my life again romantically, so I have to move on... again. Ouch, damn this hurts. It doesn't look that great so far hopefully the end result will look better. Whitney what are you doing girl? You are getting this tat, spending his money, and enduring this pain all in vain.

But I don't care I've wanted this tat for years, so stupid or not I'm gonna finish getting it, and just live with whatever happens in my life afterwards.

Forty-five minutes later Whit jumps back in K.C.'s car.

"Done..." he asks. "Yeah, let's go." she replies. He drives off quickly headed towards *Giraffas*.

"Okay so I know this is not a date," Whitney says, "your fiancé made that more than clear before we left your house, but to what do I owe the pleasure of this evening?"

"We are celebrating your new house of course," K.C. explains, "And honestly I miss you. Not in a sexual way, but you used to be my closest friend, and for years you were the only constant in my life... my comfort zone."

"Awe," Whit moans, "I miss that too. I regret trying to handicap you, but baby you have to understand..."

"I understand completely," he interjects, "trust me I know why you were, the way you were. You didn't want me to become independent, because in your mind if I became a real man I would no longer need you. You were absolutely right. I would not have needed you to care for me like a helpless child anymore. But I would have still needed and wanted your love and presence in my everyday life."

"Wow," Whit blushes, "that was beautiful Keldrick. What has gotten into you?" K.C. smiles and shakes his head to himself. "My God," he says, "I am so much closer to the Lord than ever before.

And that's why I feel so bad about the hatred I've held in my heart for you for the past five years. I also mentally and emotionally destroyed Cameron yesterday in the middle of a store in the Aventura mall."

"Wait," Whit says, "What do you mean you destroyed her, your fiancé seemed happy when we left the house two hours ago…" "Yeah," he replies, "My fiancé is happy," he says, "*but*… my fiancé is not Cameron." "What?" Whit asks.

"Cameron Jiles has an identical twin named Megan Jiles," he explains to her, "Cam was on the island with you and Carlos, but her twin Megan has lived here in Florida her entire life. I met her one day at the movies in Orlando, and when I saw her of course I thought she was Cam."

"And so, what happened when you approached her," Whit asks, "I know that had to be crazy." "I was so nervous Suga Mama…" he admits.

"Don't do that." Whit says. "Don't do what?" he asks. "Don't call me your Suga Mama." Whit says.

"You will always be *my Suga Mama*, Whitney Powell," he vows, "No matter what foolishness you ever say or do now, the girl I fell in love with years ago was still my first love, *my Suga Mama*."

As Keldrick pulls around to the back of the restaurant to park his all black 2015 Mercedes S class coupe he can't help but feel conflicted about this evening. On the one hand, he has every intention to marry Megan, but in the back of his mind he knows Whit will always have a piece of his heart. He also knows that Megan's twin Cameron is the only woman he is truly in love with.

After parking the car Kel hops out, and makes his way around to the passenger side of his car to open Whit's door for her.

"Keldrick," she starts, "I have to admit I am very proud of you and the man you are becoming." "Thanks that means a lot coming from you Whit." he says. "And why is that?" she asks.

"Because," he looks at her, "you were there before I had anything,

187

baby you were my high school sweetheart. And I am now finally living everything we dreamed of together as kids."

"Without me." she says.

K.C. looks into Whitney's eyes as they both walk towards the front door of *Giraffas*. "Our entire lives," he admits, "were supposed to be filled with nights just like this one, but life happened." K.C. politely opens the door to the restaurant for her.

On their way to their table following closely behind one of the hosts K.C. waves to several gushing fans as he and Whitney pass by their tables.

"Here you are Mr. and Mrs. Cole…" the hostess holds her thin arm out to signal which table is theirs for the evening. "No, she's not…" Kel starts.

"Thank you, ma'am," Whit interjects quickly, "Mr. Cole and I will be ready to order shortly." K.C. looks down at Whit, and then decides in his mind that this is only for one night so it's not necessary to argue with her about what just transpired.

As they sit down at their table, they both can feel the energy between them growing. "So, tell me about how you met Megan." Whit says.

"I was in line to get tickets to that movie *"Phoenix Rain"* by Delure," Kel tells her, "and when I looked at the cashier in the ticket booth, I nearly lost my mind. For years I thought you and Cam were dead, so to see her standing right there in front of me was mind blowing."

"I bet." Whit agrees. "Yeah," Kel continues, "So I was standing there in line nervous as hell. And then it was my turn to buy my ticket, so I approached her window. Of course, Megan didn't recognize me. I was flashing money and what not trying to persuade her to quit her job and move home to Miami with me. Megan refused me though."

"Wait," Whit says, "Why did she refuse?" "She didn't know me

188

Whit," he reminds her, "but after my movie was over she was sitting in the lobby waiting for me. We've been together ever since."

"Wow," Whit smiles, "that's amazing. So, you said you were nervous when you saw her right?" "Hell yeah." he replies through a magnetic smile of his own.

They share a good laugh together like old friends. "Okay," Whit says, "were you more nervous than you were the first time you talked to me?"

"No," he admits, "I wasn't nervous with you. Suga I was terrified. You were a cheerleader, and the prettiest girl in school."

"So…" Whitney blushes slightly.

"So," K.C. repeats, "that's a lot for a young dude to deal with, I had a lot of pressure on me to get your number." "You wanna know a secret?" she asks.

"What…" he replies. "I had a huge crush on you, months before you ever tried to holla at me." Whit tells him. "Are you serious?" he asks.

"Hell yeah," Whit laughs nervously, "How could I not? We were only fifteen then but you were already like 5'11, dark skin, perfect teeth, perfect body, just perfect period. And your name was already all around the school and the state, you were already a legend. In fact, I remember hearing your name like a thousand times before I ever saw your face."

"It was all hype though," K.C. reflects, "my freshman season really wasn't all that good."

"Are you kidding me," Whit asks, "boy please… you were a beast. You had like 1,700 yards that year. You broke like three school records with your single season receiving stats, within the first half of that season. You had more receiving yards in the fourth game of the season, than all of the other receivers on the team had combined that entire season."

"Damn Whitney," K.C.'s unable to take his eyes off her, "you remember all of that?"

"I don't think I could forget if I wanted to." Whit admits.

"It's just crazy because back then I had no idea you were such a football fan." K.C. tells her. Whit laughs that adorable laugh, as she begins to blush. "I was never a sports fan period," she admits, "I was a K.C. fan. I was at every one of your track meets, basketball games, football games... I even came to that Academics bowl thing you were in our sophomore year." They both burst into laughter together.

"I'm not giving you any credit for being at all my games Ms. Powell," he grins, "you were a cheerleader so you had to be there. But remembering my stats, that's impressive." "You matter to me... you always have." Whit admits.

K.C. feels something inside of him that he can't quite explain, or define in the slightest bit. "Um," he starts, "I need to go use the bathroom now."

"Uh, okay..." Whit says; "I'll be right here waiting for you." she smiles. "And," she continues, "I won't give some random guy a business card while you're gone."

K.C. smiles back at her. "Hmm, maybe you should Whitney," he tells her, "I mean *that is* how I originally met my Cam." Then he excuses himself to head towards the restroom.

Minutes later as he heads back towards the table Whitney is locked in on him and no one else. She licks her lips slowly. Whitney remembers she used to always love to watch him walk. She thinks to herself how much K.C. looks like a *regal* giant made solely of black concrete taking powerful strides headed to sit on his rightful royal throne.

K.C. sits back down pretending not to notice the way Whitney is staring at him. "I'm back." he announces to her as if he is invisible. "What took you so long?" she asks sipping some of the wine the manager had delivered to their table while K.C. was in the bathroom. "I had to make an important phone call, but its fine

everything
is fine." he assures her. Whit continues to gaze at K.C. without even
blinking once.

"Hey…" he breaks the silence. "Yeah…" she replies. "Do you
remember Hectoria Santos?" K.C. asks.

"Nigga do you remember Hectoria Santos," she returns his
question through a crooked smile, "hell I had a black eye for a
week. Of course, I remember her ass."

"Yeah but you won that fight though." K.C. says. "Thanks to
you," Whit says, "you were my teacher, my lover, and my best friend.
I remember the night before the fight like it was yesterday."

"Yeah," Kel says, "Me too." "I snuck out the night before and
ran all the way to your house." Whit reflects. "We stayed up till like
3am," Kel says, "just so I could teach you a couple combos before the
fight."

"It worked," she reminisces, "you walked me to school that next
morning, and held both my hands right before the fight, just so no
one could tell how bad they were shaking."

"I remember," he says, "I was so proud of you babe. Not for
fighting, but for standing your ground. Hectoria disrespected you,
she deserved what she got."

"I agree," she smiles, "but those combos weren't the only thing
you taught me that night in your room."

Whit reaches under the table to caress K.C.'s knee as she takes
another sip of her wine. He gently removes her hand.

"Whitney, don't start anything you can't finish." he says.

"You're the one who can't finish sir." she wets her full pink lips.
"Oh, I can finish," he says, "You know I can finish, but I won't.
I'm engaged now Whitney, please respect that."

"Hell no," she whispers across the table, "it would be one thing
to lose you to Cam, hell I've been there done that. But to lose you
to her twin… who *tricked you* into thinking *she was* Cam. That's way
too much to swallow Keldrick. It's not fair to me."

"Come on now Whit," he says, "you know you can swallow anything no matter how big or small."

"Boy, don't play with me right now," she demands, "I don't wanna play anymore. I'm very serious right now. It's not fair Keldrick, and you know it."

"How's the food?" a young white waitress asks as she refills their glasses with more wine. "It's perfect." K.C. tells her. "Awesome," the waitress replies, "if you need anything else just let me know." "Thanks, will do." he tells her.

As she walks away, K.C. grabs the napkin out of his lap, and wipes his mouth. "Whitney Michelle Powell," he says, "I know damn well you didn't just say what I think your ass said."

"Yes, hell I did," she said, "It's not fair. You will always belong to me, and I refuse to lose you to a fake ass Cam."

Keldrick smiles at Whitney, trying to hide his true sentiments. "First of all," K.C. starts, "I am not engaged to a fake Cam, I am engaged to the real Megan Jiles. She is more woman than you or Cam will ever be. No, she's not perfect, but she would take a bullet for me without hesitation. She already proved that."

"Of course, she would die for you, *dumbass*, she had no life period before you," Whit says, "didn't you find that hood rat working at the movie theater or something? You're her meal ticket."

"Yeah, I did find her working at a movie theater," he replies, "and now she's a rich Miami housewife, with a black card. Her position in life is a major step up from your current situation. Damn it Whitney, I'm paying your rent, so you have no room to talk about my fiancé."

"K.C. can you please just shut up, and spend the night with me tonight... one last time?" Whit asks.

"This dinner is over," he says, "Come on I'm taking you home, to the house that my fiancé is paying for... yeah she handles all of my business expenses."

192

K.C. stands up. "So that's what I am to you now," she asks, "a business expense?"

"Let's go Ms. Powell." he places a crisp hundred-dollar bill on the table.

"*Ms. Powell*," she yells, "nigga don't you ever call me that! I'm Suga Mama. My sugar is the first and last sugar you will ever taste. I'm the only Mrs. Keldrick Jermaine Cole!"

"You're drunk Whitney." he tells her. "Sit back down!" she demands. "It's time to go Whiney." he says.

"I am not ready to leave yet." she says pulling her left breast out, and removing the covering to expose her new tattoo. Whitney's new tattoo is a bright red heart dripping blood. Inside the heart, the tattoo reads "*K.C. & W.P. 4EVER & ALWAYS*."

"Now, Keldrick sit your ass back down… please!" she begs.

"You shouldn't have gotten that Whitney." K.C. shakes his head at her, and then heads towards the exit without looking back.

Chapter 15
The Best Man

Ty and Jay both dressed in old sweat pants and tank tops are sitting in their den watching reruns of the hit 90's television show "*Family Matters*". "Did Steve Urkel ever actually marry Laura Winslow?" Jay asks.

"Uh... I don't remember," Ty says, "I think she married *Stefan*."

"Yeah I think you're right." Jay replies. "Who was the best man?" Jay asks. "I don't know Jay," Ty says, "I guess Eddie Winslow. You've been asking a lot of questions about weddings lately. What's going on bro? *I know you*... you wanna tell me something so bad, but you don't know how."

"Na," Jay says, "I was just trying to remember what happened on the show bro." Jay insists. "Jay..." Ty says. "What?" Jay responds.

"Nigga what's up?" Ty asks. "Nothing," Jay says, "Aight... man look K.C. is engaged again." "Aw man that's awesome news bro." Ty says. "That's not all though." Jay says. "What else?" Ty asks.

"He uh..." Jay starts, "he kind of asked me to be his best man this time."

"Oh," Ty hesitates, "that's cool." "I mean if you don't want me to do it bro..." Jay starts. "Don't be stupid," Ty interjects, "It's an honor and a privilege to be Keldrick "*Kool Hands*" Cole's best man. Bro you gotta do it, besides if you ruin his wedding he'll probably kill

194

us both." They both laugh. "You sure bro…" Jay asks. "Hell, yeah bro have fun." Ty tells his friend.

"You think you'll ever get married Ty?" Jay asks. "I don't know bro," he replies, "but I doubt it." "Why is that?" Jay asks. "Everybody I ever knew that got married is now divorced, unhappy, and broke." Ty tells him.

"Wow." Jay says. "Yeah," Ty continues, "And none of them were in that terrible situation before they decided to take that step. It's just scary that's all I'm saying."

"No, I agree bro," Jay says, "I was reading in a magazine yesterday that ninety percent of married men possess one of three marriage ending qualities."

"What three qualities?" Ty asks. "Let's see," Jay says, "they cheat, they bore the shit out of their wives after about four months of marriage, or they end up being gay on the DL."

"I agree," Ty says, "That's pure truth. A lot of times even the flamboyant, charismatic, fun husbands eventually grow tired of just surprising their own wives, and only their wives. They start wanting more, so eventually they cheat too."

"Marriage is a tricky game," Jay says, "but whenever I take that dive, I'm never gonna step out on my wife. But I am gonna wait until I know I'm good and ready to make that transition in my life before I actually do it."

Chapter 16
Old Habits

(Cameron)

We do not choose who we love, or the amount of love we accumulate over the years for that one person. Love has never been voluntary, it sneaks up when we least expect it, sometimes when we don't even want it. And then it takes its time to choke the life out of us, crippling us… and blinding us until the only thing we can still see is the person we love. Some people are lucky enough to have this insane love reciprocated back to them, but in most cases, it's not that simple.

We sometimes play stupid mental games in our relationships, thinking that we are in turn heightening our importance in our lover's lives. These games are intended to solidify our stake in our mate's future. In actuality, these games usually only make things worse. And we only play these games because we become one of two things. Some of us become insecure, and in turn we panic and try all kinds of things to make our partners believe they still need us. Some of us become arrogant in our relationships, and momentarily we relax and take our significant other's for granted. Terrible idea…

What we should do is try our best to be everything our mates could ever want and need. We have to dive into the love we want head first and never look back. Forget the past, we have to apply, and indulge ourselves in each new relationship as if we have no recollection of the failed relationships that we were in beforehand. If we bring our old pains and mental baggage into each new relationship, we will continue to get the same end results.

Once a relationship is truly over... and you know when it's over, beyond the denial and momentary insanity you know when your mate is finally over you. At that point, you have to be strong enough to accept the pain. Accept the pain, feel it, endure it, and then overcome it. That pain can only build you up, and make you that much stronger, especially if you understand why the relationship did not work.

I should be listening to my own advice right now when it comes to K.C., but forget that. I don't wanna be sensible right now. I need him, I want him... I have to be near him right now! I cannot breathe or exist without that man. Lord he is perfect for me.

Cam looks over at Charlie to make sure he's still sleeping. Once this is confirmed she slips out of bed, and throws on some black leggings, a tight black half shirt, and a pair of all black air max shoes.

On the table, next to the bed she finds the keys to the Phantom. As quietly as she possibly can, she makes her way out of the hotel door, and then she runs down to the car. She pulls off in seconds.

In an email, a couple of years ago K.C. sent Cam the address to his Miami mansion and asked her to pay him a visit, but of course Cam had no choice but to decline because she was stuck on the island with Carlos and Whitney.

Cam quickly pulls up that old email and then copies and pastes the address in her phone's GPS system. The GPS says she's twenty-seven miles away from K.C.'s house.

She steps down hard on the gas and heads in his unsuspecting direction. The possibility of Charlie waking up does cross Cam's mind but she really doesn't care one way or the other. The only thing she does care about is K.C.

Good Charlie left his gun in here. That will come in handy on this mission. Damn it, I forgot to wash my face and brush my teeth. I feel disgusting, and so unstable. When I get to K.C.'s house I don't know if I'm going to kill them all, or just watch my baby K.C. from a distance just to feel close to him again. I know I did this with Carlos years ago but that was different, I wasn't stalking him I was just making sure he was okay. Fifteen minutes later she reaches the address. Cam passes the mansion several times before she finally parks the car. After getting out of the car, she makes her way down the street to the house without much hesitation at all.

Then Cameron quickly walks around to the back of the house through the wide-open iron-gate, and crouches down in the bushes to see what she can spy.

There is absolutely no one in sight from where she's positioned. She moves closer, now she's right below one of the downstairs bathroom windows. She stands up to peak through the window.

As soon as she looks inside she gasps. Megan is bent over with her head in the sink, with K.C. behind her giving her everything she can handle. She has her right foot planted firmly on the toilet seat. That used to be Cam's favorite position with K.C. years ago.

Watching the two of them enjoying each other is breaking my heart. No, to hell with my heart this is actually killing me. But killing them won't fix the problem. My problem is I'm empty without him. He loves Megan now though, so winning him back isn't possible for me. It's not possible for me... The only person capable of taking him from Megan now is Megan herself... I got it. I'll just steal that bitch's move. All I have to do is get rid of her and take her place nobody will ever know the difference. Cam smiles mischievously.

"Ms. Cam..." a tiny voice says from behind her. "Oh Jaze," Cam whispers, "Come here baby, how are you?" They hug. "I'm ok Ms. Cam," she replies, "but why are you whispering?" "I'm not supposed

198

to be here right now," Cam admits, "but wait a second Jaze... baby how did you know it was me and not my twin sister Megan?"

"I don't know about my dad, but it's easy for me to tell the difference between you and her," Jaze claims, "and plus *you're* outside the house peeping through the window, and Megan is *inside* the house having sex with my dad."

"Little girl," Cam laughs in silent shock, "You are just too grown for me. Please Jaze whatever you do, don't tell K.C. you saw me out here." "I won't," Jaze promises, "So this has to be our secret, right?" "Yes, good girl," Cam says, "you never saw me."

"Cool," Jaze replies, "Um Ms. Cam, can I ask you something..."

"Anything *love*..." Cam replies.

"*Uncle Love*," Jaze spins around quickly in obvious fear, "where?" "Calm down Jaze," Cam says, "I was calling you love... Wait... why are you so afraid of your Uncle, did he... *touch* you?"

"Hell no," Jaze says, "he... I saw him kill my Grandma."

"What..." Cam covers her mouth. "Yeah," Jaze continues, "and he was going to kill your sister Megan, and my daddy the same night but my little brother stopped him."

"Are you serious," Cam asks quickly peeping in the window to make sure the love birds were still occupied, "Well how did your little brother stop him?"

"I really don't know Ms. Cam," Jaze tells her, "I was scared frozen standing down the hall in the dark. After I saw what my uncle did to my Mama Cole I snuck back down the hall to hide in my room. But all I know is when my little brother looked up at Uncle Love, he changed." "Who changed Jazemene?" Cam asks.

"Uncle Love," she replies, "he fell to his knees in front of K.J., like he was the baby Jesus or something. Uncle Love had tears in his eyes and everything."

"What does K.J. look like baby?" Cam whispers. "He's my color," she explains, "with short curly hair, green eyes..."

"Green eyes…" Cam repeats. "Yes Ms. Cam," Jaze replies, "they're so pretty. I wish my eyes were like his."

"He has his father's eyes." Cam reflects. Jaze laughs quietly. "No Ms. Cam," she says, "you know my daddy has brown eyes."

"Jaze," Cam says, "baby I have to tell you something that I know you haven't realized yet."

"What is it Ms. Cam?" she asks "Uncle Love is your brother's father Jazemene, *not your daddy*." Cam tells her.

"Do you know your Uncle's number baby?" Cam asks. "Yes ma'am," Jaze thinks to herself, "It's, (407)221-0438." Cam pulls out her cell phone. "Okay I got it saved." Cam says pressing a few more buttons on the screen of her brand new smart phone, "thanks baby girl."

"Jaze," K.C. yells from the front of the house, "baby, where are you?" "Coming Daddy…" she yells back, "Okay, Ms. Cam when I go around to the front of the house this way, you leave that way and nobody will see you leaving."

"Okay," Cam says, "thanks again baby. And remember this is our secret." Jaze hugs her old baby sitter tightly. "I want my daddy to marry you, not your twin." she admits.

"We'll see what we can do baby girl," Cam smiles, "Now run along before *we* get me caught." "Yes ma'am." Jaze says before running around to the side of the mansion to play some hoops with her old man.

Once Cam is safely, back in Charlie's brand-new Phantom, she shoots Love a quick greeting text, and tells him she needs to speak to him soon. Then she cranks the car up and high tails it all the way back to the hotel with a new smile, and a new deadly plan.

Chapter 17
Death Trap

(K.C. & Megan)

Megan is a new person now that she no longer has to hide who she is. The days of pretending to be her twin sister Cameron, are finally over. She delighted in calling the expensive wedding planner and telling her to change everything from invitations to the cakes, from the name Cameron to Megan.

She can tell Keldrick is still conflicted by the fact that she tricked him, but he's coping well. He hasn't mentioned it verbally, but that man's eyes can make you feel things you never even knew you could. The guilt would be overwhelming to most women, but not to Megan. She's built differently than most women, and honestly only cares about her own well-being.

(Megan)

Now that I am the queen of this castle, its time I make my presence and power known. Keldrick will do whatever I say, I am his last chance at a happily ever after with his only true love, my sister Cameron. This doesn't unnerve me at all. He can continue to imagine I'm my sister, as long as I get to enjoy this fairytale lifestyle.

But I have to make sure she doesn't make her way back into his life, and I have to eliminate all possible distractions.

Any woman, who is smart enough to make her man, make her his main priority will never have to worry about being lonely, cheated on, or heartbroken. I have studied men, women, and relationships for a very long time during my own sabbatical from relationships.

Women, we need men like we need air. But at times we fear letting them know how much we need them, as not to become his stepping stone. Whenever most men realize a woman feels as if she can't live without them, they take total advantage of that fact, and the relationship. At that point, you no longer have a real relationship… he is king, but you are not his queen, you just become one of his loyal peasants. Once you become his stepping stone, he can and will walk all over you… until he finds a new queen, who he feels like he actually needs. Whether he realizes it or not, every heterosexual single man is searching for the kind of woman who can add something to his life that he doesn't already possess...

"What are you in here doing Mrs. Cole?" K.C. enters his bedroom with a huge smile. "That's right," Megan agrees returning his smile, "I am Mrs. Cole, and you better not forget it."

"Not in a million years," he tells her, "let's fly to Atlanta tonight." "That sounds great baby, for what though?" she asks.

"Just because we can baby…" K.C. says. "We can hit *Sacs* first and do some shopping," he continues," then check out Lenox mall, and finish the night at one of the hottest strip clubs." "Okay." she replies dryly, walking towards the bathroom.

As she walks, Kel proudly watches her gorgeous dark-skinned shape from the back. He follows closely behind her.

"Okay," he repeats, "that's it? I mean if you'd rather fly out to Houston, or maybe Paris that's fine too."

"Wherever you want to go is fine, *I* might not go with you though." she tells him as she brushes her long dark hair in the mirror.

K.C. laughs lightly. "What are you talking about… of course you're coming with me." he says.

"No, I'm not Keldrick." she turns to look at him, while pulling her hair into a tight ponytail. "We have matters here at home that need to be dealt with." she tells him.

"What matters at home…" he asks folding his arms tightly across his broad chest. She hesitates. "We don't have room or time for distractions Keldrick." she says.

"What distractions do we have Megan?" he asks through a curious irritated glare. "We are not ready for kids." she tells him. Kel immediately bursts into laughter.

"What the hell are you talking about Megan," he asks, "I already have two kids. I have… no we have no choice but to be ready for kids, they're already here. And aren't you pregnant *now*? Or was that yet another lie?"

Megan throws her expensive hairbrush down on the hard bathroom floor breaking it into two pieces. "Finally," she screams, "come on damn it Keldrick let's do it. You've been just waiting for the opportunity to throw this all in my face. Yes, I lied. I pretended to be Cam, because I wanted you for myself. Damn it, I'm sorry. But I feel like I did you a huge favor, that bitch is… and has always been a train wreck. Boy, I saved your black ass."

"Yea maybe so," he replies, "but saving me was not your intention. You were trying to save yourself, and you used me and Cameron to do so."

"I'm sorry," she says, "one thousand times over I'm sorry. But if you never let this go we will never be happy together."

"You know what," K.C. says, "You're right. You're right but this conversation was definitely necessary." "So is the conversation about the kids." she tells him.

"And what about my kids Megan…" K.C. inquires. "I think we should send them away to school," she tells him, "well not K.J. he's too young but Jacqueline we need to send her away for some formal training, both etiquette and education as soon as possible."

"My daughter's name is Jazemene, and are you suggesting I send my baby girl away to a boarding school?" Kel asks.

"Right Jazemene," Megan laughs to herself, "my bad. Look babe, I've already researched several beautiful facilities online, and they're not really that expensive."

"Facilities," K.C. says, "it sounds like you're talking about some filthy ass prison." "No not a prison babe just an all girl's preparatory school." Megan tells him.

"Woman, are you out of your damn mind?" Kel says with a hand on each of his muscle-bound hips. "No," Megan says, "I'm trying to help. Sending… *Jazemene* away to one of those schools will really help her out in the long run, and it will give us a lot of extra time to work on our lifelong bond with each other."

"Megan," Kel steps back away from her, "my daughter is a part of me, and I already have a lifelong bond with her. If you don't want to be married to my kids along with me, then we can end this now, and I can just…"

"Never mind baby…" Megan says. "You know Megan," he says, "you really just sounded like what everybody else is already saying you are, with that crazy ass idea."

"If you will judge me," Megan says, "judge me for what you know of me, not from the mouth of someone who knew my past, or nothing of me at all."

"Just tell me one thing Megan," Kel says, "tell me that you see *me,* and you're here for me… and not my money."

Megan falls to her knees in front of him. "Boy you and I meeting was never a mistake," she says through convincing eyes, "and I will continue to love you more every single day until I stop breathing."

"What are you doing Megan?" he asks. "Baby shut up…" she

says with her eyes fixed on her bulging prize. Pulling the left leg of his gym shorts up, she pulls his throbbing member out through the bottom of his shorts, and begins kissing it softly. Keldrick wraps her long ponytail around his large hand, and begins showing her exactly how to please him.

(Whitney)

Whitney's home is much nicer than it probably should be, but she is the mother of K.C.'s children, and his high school sweet heart so he wasn't going to just put her in the projects.

Whit's three-bedroom house is right in the middle of one of the better neighborhoods in North Miami. She is silently very grateful for the house because she hasn't had her own money or income since she ran away to the island to be with Carlos.

In the near future, she wants to have the kids over to spend the night with her. But right now, her focus is getting rid of Megan. Whitney realizes she will never be able to get rid of Megan herself, for several reasons.

If she does something to her it would be way too obvious, and she doesn't have the capacity to kill another human in the first place. She knows she has to find somebody else who hates Megan just as much as she does.

Whit pulls out her cell phone and begins searching Facebook. Luckily Cam has reactivated her page. After several intriguing messages, back and forth between the two ex-lovers, Whit sends Cam her new cell number.

Whit's phone rings. "Hello Cam…" she says, "Yeah, we need to talk about this Megan problem. Now I know that's your twin but…" Cam cuts Whitney off yelling into the phone. "I was hoping that's what you would say baby," Whit says with a relieved smile on her face, "Now I'm texting you my address, GPS me and come over here ASAP." Cam starts yelling again.

"Wait," Whit says, "calm down Cam, *now who* are you bringing with you?" "No," Whit continues, "Cameron, you know I don't like surprises… Hello, hello…" She's gone. Whit throws her cell phone down and rushes to go change clothes because she has no idea who Cam is bringing to her house as a surprise.

(CRAZY OLE UNCLE LOVE)

A fire red Camaro pulls up in the parking lot at the Millenia Mall. After circling the lot a few times Love finally parks close to the main entrance. "Why are we at the mall Uncle Love?" K.J. asks looking out of the window from his car seat strapped tight in the backseat of Love's car. "Yeah," Jaze agrees in the front seat, "I thought we were going to Wonder Works'."
"We are," he says, "we just have to meet Ms. Cam here at the mall first." "Ms. Cam is going with us?" Jaze asks. "Who is Ms. Cam," K.J. asks, "my daddy said to call the pretty black lady Ms. Megan now." "Ms. Cam is Megan's twin *squirt*." Jaze tells her baby brother.

"Oh okay," K.J. replies with his brows wrinkled tightly, "what's a twin?" Love smiles at the adorable child in his back seat. Jaze shakes her little curly brown head. "Twins are two people with the same birthday and the same face." Jaze explains to the best of her ability.

"Uncle Love I look like you," K.J. admits, "are you my twin?" Love ignores the question.

"No dummy, he's your real dad!" Jaze blurts out.

"Oops…" she covers her regretful mouth. Love's eyes triple in size as he looks down at his young talkative niece. K.J. brows   are wrinkled even more than before now.

"Uncle Love… Are you my real daddy?" the young boy asks. Love looks at Jaze, and then back at K.J. He hesitates, as his

206

momentarily incapable mouth tries hard to form words. "I um," he stutters, "I am your Uncle and I love you very much. And… one day you and I will sit down and talk about life, and… a lot of other things. When you are much older, for now don't worry about the future just continue to love your daddy, and your big sister, and continue to be a good little boy." Love tells K.J.

"Okay Uncle Love." he replies.

A black Rolls-Royce Phantom with dark tinted windows pulls up next to Love's car. The engine shuts off, and the door opens. Wearing a short purple dress, classy black heels, and adorned with expensive black jewelry Cameron steps out of the car looking like she's ready to become America's next top model. Her hair is laid to perfection, with a light brown tinted bang just slightly falling over her left eye.

"Damn." Love whispers. Then he unlocks his car doors, and reaches over to unfasten Jaze's seatbelt. Cam opens the back door and begins to help K.J. out of his car seat. By the time she picks him up to take him out of his car seat, Love is standing close by on the passenger side of the car opening Jaze's door.

Cam lustfully looks Love up and down without him noticing. "Damn." she whispers. She fears and respects this deranged serial killer, who happens to be the younger brother of the man she loves, but she can't deny that he is a beautiful man.

"So, what's the plan?" Cam asks, holding K.J. comfortably on her hip. Love takes Jaze by the hand and begins to lead them all towards the mall's entrance.

"Well I have the kids all day," Love tells her, "because K.C. and Megan are in Atlanta for his big game against the Falcons. But I just wanted to stop here and get something for K.J. and I really quick. After that we can all head towards Wonder Works' to have some fun."

"Cool," Cam replies as they all enter the mall, "Well you and

K.J. go shop, and I'll take my princess to the ***Millenia Nails &
Day Spa*** so we can get our nails done and talk about boys."

Jaze blushes, as she looks back at Cam, and then up at her Uncle.
"Jaze better not be talking about any boys but me, her daddy, and her
baby brother." Love smiles down at his bashful niece. "That's
right."
K.J. agrees shaking his tiny finger at his big sister.

(Atlanta)

"The revitalized Miami Dolphins have just defeated the
Atlanta Falcons forty-nine to fourteen." a host for the post-game
press conference announces to a crowd of reporters and a few fans.

"First," he continues, "we wanna bring to the stage the reason
for some of the recent success the Dolphins have been having as of
late. You know the number… thirty-three, and you know the name
"***Kool Hands***". ***Mr. Keldrick K.C. Cole!***"he announces.

K.C. walks up on the stage with Megan close by his side. They
both take a seat before the reporters. "*Kool Hands*," one reporter says,
"let me start by congratulating you on an amazing game. Nine huge
catches, for five touchdowns, and 317 yards. What goes through your
mind when you're in an unreal zone like that Kool Hands?" he asks.
"It's just a blessing to be able to play the game I love and be
successful, all glory to God." K.C. tells him. "Amen," the reporter
gushes, "One more question Kool Hands. You are going to
undoubtedly leave your mark on the game of football forever… and
not just by your stats, and your level of success, but you are a strong
man who seems to delight in being different. I notice you have your
wife with you. That is not something we see at most NFL post-
game press
conferences."

"That's a shame." K.C. replies smiling at Megan. She happily
returns his warm smile. "That should change," K.C. continues, "I

love my coaches, our entire staff, the fans, and all of my teammates…
but this woman right here is a piece of me that I cannot function
without. *Love is life*."

Kel nods to the conference host. The host immediately
acknowledges the big man, and steps forward with his wireless
microphone. "There will be no further questions for Mr. Cole at this
time." he tells the people.

"Thank you for your time Mr. *Kool Hands*." he says as the super
star begins to leave. K.C. politely waves to the crowd as he escorts his
gorgeous life partner out of the room.

(Wonder Works')

Wonder Works' is a child and adult favorite in Orlando. It's
basically an indoor theme park, filled with unforgettable attractions
that teach you, and entertain you all at the same time. The building
is magical inside and out. If you're ever in Orlando and you drive
down International Drive, you can't miss Wonder Works'. The entire
building is upside down.

Love has been to Wonder Works' at least a hundred times over
the past fifteen years. Mostly trying to relive the childhood he feels
he never really had. He's mentally trying to cheat time and snatch
those precious years back from his clouded memory. Today though
is not like the other ninety something times he's entered this
building. Today he has Cameron, K.J., and Jazemene with him.

"To what do I owe the pleasure of your text… and now your
company Cameron Jiles?" Love asks. "Is it a pleasure?" Cam asks
teasingly. "Well that's yet to be determined I guess," Love says, "but
it is weird because you never took any interest in me before."

"I always thought you were fine as hell," Cam admits, "but
you're Kel's baby brother."

"So is Ty." Love says through a coy smile. "That's not right
Love…" Cam tells him returning his smile. "No, I'm just kidding,"

he says, "but thanks for the compliment."

"Uncle Love," Jaze tugs on his pant leg, "I wanna go get on the bed of nails." "The **Bed of Nails**," he mimics playfully, "And what do you know about the **Bed of Nails** little lady?"

"My Mama Co…" Jaze hesitates and then looks at Cam. "Your Mama Cole what baby…" Love asks noticing her nervousness. Jaze hides her hands behind her back so her Uncle won't notice how badly they're shaking.

"Mama Cole used to bring me here when I was little," Jaze says, "Well she brought me once." "I miss my Mama Cole…" K.J. cries. "Come here little man." Love scoops his little look alike up in his arms.

K.J. is matching Love from head to toe. Love made that special stop on the way here, by the Millennium mall just to pick out outfits for him and his little boy. Love whispers in K.J.'s ear, and he almost immediately stops crying. The two of them seem to have a unique bond that time could never create. What they have together is a natural connection.

As they head upstairs to the area where *"the bed of nails"* is K.J.
never leaves Love's side. "Who's next to try the deadly *bed of nails*?" a young Asian girl says, wearing a bright yellow Wonder Works' shirt. "How about you little lady?" she points to Jaze. Jaze steps back and hides behind Cam.

"What are you doing lady bug," Uncle Love says, "I thought you said you have been on the **Bed of Nails** before?"

"It's been a long time." Jaze tries not to blush.

"Okay how about me and K.J. go first?" he asks. Jaze nods her pretty little head up and down. "No!" K.J. screams.

"I don't wanna die Uncle Love." K.J. continues. "Listen son," Love says, "I'm going to lie on the **Bed of Nails** and you just sit on my stomach the nails will never touch you. I want you to always remember what I told you. I will never let anyone or anything hurt you. I will die first son."

Love turns to the employee. "Can we do it that way, Christina?" he asks after reading her name tag on her shirt. "Sure." she tries to hide the fact that she's utterly stunned by his eyes, lips, and dreads.

Love looks down at K.J. "Are you with me son?" he asks with a comforting smile on his proud face. "Okay." K.J. says. Love lies down flat on the glass table. Then Cam picks K.J. up and sits him on Love's stomach.

"Ready sir?" the employee asks. "*Turn up*." Love says. The employee presses the button to release the nails. As they begin to raise,

K.J. with his eyes wide open stares down into Love's eyes. "Are you okay Uncle Love?" K.J. asks patting Love on his strong chest.

"Never better son." he replies.

"Catherine… Catherine Whatley is that you?" a voice says nearby. Love feels his entire body begin to tingle, and his mouth is watering as well.

"Judge Whatley…" he whispers to himself. "What did you say Uncle Love, I couldn't hear you?" K.J. asks.

Love doesn't respond. The nails are lowering back into the table now, bringing Love and K.J. back down as well.

As he climbs down off the glass table Love hands K.J. to Cam, and quickly surveys his surroundings. There she is. He has her in his deadly sights. "So how many convictions did your court room see last quarter Cat?" a man asks the heartless judge.

"Well," Judge Whatley replies, "let's just say if their color *wasn't right*, and their money *was tight*… hell I tried to give em *life*!" Judge Whatley and her friends all find this sick joke more than amusing, as they all join in with her avid laughter.

"Hey Cam…" Love reaches in his pocket. "Wassup Love, are you okay?" she asks. "Yeah, yeah, I'm great," he lies, "here's a twenty take the kids down stairs to get some pizza. I'll meet ya'll down there in five minutes. I just wanna make my presence known

211

to an old friend."

"Okay," Cam reluctantly takes the twenty, "come on kids, let's go get some pizza." Holding Jaze and K.J. by the hand Cam leads both children towards the stairs. Cam saw the poisonous look in Love's eyes, now she's sure he's the man she needs to eliminate her own pesky problem.

Love watches the three of them until they are completely out of his sight. "I'll be back Deb and Andrew, I'm just gonna go use the little girl's room really fast." Judge Whatley says.

"Me too oh honorable Judge," Love whispers to himself, "hope you won't mind a little company." Love swiftly makes his way to the men's bathroom to prepare himself. Inside one of the stalls, he quickly puts on his tight black gloves he carries in his back pocket at all times, and then strips the shoe lace from his left shoe.

As he exits the restroom he pulls his hood down way over his face, and tries not to move too fast as not to lose his unlaced shoe off of his left foot. After making sure no one is watching him, he stares up into the camera right above his head, and then rushes into the woman's bathroom anyway.

Once inside, the foul smell of the honorable Judge's bowels and gas, begin assaulting his nose immediately. Love knocks softly on her stall door.

"Just a minute." she says. The toilet flushes, and then the Judge, emerges from the stall. When she sees his unforgettable green eyes she tries to scream, but the fear is too heavy on her heart to even make a sound.

"I called you several times, and wrote you thousands of letters while I was locked up Judge Whatley." he growls. "I'm sorry." she whimpers. "When Love called bitch, you should have answered." he growls.

"Come here!" he growls. Wrapping the strong shoe lace tightly around her neck twice he pulls her back inside the stall she was just in, and chokes her until he smells her defecating on herself.

"Damn," he gags, "I guess she was finished when I knocked." Love then locks the stall from the inside, and crawls underneath the door. After exiting the women's bathroom, he returns to the men's room once more. After removing his gloves, washing his face, and lacing his left shoe back up, Love exits the men's room and makes his way down to the concessions area calm, cool, and collected.

(Two days later)
(Cam & Whit)

Whitney is still at home sitting nervously on one of the brand-new couches K.C. furnished her new home with. She hasn't seen Cameron since days before she left the island. Now that they're back in the states, Whitney wonders if their mutual love for Keldrick will make them enemies once again. The hatred they once had for each other was all but deadly. Whitney hopes they can keep all that dangerous hate behind them and just focus together on getting rid of Megan.

The doorbell rings. Whitney jumps as a sudden chill goes down her spine. As she makes her way to the front door she swears she hears somebody in the back of the house, but she realizes she's just being paranoid in a new house, because she definitely is here all alone.

Whit opens the door. "Hey girl…" Cam says through a cute smile. "Hey baby." Whit replies. They hug tightly. After they hug Whit takes a couple steps out towards her front lawn to look down her street. "Do you know whose red Camaro that is parked down the street?" Whit asks.

"Um no," Cam laughs nervously as she lies; "remember you live out here babe not me." "Right," Whit laughs nervously, "silly me. It's just that, that car has been parked in front of that house for over an

213

hour and nobody lives there. Oh, nice Phantom by the way, is it yours?"
"Girl I wish," Cam laughs, "It belongs to Charlie."

"*My Charlie?*" Whit asks. "Yes girl… *your* Charlie."

"He's here… in the states?" she asks. "Yeah Whit he brought me back himself." Cam tells her.

"Wow, okay well come on inside and tell me all about it." Whit tells her. Whit looks down the street at the mysterious Camaro one more time before stepping inside. She quickly closes and locks the door after they walk in.

"You want something to drink Cameron?" Whit asks. "Yeah," Cam smiles, "a tall glass of your fine ass. Come gimme some suga, Suga Mama."

Whitney, wearing some skintight pink leggings, and a green A.K.A. tank top with her tiny nipples protruding beneath it, makes her way to the couch slowly. "I love to watch you walk babe." Cam says.

"I know you do." Whit brags playfully. Whit slowly straddles Cam on the large sofa as they begin kissing each other passionately. Whit holds her hands straight up in the air, as Cam pulls her tank top over her tight blond curls and then throws it on the floor. Whit sits back on Cam's lap, as she squeezes her own bare breasts.

"Wait Cam," Whit says, "we can't do this." "Yes, we can," Cam says leaning in for another kiss, "come here babe."

Whit stands up. "No, I mean we need to handle our business before we give each other *the business*; you feel me? We have all night for this." Whit says. Cam wipes her wet mouth. "Yeah, I feel you babe," Cam reluctantly agrees, "so where do we start?"

Whit takes a seat on a comfortable reclining chair across from the couch that Cam is seated on. "First of all, how attached are you to your twin?" Whit asks. "If I wasn't scared of jail I'd kill the bitch myself." Cam replies. "Perfect," Whit smiles, "so we just gotta figure out how to get rid of her and not get caught."

"Um…" Cam starts.

"Just listen Cam," Whit continues, "I've been watching a bunch of cop shows, and I even Googled some information on how to get away with murder."

Cam laughs loudly. "Wait bitch," Cam says pleasantly amused, "you did what baby…" "Girl…" Whit says, "Google has *everything* honey, trust me. I can also make you and I both squirt one hundred and seven different ways, at the same time."

"*Well amen*," Cam screams, "don't talk like that baby you gone have me side tracked all over again. And please put your lil ugly *akuh* tank top back on because your breasts are distracting me too."

They both laugh. "*Akuh*…" Whit says still giggling, "I forgot you are a *paper* Delta. Hmm, get it right boo, its "*A.K.A.*" *Alpha Kappa Alpha Sorority Incorporated*. You could have made the right choice as well, but you allowed yourself to be sadly misguided to the wrong side."

"Oh, I made the right choice baby," Cam says "never have I been a stuck-up air head, nor do I enjoy wearing clashing colors on purposely. Soooo, back to the matters at hand though." They both burst into adamant laughter together again.

"Girl you really just tried me," Whit says, "it's cool though, that was cute. Don't let it happen again."

"Girl whatever," Cam smiles, "So look I'ma be honest babe."

"Go head." Whit says. "I wanna hire Love to kill my sister." Cameron tells her. "You what…" Whit stands up to put her tank top back on.

"You heard me Whitney." Cam says. "Are you crazy Cam," Whit says, "That dude wouldn't hurt a fly. You gotta break his heart or call him gay just to get his little psychotic split personality to come out just so he will do something."

"Wrong." Cam says. "What do you know that I don't Cam," Whit says, "because I know Love to be a really *sweet* dude literally, and that's about it. I mean he shot my daughter when she was five,

215

complete *bitch* move."

"Yeah," Cam says, "That was pre-prison. Literally everything you're remembering and speaking on was before Love did five years in a cage, locked inside his own mind. He completely buried himself physically and mentally in pain, regret, and now revenge."

"I've seen dude though," Whit says, "a couple times at K.C.'s house. He still looks the same. Well he's much bigger now, still fine as hell, but he ain't a killer Cam."

"He killed Mama Cole Whitney," Cam says, "Ask your baby Jazemene, she watched him kill Mama Cole in cold blood in her own room."

"Are you serious?" Whit asks. "As a serial killer baby," Cam says, "Love is the real deal. I've been doing my research I think he also murdered K.C.'s father Paul, his old landlord Marco Ligetti, and several other people too. That judge that got murdered in Orlando at Wonder Works, it was all over the news a couple days ago... Ms. Catherine Whatley..."

"Damn... Whatley *was* Love's judge, wasn't she?" Whitney gasps in real fear. "We were there that day." Cam tells her. "Who girl..." Whit inquires.

"Love, Jaze, K.J., and I," Cam says, "we were all upstairs near the *Bed of Nails* when Love heard the Judges' voice, and then when he saw her... Oh my god the look in his eyes was priceless Whit. The man is like a skillful, trained assassin. That's why I didn't show up here two days ago, I had so much on my mind."

"So, what's gonna keep him from killing us Cam?" Whit asks making her way back to the sofa to sit closer to Cameron. "If he wanted us dead Whit," Cam says, "we would have **been** dead. We obviously aren't on his shit list."

"I'm not so sure Cam..." Whit admits. "Why what happened?" Cam inquires. "Well nothing really happened," Whit admits, "but ever since I moved in here, I've always felt like someone is here watching me."

"Mmmm I can't say I would blame em' baby." Cam teases as

she rubs Whit's thick left yellow thigh as she licks her own full lips.

"I'm so serious right now Cameron." Whit cries with true terror in her eyes. "I'm sure you're just paranoid Whit," Cam consoles her, "okay babe?"

Two tears stream down Whit's panic-stricken face.

"No baby, please don't cry," Cam begs, "you're killing me love." Whit jumps. "No," she screams, "do not call me that *ever*, and don't say that name in my home or I will have to ask you to leave."

"Okay," Cam giggles nervously, "Um babe you're really starting to scare me. Why are you so shaken up right now?" Whitney is crying full force now. "Whitney talk to me baby." Cam begs.

"You just told me a man that I mentally mistreated and eventually destroyed has become a violent, tactful serial killer," Whit tells her, "Why the hell wouldn't I be afraid? If he has a list Whitney Michelle Powell is the crowning jewel on that list... *trust me*."

"No, you are not Whitney, don't say that." Cam tells her. "And if you are on his list," Cam continues, "I will personally take you off of it. I will kill him myself, or die for you to live." Whitney falls freely, into Cameron's loving arms. Cam rocks Whitney back and forth for about twenty minutes.

"Whit..." Cam says. She doesn't respond. "Whit baby..." Cam repeats.

"Yes..." she replies.

"Come with me..." Cam tells her. "Where are we going?" she asks. "To the bathroom," Cam tells her, "let's go wash your face, Love will be here soon."

Whit leads Cam to the bathroom still in tears. "Damn it Cameron," Whit cries, "You already told him where I live didn't you. Damn it... damn it... damn it..." "He is not after you baby, you'll see." Cam assures her.

217

In the bathroom Cam stands behind Whitney wiping her red face with a warm wet towel. Cam's heart stops when she notices the reflection in the mirror. In the mirror's reflection standing behind her, Cam can see him standing there silently in the bath tub hiding behind the shower curtain with his dreads hanging all around his yellow face.

He has one finger up to his lips and a black gun in his right hand. "Um I left something in the car babe," Cam mumbles uneasily, "I'll be right back." Cam sits the towel down slowly, kisses Whit on her lips one last time and then hurriedly leaves the bathroom. "Wait Cam…" Whit cries.

Whit realizes what's going on. She quickly looks in the mirror. She opens her mouth but nothing comes out of her dry throat. The look in Love's eyes could leave anybody's blood curdling cry forever stuck inside their throat.

"I knew it…" she cries softly. Love steps out of the tub and places his gun to the back of her head. "I called you, and wrote you a thousand times from prison." he claims. "I didn't know." she lies.

"You answered the phone a couple times," he recalls, "but you would always hang up." Whitney continues to cry.

"Why didn't you respond to me when I reached out to you for moral support?" he asks. "Love," she starts, "you were in there for kidnapping and shooting my five-year-old daughter, and also for attempting to kill me. If you were searching for moral support, I was the last person who should have been on your list."

"I guess you're right Whitney," he smiles, "But when Love calls you should always answer. But you didn't, and prison made me hate being ignored, it's my number one pet peeve now. I would *kill* about that."

He laughs his sickening laugh. "Why now?" she asks. "Why now what Whitney?" he replies snidely.

"You've had multiple opportunities to kill me," she cries wiping more of her tears away, "why did you wait so long?"

"Why not?" he asks with his head tilted curiously to the side. "Why are you looking at me like that," she asks, "don't play with me Love. You're really creepin' me out. Just kill me and get it over with."

Love cocks his gun close to her tiny yellow ear. With his finger on the trigger Love closes his eyes and kisses Whit on the back of her blond head. "Goodbye…" he whispers.

"Put the gun down *now* Bruh!" a man demands from the doorway. "Who the hell are you?" Love asks. "It doesn't matter," he says, "put the gun down or we're all gone be some dead mother fucker's in this little cute ass bathroom."

Whitney recognizes that voice but is scared to move. "Charlie…" she whimpers. "Why the hell do you care if she lives or dies dude?" Love asks. "Because *dude,*" Charlie replies, "she gives me life. I am undeniably head over heels in love with the woman you're holding at gunpoint. So, do us all a favor and please remove it."

Love can't win so he does as he's instructed. "I really don't even want you dead Whitney," he admits, "You're K.J.'s mother. But when I heard you up front talking about me, something snapped. You said I was weak."

"If you didn't want me dead," Whit starts, "then why the hell did you break into my house, and hide in my bath tub?"

"All I really want to know," Love says, "is K.J. my biological son or not?"

"What…" Whit asks. "Is your son… *our* son?" Love asks. "Are you all really that blind," she asks, "the boy looks just like you Love. And around the time he was actually conceived I was only sleeping with you."

"So that means… he *is* my, K.J. is…" Love tears up as he finally receives the only confirmation he truly needed.

"So yes Love, K.J. is your biological son, not Keldrick's," Whit admits, "his little gorgeous green eyes were part of the reason I ran away. It was killing me to know that deep down Keldrick knew

219

K.J. was not his son. Our marriage would have never worked, so I left on that basis alone."

Love leaves the bathroom taking Cam who was hiding behind Charlie by the hand. Whitney runs to Charlie Breeze. *"**Charlie**,"* she cries, "you saved my life… again." "Perfection only shows you its face once in a lifetime." he tells her. "I never even understood what that means Charlie." she admits.

"You Whitney Michelle Powell," he says, "are an extraordinary woman. When I look at you I see the only way I want my future to be, and the only person I want to spend every day of the rest of my life with. You may have been another man's painful past, but you are, and will forever be my perfect match."

"Aw thank you Charlie…" Whit moans. "Listen Whitney," Charlie says lost in her conflicting eyes, "I wanna be your man, **your only man**."

"I know." Whit replies. "I'm serious Whitney, forget K.C." he tells her.

"I can't just…" Whit starts.

"Yes, you can," Charlie interjects, "he already forgot about you. He's so in love with Cameron… hell he's married to her identical twin." Charlie laughs to himself. "Don't you see," he continues, "I wanna show you things you've never seen before, tell you things you've never heard before, and I wanna be to you what no one else has ever been to you *in your life*."

Lost in the cadence of his words and the tone of his voice, Whit can barely control her sputtering heartbeat. "And what is that Charlie?" she questions. *"**Your forever**…"* he tells her with pure confidence in every single word.

In the front room Love and Cameron are going over the specifics of their secret contract. "This conversation never happened, Cameron." Love tells her. "Okay." she replies. "I'm as serious as brain cancer Cam." he tells her.

"Who has brain cancer?" Whitney asks as she enters the front room. "Nobody," Cam says quickly, "you okay babe?"

"Yeah," Whit replies, "no thanks to you. Bitch you left me to die!" Cam stands up quickly, and puts both of her hands defiantly on her well-defined hips.

"Are you serious," Cam asks, "I saved your sorry ass life. What the hell was I gonna do he had a gun?"

"You left me to die." Whit repeats. "No, I left you to run out to the car and get Charlie, who I knew had a gun." Cam explains.

"Yeah Whit," Charlie interjects, "Cam did the right thing. I was right outside in the car bae." "I apologize, Whitney..." Love says, "I told you I don't want you dead. I want my son to have his mommy. A boy's relationship with his mother is almost as important, to his development as his relationship with his father is."

"That's beautiful Love, and so true." Cam agrees.

"I respect your love for our son," Whit claims, "but Love you scare me, so I'm not sure yet how we move forward at this point. And what about K.C..."

"What about my brother?" Love asks. "Somebody has to officially tell him the truth about K.J." she says.

"Yeah well let's wait till after the wedding, and then we can break the news to him." Love suggests. "Yeah Whit," Cam agrees, "That would be best."

"Fine..." Whit agrees, "so Love you're going to take care of our problem right after the wedding, right?"

"No, not quite..." Love says. "We came up with something even better girl," Cam claims through an excited toothy smile, "wait till you hear this."

Love puts a hand on Cam's left thigh. "Now one last time are you sure you want your sister, your own twin... dead?" he asks.

"Is Dr. Carlos Sanchez richer than God?" she asks.

"I'll take that as a yes," Love replies, "one last request though, you tell nobody the exact plan until it's already done. And tell Whit my other condition *right* now."

"What other condition?" Whit inquires. Cam exhales heavily. "Whit," Cam pauses, "Love wants joint custody with you for K.J."

"Definitely not…" Whit responds without hesitation. Love stands up and shakes Cam's hand. "Well Cameron looks like there is no deal, but thanks for your time, have a great night…"

"Wait." Whit interjects. "I can't let that fake ass Cam marry my Keldrick." she explains. "Then agree to his terms Whit." Cam tells her.

"Come here Love we need to talk before I make this decision." Whitney motions for him to follow her to the back. "If you need me I'll be right up front Whitney." Charlie promises. Then he takes a seat on the couch and begins talking to Cam while they wait.

Love follows Whit back into the bathroom. "What's up Whit?" Love asks. "Take your hood off." Whit tells him. "What…" he asks. "Do it." she demands. He obeys.

"Let your dreads down." she demands. Love unties his dreads and allows them to swing down around and in his face. "Now what…" Love asks.

"Don't speak," Whit licks her succulent pink lips, "take your hoodie off." Love obeys. "Pull your tank top up." Whit tells him. Love obeys. Whitney kneels down in front of him and reaches up to run her long nails up and down his well-sculpted stomach. "Take off your pants." she demands. Love obeys once more.

In nothing but his tight red boxer briefs exposing the shape of him, Love waits on his next instruction. Whitney can't help but stare at his gorgeous bulge. "You want joint custody of K.J.?" she asks caressing him as he grows stiff.

"Yeah I do." he moans. "Then fuck me for it…" she tells him. "What…" Love wrinkles his brows tightly. "You heard me," she confirms from her knees, "Fuck me better than you ever have before right now, if you want joint custody of our son."

Love grabs her by her curls, pulls his strong member out and shoves it all the way in the back of her throat. With her hands on his waist, and his hand pushing her head back and forth, Whit takes pleasure in his oral intrusion. She chokes several times.

She pulls back to quickly spit in the toilet then starts back again where she left off. "You want me to close the door?" he asks. She pulls back again. "For what we're grown…" she replies. Then she forces him in the back of her throat again.

"What the hell…" Charlie growls from the doorway. Whitney doesn't budge. She's hypnotized by Love's long strong hardness. Love looks back at Charlie with a friendly grin. He motions for Charlie to come closer. He does. Charlie begins to stroke himself through his jeans, as he watches his girl pleasure Love.

Once he's at full salute he unzips his pants and pulls himself out. With his tip on the side of Whitney's rapid moving face Charlie continues to stroke himself as Whitney continues to satisfy Love.

With her right-hand Whit takes control of stroking Charlie as she continues to swallow Love as much as humanly possible. With a swift motion Whitney switches positions, forcing Charlie's member down her throat while stroking Love with her left hand.

"Whit, what the hell are you doing?" Cam asks. "Come here baby." Whit tells her after pulling Charlie out of her throat. Cam obeys. Down on her own knees Cam begins to engulf Charlie Breeze, while Whitney licks and softly bites Love's huge tip. Both men switch positions, Cam and Whit have no objection as they allow the men to take over complete control.

Charlie grabs the back of Whit's head with both hands and holds her mouth all the way down on him until she can no longer breathe. Then he pulls her head back as she gasps for air and turns to spit in the toilet again.

Charlie then picks Whit up by her hair and carries her to the front room. Whit bends over on her luxurious sofa, waiting for him. Charlie pulls her leggings down to her ankles. Then he quickly snatches off all of his clothes and throws it on the floor in a messy pile. In his back-pant pocket on the floor he finds a small gold packet. He rips it open with his teeth and slides his condom on securely. He loves Whit but doesn't need any kids or other distractions in his life right now, so he takes the necessary precaution this time.

Charlie wets his left hand thoroughly, and then uses it to further moisten Whit from the back. With his hands on her slim waist he enters her slowly from the back. He can barely contain himself, he has dreamed many nights about being with her like this again.

Cam and Love eventually follow suit and line up next to Whit and Charlie on the sofa. Love doesn't have a condom but he doesn't really care at this point. As Charlie continues to make sweet Love to Whit, Love pounds Cam as hard as he possibly can. While they both take it from the back, Whit and Cam are kissing each other with open mouths.

Love notices how slow Charlie is working Whit, he laughs and then abruptly comes out of Cam, pushing the black china doll down on the sofa like she means nothing to him. "Watch out homie," Love laughs, "Lemme show, you how to *pain* Suga Mama."

Charlie pulls out and steps aside as Love enters Whit hard from the back and pushes her head all the way down to the sofa. Whitney arches her back as much as she possibly can to invite him in even more. "Love, baby I missed you, *daddy*!" she screams.

Charlie makes his way over to Cam, and picks her up in his arms putting all of himself in her, as he walks around the room bouncing her up and down on him. Cam can't take it all, she feels as if she's about to pass out. But just before she passes out, an intense orgasm snatches her back to consciousness.

Chapter 18
The Surprise

(K.C. & Megan)

Keldrick and Megan received word via email from his agent that he has just been offered three of the largest endorsement deals of all time. The deals will continue on into his retirement. The total he will net from all three deals is a little more than seven hundred and seventy-five million dollars. First *Nike* is giving "Kool Hands" three hundred and fifty million dollars. He will have his own line of shoes, cologne, sports water, and football gloves. *BMW* is giving him two hundred million dollars for the 2015 BMW 329i *"Keldrick Cole"* edition. BMW boasts over a hundred of these cars already presold internationally.

Last but not least *Wal-Mart* is giving Cole two hundred and twenty-five million dollars for the sale of his autobiography *"From Behind Bars to Billions,"* as well as a line of "Keldrick Cole" grills, and grill utensils, all to be sold exclusively at Wal-Mart stores.

With these endorsements, his current stock trade money, along with the money Love gave K.C. that he stole from their late mother's accounts, K.C. is now officially a billionaire. As soon as the checks hit the bank K.C. sent Love and the kids to a Disney Resort all expenses paid for the weekend.

The house is quiet and immaculately clean. K.C. gave all the help the weekend off, so with the kids away with Love on the Disney Resort for the weekend, Keldrick has his wife all to himself for a few days. This night unbeknownst to Megan was planned a week in advance.

In her huge walk in closet hanging there in the middle of

everything else Megan finds the prettiest tight blue dress she has ever seen.

"Have you seen the shoes yet?" Kel asks walking in behind her. "Where did you come from baby?" she asks trying to hide the surprise in her voice.

"Downstairs," he replies, "do you like the dress?"

"Of course," she gushes, "it's gorgeous. Who made it?"

"Charles Andrews of course," K.C. boasts, "he designed this dress, the matching heels, and all the accessories *just for you*."

"For what occasion, though?" she asks. "I don't need an occasion to have one of my closest friends who just happens to be a top of the line fashion designer, create something exceptional for my own wife." he tells her as he massages her tight shoulders.

"No, you don't," she agrees, "but I'm sure you didn't have Charles create this masterpiece for me to just wear around the house."

"Yea I thought you would look cute washing the dishes with it on." K.C. says with a coy smile. "Don't play with me Keldrick." Megan whines returning his sly smile before taking a closer look at the gorgeous dress.

"I'm not playing. I really don't have anything special planned for tonight." he walks towards the bedroom. "But baby," she whines, "the kids are finally gone, we can go anywhere we want to, and do anything our hearts desire for seventy-two hours straight."

Kel dives across the bed. Megan walks towards him and stands near the edge of the bed with her arms folded tightly. "Keldrick Jermaine Cole…" she says.

"Girl, go get dressed already," he says still lying down hiding a new smile, "we got enough money for three lifetimes and only one life to live… of course I'm taking your pretty ass out tonight."

Megan screams. "Yes baby," she exclaims, "so where are you taking me this time. Wait… lemme guess, Bora Bora, or the French Island of Corsica, no… the Split's Diocletian Palace in Croatia…"

"It's a surprise baby girl just go get dressed." he tells her. As

Megan happily makes her way back to her closet to prepare for the wondrous evening ahead of her, K.C. is left alone with his haunting thoughts.

(K.C.)

Damn it. Kel what are you doing to yourself and this woman? You are married to, and living with a complete stranger. A woman you don't even know... your wife, is carrying your child inside of her right now.

I have somehow been stupid enough to...fall in love with the idea of a woman. So, in love in fact that something that only resembles the actual woman is enough to take over my whole heart and mind.

Every time I touch, kiss, make love too, or even look at this woman I have to restrain from calling her Cameron. Cam is my one and only true love, I can fight it until I stop breathing and it won't change or matter because only Cam has the power to give me life, and in turn the control to take my breath away.

I can admit to myself that I love that woman with all of her flaws and screaming imperfections, and I wouldn't change her for the world. The world... I can't even tell the world how much she means to me, and that she's the only one I want the one I truly need, and dream about.

This woman, her twin Megan tricked me and allowed me to believe she was Cam, so of course I loved her fiercely. She was my last chance to be with my soul mate in the flesh. I want to take back every terrible thing I ever said or did to Cam, but my pride is in my way. I can't go back now. I've already said and done way more than Cam will ever be able to forgive me for.

At this point I realize if by some kind of gigantic miracle Cameron and I did reconcile our differences and our relationship, we would

never be able to coexist for long. We would both live with those old pains, words, and regrets forever. But my God how much do I love that woman that she has become a part of every single thought I ever have? Doesn't matter now, I have to live forever inside of a lie with a woman who looks exactly like the woman I actually live for. Lord your will be done.

An hour later K.C. and Megan both dressed to the nines are standing in front of their luxurious mountain of a home, as the stretch limo pulls up like clockwork.

The driver parks and jumps out swiftly making his way to the back door. "Good evening Mr. and Mrs. Cole, my name is Bennie and I'll be your driver this evening." he says as he opens the door for the couple and then shuts it behind them after they climb in.

Inside the limo a handsome man, with a well-kept low-top fade, wearing a black servant's suit is seated and waiting for his affluent patrons for the evening.

"Good evening Mr. and Mrs. Cole." he says nodding his head in appreciative servitude.

"Good evening to you my brother," K.C. replies, "what is your name sir?"

"Desario Caldwell sir thanks for asking…" he replies, "but you can call me Desi if you like." "It's very nice to meet you Desi." Megan smiles at him.

Old school R & B jams are wafting through the limo speakers, setting the perfect mood for tonight's surprise romantic excursion. Kel points to the tiny fridge and full bar close to Desi's right side. "Are you hungry or thirsty baby?" he asks his wife.

"I am…" she replies. "Desi," Kel says, "if you would can you please make my wife a light *Mary Pickford* with a twist of mango?" "Yes sir, and what can I get for you sir?" Desi asks. "I'll have a *Nick & Nora Dry Martini* on the rocks." K.C. replies.

Desi hands Megan her drink first. Megan studies the beverage; she smiles at its delightful strong pink color. "What's in it baby…" Megan asks Kel. "Well, let's see if I remember correctly," K.C. pauses to think, "it's a rum-based cocktail. It's supposed to be tantalizingly sweet but with a real kick. The pink tipple calls for pineapple juice, grenadine, and just a hint of maraschino liqueur."

"Very good Mr. Cole..." Desi smiles acknowledging K.C.'s impressive drink mixing knowledge. Desi hands Kel his drink with a green olive in the bottom of his glass.

"This is one of the best drinks I have ever tasted." Megan admits. "I'm glad you like it love." K.C. replies.

Megan takes a moment to sit back and stare at her handsome husband. Kel smiles as he notices her smiling at him.

"Are you okay baby?" he asks. "Nope," she laughs to herself, "I am not okay. I am **blessed** by the best, to even be in your presence right now. You really are something Keldrick Cole." "Well thank you Mrs. Cole." Kel leans over to kiss his woman.

"I'm serious K.C.," she continues, "You really are an extraordinary specimen of not just a black man, but a man period. You are what every young boy dreams of being. *My lord...* you came from the absolute bottom and made all your dreams come true. No, I believe you surpassed even your own dreams, baby you are a self-made black billionaire. And I know I didn't know you before you became rich, but I'm sure you were not what you have become as a person."

"I'm sorry I don't think I follow that last part." he says. "You give millions and millions of dollars to so many charities and causes anonymously," she explains, "You have researched so many things, and have become so well rounded and cultured."

Megan smiles genuinely. "No offense," she continues, "but I'm sure as a poor little black boy from Orlando, you didn't grow up with much knowledge of polo, croquet, or *collecting ascots.* You ride horses well, and you wear, drive, and eat only the finest things. That takes practice to truly become classy to the point of it actually being natural."

"Thanks again baby." K.C. returns her proud smile.

"She's right Mr. Cole," Desi agrees, "I'm sorry to interrupt your conversation and I know I don't know you personally, but when the

news hit about the deals you made with Nike, BMW, and Wal-Mart last week I cried *my damn self.* That was the first time I had ever been proud of someone I had never met before." Kel nods in appreciation. "Honestly guys," K.C. tells them both, "I've realized that about ninety percent of the Americans I know are all satisfied with just surviving. I never again want to just survive and exist in my own life… I want to thrive and maintain an eternal state of happiness
anchored by my own talents and my own supreme work ethic."

"Some people just weren't born to think that way Mr. Cole." Desi tells him. "You're right," K.C. agrees, "but I thank God that I was and I'm going to make sure my children grow up to think the same way."

"Oh, my how your children are blessed…" Desi gushes. "They are," K.C. agrees, "but people should also never try to ride on someone else's coattails whether they are family or not. *If a person does not invite you along to be a part of their dream… then you must build your own dream or accept eternal mediocrity.*"

The limo stops. "We must be here." Desi says. Megan looks out of the window at the large building, and the huge crowd outside waiting to get in. "Grand Central," Megan asks, "what's going on here tonight?"

K.C. places two tickets in Megan's lap. She looks down, and then picks them up. She screams out at the top of her lungs, and then jumps in K.C.'s lap kissing him fiercely.

"Maybach Music Group… and Omarion is performing *live tonight*," she screams, "How did you know baby? Cam and I were the biggest B2K fans on the planet." "*I know.*" Kel replies looking down. Megan reads his facial expression. "It's okay," she tells him, "I love you and our life together Keldrick. If you need to, or just want to pretend I'm… Cam then do it baby. You can even call me her name if you want I don't mind, I just want you and everything that comes along with you."

The door opens. The driver helps Megan step out, and then

stands back as the larger K.C. steps out. "Thank you, Bennie."
Megan smiles at the friendly driver. "You're welcome Mrs. Cole," he
replies, "Now Mr. Cole shall I just wait for you here or would you
rather call my cell, when you want me to come back?"

"Um," Kel hesitates to respond as he studies his woman's face,
"yeah the second one. Who knows, me and the wifey might take a
walk after the concert and get some fresh air."

"Perfect," the driver replies, "Say no more. Now you're paid up
for the whole weekend so this is your limo Mr. *Kool Hands* so if you
call me I'll come instantly."

"Awesome thanks Bennie." Kel shakes the driver's gloved hand.
"And thank you too Desi." he says looking back inside the back of
the limo. Desi salutes him. The driver tips his hat, closes the back
door and then returns to the driver's seat to take off.

"This line is monstrous." Megan says looking at the crowd in
front of them. "Not for us it's not," K.C. says, "follow me babe our
tickets say V.I.P. for a reason."

"Yes sir…" Megan replies, "just lead the way." K.C. pulls his hat
brim down low, and throws on a pair of *Ray Bans*. Tonight, is not
an autograph signing paparazzi kind of night. It's all about his wife
tonight.

"Come on." K.C. takes her by the hand. She realizes she's mostly
living a lie, if not someone else's life all together, but Megan would
follow this man to Hell and back if she had to. They head towards
the front of the crowd.

As they get towards the middle of the line K.C. sees Jazemene's
teacher Cidra Bell. "Cidra." he whispers in her ear.

Megan snatches her hand away from him and puts both hands on
her hips. "K.C.…" Cidra says trying to see through his disguise
without causing a scene. "Yeah, it's me," he says, "This is my wife
Megan."

"Yes, I know," Cidra tells him, "I saw her on your Facebook
page and in a couple magazines with you." The two women wave to
each other nonchalantly.

"Oh okay," Kel replies, "who are you here with?" "What's up big bro?" Jay says from behind Cidra. "Jacody," K.C.'s brows begin to furrow, "What the hell are you doing in Miami, and with Ms. Bell?"

Megan exhales loudly. Jay laughs nervously. "We uh…" Jay stutters. "He added me on Facebook after I liked a few of your island wedding pictures."

"Yeah," Jay says, "something like that." "Oh really," Kel asks, "so he's your boyfriend Cidra or what…"

Megan exhales loudly again. "Look big dog," Jay steps forward, "don't question my date. We are together right now, and that's all that matters." "What…" Kel responds with wide eyes.

"I mean damn," Jay continues, "somebody has to eventually date the women you discard, right?"

With that said Kel doesn't panic, he turns around and kisses Megan passionately. Looking deep in her eyes he says, "I'll always be yours."

Then he looks back at Jay. "Don't be late to my second wedding *Mr*. Best Man." he tells him. Then he takes his wife by the hand and heads towards the front of the crowded line. They can finally see the front door. They show their tickets at the door as a security guard ushers them both in.

(Megan)

I can never stay mad at him because I know I don't deserve him. He is everything I always dreamed would happen to me. When you luck up on a man of this caliber it's much deeper than just meeting someone. This is a drastic lifestyle change that would force some of the strongest women to compromise themselves, and everything they have ever claimed to believe in.

A lot of women will say they don't want rich, popular men, who are always on the go. But those same women are also immensely unhappy with the broke, unwanted; going nowhere ass men they have now.

I've been with normal men, and now I've been with an extraordinary specimen of a man, I think I'll stick with what I got.

Everything is moving so fast. There are so many people all around them moving and acting sporadically, obviously excited about the show.

Moving through this heavy human traffic, amazingly K.C. is able to keep anybody from even so much as bumping into or touching Megan. She feels like an actual black American queen. One of the things she loves the most about him is the fact that he's the star but he treats her like she's the famous one.

"You ready baby girl?" Kel asks approaching the entrance to the back of the stage. Megan reads the door and then steps back with her eyes wide open, covering her mouth with both hands.

"Are you ready bae?" he repeats. "Since I was twelve years old…" she admits. Once in the back-stage area, K.C. stops to speak to several Maybach Music Group giants; first Meek Mills, then Gunplay, last but not least K.C. shakes hands with the big homie Ricky Rozay.

"Ayo Rick," K.C. says after they hug, "Where O at?"

"Uh… O should be down the hall, third door on the right. Go holla at him he

getting ready to do his set in a few minutes."

"Cool." K.C. takes Megan by the hand again and leads her further down the hallway.

Megan can't believe this is really happening. She knows this has to be a dream. Her heart is beating loudly in her ears; her entire body is sweating but she feels so cold. Her feet are moving but she doesn't remember how to walk or talk anymore.

She looks up. The door up ahead on the right reads the name *"Omarion"*. She puts her head back down and continues to try to take confident steps.

"You wanna knock?" K.C. asks. Megan keeps her head down and shakes her head quickly. K.C. laughs to himself at just how adorable his wife is and how much she looks exactly like his only true love,

Cameron Jiles.

K.C. knocks twice. The door opens. Wearing nothing but some fly all black Giuseppe shoes and black leather drop crotch pants Omarion opens the door.

"Damn… **Kool Hands** Cole…" he shakes hands with K.C. and hugs him briefly. "What's good O…" Kel says. "I'm just livin' life Mr. Billion-dollar man," O replies, "Na but yeah everything's good homie. I'm about to go wreck this stage in a minute though."

"Cool," Kel looks down at his lady, "Well before you go I want you to meet somebody very special to me. This is my wife Megan, and she's been a fan of yours since your old B2K days."

Omarion takes Megan by the hand. "It's nice to meet you love." She smiles but can't respond no matter how hard she tries.

"Your wife is gorgeous K.C.," O tells him, "hold on to her homie." "Thanks." Megan mumbles.

"Wait a minute now," O flashes his signature smile, "Ms. Megan, you been rockin' wit me since **Pandemonium** and all that way back in the beginning, so I know you not up here acting shy on me. We family boo, come here gimme a hug."

In his arms, she can no longer control her emotions. The warm tears rush her face before she can stop them. Omarion can feel her body shaking.

"Now that's love," he says, "I want you both at all my shows when I'm in town. Megan, fans like you are the reason I go so hard and never stop."

After hugging Omarion and actually looking up into his eyes all of Megan's nerves seem to be slowly melting away. "You good?" he asks her handing her some tissue.

"Yeah I'm good." she returns his smile as she wipes a few tears away.

"Come on in ya'll," O walks back towards the huge mirror in the front of his dressing room, "I gotta finish gettin' dressed."

"Okay." K.C. steps back to let his wife walk in first. Megan

234

looks over at O, and then up at K.C. He nods in approval.

She lets go of her husband's hand and walks close to Omarion, as he puts on his shirt in the mirror. "Omarion…" she says.

"Wassup love…" he replies putting in his expensive earrings.

"Can I ask you something?" she walks a little closer.

"Of course…" he replies. "You are one of the most talented, handsome, amazing artists that have ever come out… what's holding you back from reaching that next level?" O turns around to look at K.C., they exchange a respectful smile.

"Man K.C. where did you find this girl, I need me one just like her." Megan laughs to herself. "You got a twin Megan?" O asks with a comforting smile, "Because if you do I need her number *now*." he tells her. "Actually I…" Megan starts.

"When's the next time you gone be back home in Cali O?" K.C. hastily interjects. Megan turns to look at her husband with a sad face.

"Um okay," O laughs nervously, "I don't know what just happened, but I'm not getting in that. I'm going home tomorrow actually, you going to the West coast anytime soon K.C.?"

"Might be buying a couple houses in Cali, but nothing's final yet." he tells him.

"Cool." O looks back at Megan.

"So, Ms. Megan," O continues, "you got any more questions before I hit this stage?" "Just one," she says, "What is the difference between *love* and other *drugs*?"

Omarion can't stop smiling at this seemingly polite, curiously gorgeous, dark skinned goddess who possesses the heart of a child.

"You tell me Ms. Megan," Omarion says, "Because I'm more than sure you have your billionaire husband addicted, afflicted, and convicted in all kind of different ways."

"You better know it." Megan turns around to smile at K.C. They all share a good laugh together.

There's a knock at the door. "Yeah…" O yells. The door opens, a young Hispanic girl peeps her head in.

"You're on now Mr. Omarion." she says. "Cool," he says, "hey ya'll are welcome to chill in here, or follow me to the stage and enjoy the show."

Megan grabs K.C. by the hand and then turns back to O and grabs his hand as well. "We're following you **Mr. Maybach O**." she says.

"Cool," O says, "follow me. I got a surprise for you anyway."

From the side of the stage K.C. and Megan are so close to the actual performance the crowd can see them just to the right of Omarion performing. Megan is frozen completely solid.

After O performs three of his new hot songs, he motions for Megan to join him on the stage. She can't move at first but after K.C. gently nudges her twice she starts walking towards him.

Once she reaches him, he kisses her hand. "Aye everybody," O yells in the microphone, "this pretty lady is a good friend of mine. Her name is Megan and she's about to marry the billionaire football player Keldrick *"Kool Hands"* Cole for the second time in two weeks."

"Aw." the crowd responds.

"Yeah my homie K.C. got cash for lifetimes." O flashes that infectious smile to thousands of his loyal fans.

"So as a wedding present I wanna do something special for *"Kool Hand's"* lady," O looks in Megan's eyes, "Tell me Megan, what was your favorite B2K song?"

"My favorite B2K song was, *"Uh Huh"*…" she says into the microphone bashfully.

The crowd goes crazy in agreement with Megan's answer.

"Cool," Omarion says, "so look, everybody's been trying to get me and my old group mates back together for years but the timing and understanding was never right."

"I know…" she says sadly. "But me and my niggaz decided we'd try it anyway!" O yells into his microphone.

"Ayo Raz, Boog, Fizz… Where ya'll at homie?" The DJ drops

the beat for the hit B2K song "Uh Huh". Before Megan's very eyes, the other three members of B2K are all rising up out of the stage's floor, in better shape than ever.

These four men back on stage together again is the dream of millions of females worldwide, and Megan got to witness it up close and personal.

As they all begin to dance and sing circles around her she can't help but to start crying again. She looks over at Keldrick and mouths the words, "Thank you so much baby, I love you forever".

He nods his head. Omarion kisses her hand once more and then walks her back to her husband. O, then shakes Kel's hand, hugs Megan and then rejoins his brothers on stage. The entire performance is perfectly unforgettable.

Chapter 19
No Longer Free...
But Yet Finally Home

(Jay)

T he Loews Miami Beach Hotel is an oceanfront hotel situated in South Beach, three blocks from Lincoln Road & Miami Beach Convention Center. When throwing a surprise bachelor party for a five-star athlete you gotta book a five-star hotel, and Loews is one of the best. They boast gorgeous pools, beach access, and exquisite rooms and suites.

This is going to be a night none of us will ever forget especially the big man, "Kool Hands" Cole. Ty and I are on top of everything. Love is helping too. His crazy ass surprised us by giving us fifty thousand dollars just to throw the party. Cool, so after we paid our rent, lights, and car insurance for the rest of the year, we started planning the party. What? Man, we don't have million dollar deals or jobs; we gotta get it in where we fit in. Love is super rich he won't even know the difference.

We only had forty-eight hours to plan this whole thing so I think we did damn well. We got enough alcohol to get a small village drunk, plenty weed, and any kinda pills you can think of.

We booked the most exclusive suite they had for three days. I plan on getting both of my best friends so messed up that none of us can move for at least seventy-two hours.

(Ty)

"Where are you going Ty?" Osiana asks. Ty doesn't respond. "Is that a hard question to answer sir?" she asks. Ty still doesn't respond. "Why can't you just answer my damn question?" Osiana screams. "Calm down baby," Ty says, "It's not that deep." "Not that deep," she repeats, "nigga you…"

"What did I tell you about using that word?" Ty folds his arms tightly. "Ugh," she groans, "so you can just leave for three days without an explanation and I'm sposed to just be cool with that?"

"I'll be back." he says.

"Oh, nigga I know you'll be back," she says, "I pay all the bills where the hell else are you going?" "First of all **Becky**, Jay and I just paid most of the bills for the rest of the year." Ty says.

"You know what," Osiana says, "we are much better than this. I trust you babe whatever you have planned for K.C.'s bachelor party is none of my business. Have fun, I just wish you would at least tell me where you're going to be. I worry about you."

Ty takes his woman by the hand and pulls her close to him. "I know you worry about me baby," he says, "that's why you're my baby. Trust me I don't trust another female on this planet beyond you and my mother." "Okay." She replies.

"I'm curious." Ty tells her. "About what Tyrone?" she inquires. "You," he says, "What is it that you want?" Osiana smiles at her man. "I want you baby." she assures him.

"Deeper than that baby, what do you really want?" he asks her. His meaning not being clear to her, Osiana's response is, "I have no idea what you mean Tyrone."

"In life Osiana," he says, "What is it that you want in your life really bad that you don't possess right now?"

Osiana puts one hand on her chin and one across her chest with her brows furrowed a bit. "To be honest Tyrone," she says, "I want *amazing* never-ending fun with friends... color blinds friends of all races that do fun stupid spontaneous things together just because they can."

Tyrone smiles at his girlfriend feeling completely drawn in by her contagious excitement. "That to me is life to the fullest," she continues, "fun, loving, loyal, lifelong friends."

"Okay baby," Ty says, "When I get back from Miami I will be that friend for you.""Aw you promise Ty?" she asks. "Of course..." he says. "It would really mean a lot to me," Osiana says, "because I never had a childhood."

"It's never too late," he tells her, "So look baby me and Jay are flying down to Miami in a couple hours. We're gonna surprise K.C. with a fly ass party to end all parties. We will be there for three days, and then I'm flying back home to you love." Gripping her soft bottom, Ty proudly admires just how magnificently built his girlfriend is.

"Osiana," he starts, "you are perfect for me, and I love the fact that your intellectual matches your physical. That makes me want to know you emotionally and spiritually on a deeper level, than I do now.""I'm all yours *Tyboonie*." she says.

(South Beach)

Ty and Jay pull up to the gate of Keldrick's beach front mansion in a rented four door drop top Mercedes Benz. "This is K.C.'s crib?" Ty asks. "Yeah," Jay replies, "I guess. This is where the GPS lead us." "This nigga lives at the mall?" Ty says. "Yeah," Jay agrees, "this is a big ass house bro. I wonder how much a house like this cost.""House,"Ty laughs,"Jay this is a palace."

Kel walks out wearing Hollister denim shorts, a black tank top, and all black Louis Vuitton tennis shoes laced to the top. His black Louis Vuitton belt matches his shoes, his black LV duffel bag, as well as his LV sunglasses. On his wrist is a custom made big face black Michael Kors watch, adorned with black stones. The watch was sent to Keldrick by Mr. Kors himself in congratulations for his recent level of success.

"Here he comes," Jay whispers, "So stop actin' like a groupie and just chill."

"Nigga you stop actin' like a groupie." Ty whispers back.

K.C. opens the back door, and hops in.

"What's up fellas…" K.C. says. "What's good *"Kool Hands"* Cole?" Jay says turning around to shake the big man's hand.

"Yeah long time no see big bro," Ty says, "I mean we are blood brothers right, so I hope the past is just the past now." K.C. pats Ty on the back.

"Yeah Ty we're good little bro," K.C. says, "we've been all the way to the bottom at each other's throats, so I figure the only thing we can do now is get better, and closer."

"I'm down." Ty says. "Hell yeah," Jay says pulling off from the house, "that's what I like to hear. We're all best friends and nothing should ever come in between that. Not money, not miles, and especially not hoes." *"Bros before hoes…"* they all shout in unison. "And that's real." Jay says.

"Not trying to live in the past or even bring it up…" K.C. starts. "Then don't Kel," Jay says, "Whatever it is just don't. What that old *Lyfe Jennings* song used to say… *Some things are much better left unsaid...*"

"Yeah," Kel says, "but I gotta say this." "Say it bro." Ty says. "I did a lot of arrogant things as a kid in high school," K.C. says, "and I let you both down a lot." The big man sheds three tears in the backseat. "And man, from the bottom of my heart," he continues, "I'm sorry. I miss ya'll boys every single day straight up. We are family before any of this extra shit. Forget the fame, fortune, and lies. Man, we are brothers for life. It gets lonely at the top surrounded by blank faces and dollar signs. There are no hearts, no emotions, no history or any real friends."

Ty sheds a few tears of his own. Jay tries to hold it together but soon he follows suit. "I forgive you big bro," Ty says, "I forgive you and I forgive myself for hating you." "Why though," Kel says, "I never understood why you hated me so damn much."

"Man," Ty starts, "we were your boys' way before you even knew how to play football. But football and everything that came with it became your friends, and Jay and I just faded away into the background." "It wasn't like that bro." Kel says.

"Let me finish K.C.," Ty says, "I hated being left out of all the amazing things you were exposed to back in high school, but I had to realize that you were the star, not me so I wasn't supposed to feel like, live like, or be treated like a star. So, I sat back and played my role. I believed that after you made it big you were going to come back and get me and Jay and make our dreams come true as well. Then you got injured, and I was so angry. *I was so damn angry*! I was angry… because I had all of my dreams riding on *your shoulders*. I was depending on you, big bro. I knew I would never be shit without the greatness of my best friend Keldrick "K.C." Cole. You were the heart and carrier of my dreams bro."

"That's what friends are for bro," K.C. says, "you never needed me to make you great… but I never minded helping you either. It was always my plan to make sure my two brothers were gonna be straight forever."

Ty turns around to look at K.C. "I'm so sorry for hating you bro." he says. "It's okay bro," he says, "Hey Jay, pull over up here on the right."

"Got you boss." Jay replies.

Jay parks the car in front of a large empty lot of land. K.C. climbs out of the car and opens Ty's door. Ty steps out.

"We had the same father Ty," Kel says, "He may be dead and gone now, but we are still forever flesh and blood no matter what." Ty hugs his big brother tightly, both strong men still in tears.

"So, what do you think?" K.C. says taking a step back towards a large billboard sign behind him. "About what," Ty says looking behind K.C. at the sign.

Ty reads the huge words, on the even bigger sign. "*The perfect pure blood of Jesus...*" Ty says falling to his knees in surrender, as he starts praying and thanking God fiercely.

The sign reads, "New Theme Park coming soon, *Introducing Ride with Me Adventures." At the bottom it reads, "Owner/CEO Tyrone "Tyboonie" Carter."* Jay climbs out of the driver's side of the car and joins his two friends.

"Surprise Tyrone," Jay says, "Mr. Owner, and CEO of **Ride with Me Adventures!**" Ty gives Jay a brotherly hug. "So, you were in on this too Jay?" Ty asks.

"Well not the financial side of course," Jay says, "that was all the billion-dollar man. But yeah, I helped pick the spot. I researched how much land you would need, and got all the info about your licenses and what not."

"Man, I love ya'll niggas man." Ty says. "And K.C you are a magician," Ty continues, "how did you pull all of this off in secret for me and Jay?"

Kel smiles before turning around to survey the two hundred and eighty acres he purchased to house his brother's new theme park.

"Wait what," Jay says, "what secret was kept from me?" Ty looks back at Kel. "Can I do the honors big bro?" Ty asks K.C. The big man nods in approval.

"Check your email Jay." Ty says. "My... my email," Jay stutters pulling his smart phone out of his back pocket, "check my email for what?"

"Are you two serious?" Jay asks through an eager smile still looking down at his phone. "Serious as a heart attack bro," Ty says, "You no longer need a record deal, because you own your own label, *Jay Milli Mulah Records*!"

"Fuck the industry," Kel says, "I believe in you Jay, I always have now sign yourself and start dropping new dope music homie." "No doubt," Jay agrees, "but this address, what is the address for?"

"Every record label needs its own fully equipped studio right bro?" Kel asks. "You got me a studio built too dawg?" Jay asks.

"Yes sir." Kel replies. "Thanks man." Jay says hugging both of his brothers again. "Now it's your turn to be surprised *"Kool Hands"*." Ty says as they all jump back in the car.

(The Loews Miami Beach Hotel)

This is the bachelor party to end all bachelor parties. There's alcohol, weed, and intoxicated party people everywhere. This is the biggest party Kel and his friends have ever been to, but he just can't quite enjoy himself the way he wants to. Don't misunderstand though, Kel is happy for the most part, and he really is delighted at the fact that he's spending time with his boys. He just can't get Megan and Cam off his mind.

Every second, one of them crosses his mind, and he can't tell a soul because he knows how much exposing his true feelings would ruin everything he has been working on with Megan. He refuses to run back to Cam like a sick puppy admitting he was wrong.

"What's good big bro," Ty yells over the loud music, "you want another cold one?" "Yeah grab me two." he replies. Ty motions for one of the half-naked strippers to go fetch *"Kool Hands"* a couple more drinks. She does so with glee.

The hundred or so strippers that ended up showing up to the party were never even invited, but they all heard through the grapevine that the party was for K.C., so of course they all showed up to try to get a piece of the billion-dollar man.

These are his final days as a free man. Well technically he's already married, because of him and Megan's island ceremony in the Bahamas, but he never had a bachelor party the first time, so these are his last official days as a free man. A three-day bachelor party is a situation fit only for a king.

"Where's Jay?" Kel asks Ty. "Um… I don't know, but if he's half as drunk as I am he probably doesn't know where he is his damn self." Ty laughs.

Jay approaches them from across the room. "Come on fellas." he mumbles with a huge smile on his face. Ty and Kel follow Jay to the other half of the suite. Once inside they find only three dancers. The three baddest strippers at the entire party are sitting on the bed waiting for the intoxicated trio of Jay, Kel, and Ty.

"Oh, I like." Ty picks his girl first. He takes her by the hand and leads her to a corner chair in the room. He hands her a hundred-dollar bill and she starts dancing on him, and stripping him simultaneously. Jay looks at Kel with a crooked drunk smile on his face.

"Two left big bro, you choose first." Jay says. Kel looks over at Ty, who is now getting head in the corner with his legs up above his own head.

"Um okay," Kel says, "I'll take her." He points at a thick pretty Cuban stripper named *Cigarillo*. K.C. chooses her but he doesn't move.

"That's the one you want, right?" Jay points at *Cigarillo*.

"Yep…" K.C. says. Jay looks at him, and then her, and then back at him again. "Then take her bro." he laughs, as he pushes his tall friend towards the gorgeous young stripper.

Kel stands frozen right in front of the beautiful *Cigarillo*. Jay steps up next to him in front of the third girl, a thick Brazilian dancer named *Dawn Diamonds*. Kel stares down at *Cigarillo*, still completely frozen.

"I uh, I li… like your mole." *K.C. stutters. Dawn Diamonds* shakes her head. Then she snatches Jay's pants down and begins to give him the same treatment Ty is happily receiving in his own private corner. "Thanks, I guess." *Cigarillo* replies. "I um," she says, "I'm not usually like this. You know shy or whatever but I'm your biggest fan, and I was really hoping you would pick me."

Dawn Diamonds, who is obviously the leader out of the two, pulls Jay out of her mouth, then holding him in her hands, she glares at *Cigarillo.* "Really bitch," *Dawn Diamonds* says, "girl stop sucking up and suck some dick."

"Okay." *Cigarillo* says unbuckling K.C.'s pants. K.C. puts both of his hands behind his head in anticipation. *Cigarillo* unzips his pants and unleashes all of him.

"Damn!" Dawn Diamonds says pulling Jay out of her mouth again, now staring at K.C.'s manhood. "Bitch I know you gone let me taste that monster." she says to *Cigarillo.*

Cigarillo laughs at her coworker's raunchy comment. Then she opens her mouth to take Kel on, but he pulls back and puts himself back in his pants. Without a word Kel rushes out to the hotel room's balcony.

Cigarillo reluctantly follows him out onto the balcony. "It's okay K.C.," she says, "Can I call you that?" "What, oh yeah sure…" he says.

"Honestly, I'm new at this," she says, "so if the problem is me I understand." "No, it's not you at all," he tells her, "trust me you are perfect, I'm just not… like that anymore." "I see." she says.

"So, you're new to this huh?" he asks. "Yeah, well I've been dancing for a few weeks," she admits, "but this would be my first time ***doing it***… for money."

"Oh okay," K.C. says, "well no worries here boo. You won't be doing anything tonight, at least not with me. This is my bachelor party, I'm getting married in about seventy-nine hours and counting."

"Wow." she hides her smile with both hands.

"What…" he says.

"You're actually keeping up with how many hours it is until your wedding," she says, "that is so cute, and sweet. Your fiancé is a very lucky, girl." "Thanks." Kel says.

He smiles at her then directs his attention back out over the balcony. "So, are you really a billionaire?" she asks. "Yeah that's what they keep telling me…" he replies.

"You know at some point in a man's life," K.C. says, "we have to agree to disagree with our own bodies. You have no idea how bad I wanted to let you do that to me in there, but my marriage is more important to me than instant gratification, you know? Like… I've always heard that no man is truly faithful to his wife, and my father wasn't faithful to my mom, but if there's only going to be one faithful man on this planet… well then, I wanna be him. You know…"

Cigarillo can't stop smiling at how perfect and beautiful this man's mind is. "Yeah, no… yeah that makes perfect since K.C." she tells him.

"Hey," he says, "would you mind just sitting out here and talking to me all night? I mean I'll pay you for your time of course."

"K.C., I thought you would never ask…" she says, "I would love to, and no charge… it's on the house."

248

Chapter 20
Wedding Bells

(Megan)

I never thought any man would ever marry me, let alone Keldrick "Kool Hands" Cole. My past is not pretty; I've done and said a lot of horrible things, I'm not proud of. I was very promiscuous when I was growing up.

I stayed up all night a couple nights ago; telling K.C. some of the things I did in my past. I've danced for money... and even slept with random dudes for food and rides to and from work.

God, I feel like a real crumb and a dirty slut. I can't understand why God allows good things to ever happen to nobodies like me. This life should be reserved for good clean girls. Women who finished school, went to college, and have actual careers.

I can lie to myself all day, but the truth is I'm scared. How long is this man going to want to be married to me? He doesn't even love me. He's in love with my twin. What's worse is he may just be marrying me to spite her, and or to fulfill some kinky twin fantasy he has.

I'm not sure about anything right now, but I can't blame anybody but myself. I was so tired of... regular, and normal. I wanted to feel like an extraordinary queen for once, I just really wanted to matter.

I was becoming a robot in my old life. Every day was exactly the same. I was tired of working like a dog just to make ends meet, but I hated my off days the most because those were the days I was stuck alone in my tiny apartment thinking.

Thinking is the worst thing ever when you have no plan at all. Your mind is filled with so many impossible scenarios of how things will get better magically. Maybe I could win the lotto, become a model, or just marry rich. But eventually you chase all those stupid notions *away from your mind and escape back to reality again.*

But this man... Keldrick Jermaine Cole came and swept me away from all of that crap... like a fairytale princess. He paid me out of my lease a week later, paid all my bills off, and bought me a brand-new car last month.

I put on a good front, but I was going to be homeless in about four days, Keldrick saved me from a very dark future. I am honestly enjoying this lifetime of beautiful moments but I will never take a second of it for granted. I will protect this life by any means possible.

This wedding though... Yes, Jesus!!! All white everything. I've never seen this much white in one place in my life. This wedding is every girl, and every woman's dream. I was in control of everything and my fiancé was right there by my side helping me make all the important decisions.

The wedding specifics actually mattered to him. Lord... this man is perfect. Even if he didn't really care what flavor the wedding cake was going to be, or what color dresses my bride's maids would wear, I would never know it because he seemed genuinely interested. First, we got married on the island in the Bahamas just Kel, and

I. He flew me and Pastor White out to the island a day before he arrived himself. The alone time I had with Pastor White, before the wedding was needed.

The old man talked with me for hours, and blessed me with so many wise mental jewels that will help strengthen and lengthen my marriage for years to come I'm sure. He also prayed with me, and showed me how to repent. I needed to repent badly.

When Kel arrived on the island Pastor walked us down the beach near the water. Kel and I said our vows, then Pastor White married us right there with the wind at our back, the sun setting over the waters, and the soft white sand between our toes.

Megan secretly makes her way to a rarely used upstairs church bathroom for a moment of solitary silence. Down on her knees in her pretty white dress Megan is finally at peace, with her praying hands pressed tightly together on the edge of the bathroom   sink.

"I finally accepted Jesus Christ in my life as my Lord and Savior." Megan whispers to herself. "No, I'm still not perfect," she continues, "and I'm not *Jesus*... so I never will be, but I'm okay now. I'm not looking over my shoulders every second, with my face riddled with shame and guilt. Most importantly I no longer fear death."

The bathroom door opens. "I know whenever God calls me home," Megan whispers, "my destiny is to be by his side in *His* heavenly kingdom forever."

"Good bitch, cause you bout to see that nigga real soon." a dark familiar voice says. Then everything goes black.

(In the sanctuary)

Cameron is sitting in the very back row of the church next to Whitney. "So, are we ever gonna talk about what happened the other day?" Cam asks. "What happened?" Whit inquires. "At your house," Cam tells her, "you, me, Charlie, and Love..."

"Oh that," Whit says blankly, "what about it? You didn't enjoy it?" "No," Cam says, "It was probably some of the best sex I've ever had, well except for with K.C. that is. Daddy will always be at the top of my list, he was my first everything... But what we did that day was so random. How did you... how do you just get down like that so easily Whitney?"

Whitney smiles at the younger less experienced Cameron. "Let me teach you something," Whit says, "And after everything Carlos made us do, over the years you should be the last person I should have to teach this to." "Teach me what?" Cam says. "You are emotionally attached to your box." Whit says.

"My box... What box Whitney?" Cam asks. "Your box," Whit says, "You know your juice box, your goodies..." "Oh okay, I'm with you." Cam says. "Yeah," Whit continues, "so all you have to do is detach yourself from your box emotionally, and your life will

251

be a lot more enjoyable."

"So, you're saying be a hoe?" Cam asks. "No ma'am," Whit says, "I have a daughter, so that is *not* what I'm saying at all. Detaching yourself emotionally from your box goes much deeper than just a sexual, or even a physical level." "How so…" Cam asks.

"Once you no longer make the majority of your decisions based on whether you're going to give somebody some ass or not," Whit says, "you will free your mind and see life much more clearly." "Okay," Cam says, "you lost me."

"I bet," Whit says, laughing to herself, "Look Cam believe it or not life is a big ass chess match and damn near every move you make revolves back around to sex. We go to school, to get better jobs, to make more money, to drive nicer cars. We also attempt to make more money to dress better, look better, all just to have more and better sex."

"Wow." Cam says. "Yeah…" Whit sighs. "Whitney, you are crazy as hell," Cam laughs with a soft hand on Whit's left knee, "but I still love you though girl, you gone be my dog no matter what."

Whitney laughs with her. "Yeah, we can laugh all day, but I meant every word I just said baby girl." Whit tells her. "Okay." Cam replies. "And remember what I said, you can marry Keldrick," Whit says,
"but you will always belong to me you were *my wife* first."

"I know babe." Cam replies. "And, anytime Charlie and I want to do some… *extracurricular activities* you better be ready." Whit says rubbing Cams thigh. "I can't wait boo, all you gotta do is hit my cell phone and I'm comin'." Cam tells Whit.

"I have one last request…" Whit says. "Anything baby…" Cam responds. "As Keldrick's wife you will have access to all of his money and assets," Whit says, "because he doesn't believe in prenups."

"I know…" Cam replies. "Right," Whit says, "so, once a month just make a simple bank transfer from me to you, to make sure I never have to work again and all of our dirty little secrets will go with me to my grave." "Say no more, I got you." Cam agrees.

"Whit…" Cam says. "What's up girl?" she replies. "I really appreciate you letting me marry Keldrick. It must be really hard I know how much he means to you." "Girl," Whit says, "I am too *damn* old to still be trying to make grown men love me."

"I know that's right girl." Cam agrees. "Besides I'm not crazy," Whit tells her, "that man is *head over heels* in love with *Y-O-U*. If he was still in love with me he would have been searching for and trying to marry *my* twin." They both laugh.

"Lemme find out you got a twin too Whit…" Cam jokes. "Mmmm now wouldn't that be a twist," Whit says, "but sadly the world was only blessed with one Whitney Michelle Powell." she sighs.

"One is enough," Cam says, "I don't think the world could handle two of you babe."

"Thanks boo," Whitney says, "but seriously though I'm really happy for you and Keldrick. I'll be alright, besides I got Charlie's fine ass to keep me occupied, terrified, and satisfied all at the same damn time." They both laugh again.

Cam's phone finally vibrates in her purse. She quickly shows Whit the text she just received, and then they both exit the sanctuary with only minutes to pull off the biggest piece of their deadly plan.

(Upstairs in the church hallway)

K.C. doesn't want to do what he's about to do, and he doesn't want to have the conversation he's about to have, but he can't marry Megan without these dangerous words being spoken.

His huge palms are sweating profusely, as he makes his way to Pastor White's office. That man has exemplified perfection and righteousness in Keldrick's mind for as long as he can remember. The very thought of Pastor White doing, or being wrong shakes Keldrick's very core.

He knocks on the Pastor's door. "Come in." Pastor says. K.C. walks in Pastor's office with his head held low. "There's the man of the hour," Pastor says, "How you feeling champ?" Kel fakes a smile. "Not like a champ." he replies.

"Sit down son, tell me what's wrong. Is it cold feet? Have you changed your mind?" Pastor asks.

"Too late for that… right Pastor?" K.C. says, "You already married Megan and me in the Bahamas last week, we're already official. And I don't need to sit down, I'd rather stand thank you."

"Of course," Pastor says, "that's fine, so tell me are you having problems in the home?" "No sir," Kel responds, "home is great, the kids are well, and Megan is almost perfect…" "So then tell me son," Pastor White asks again, "What's the problem?"

"You…" K.C. replies in a dark tone. "Excuse me son…" Pastor White stands up from his desk. "I'm not your son Pastor, my father is *deceased*." K.C. tells the old man.

"Boy I have called you son since before your little black ass could walk or talk, don't you sass talk me!" Pastor demands.

"How could you Pastor White…" Kel says. "Son, what…" Pastor starts. "How could you," K.C.'s tears begin to fall; "I trusted you, and everything you've ever told me. But now finally… I know it was all a lie. *God* is a lie; *this church* is a lie and Pastor damn it… *You* are a lie too!"

"Now look boy," Pastor White tries to step closer to K.C., "I don't know what this is about but if Megan told you something…"

"She didn't have to tell me shit Pastor!" Kel exclaims. "Keep your voice down boy," Pastor White says, "Someone will hear you."

"Pastor I don't give a damn," Kel says, "maybe some, of them need to hear me, so they can know the truth." "What is the truth boy?" Pastor inquires. "Don't play dumb with me Pastor," he cries, "Not anymore."

"Boy what the *hell* do you think I did to you? Spit it out son!" he says. "Pastor," Kel starts, "you had sex with my wife in the Bahamas." "Boy, are you crazy," Pastor White wipes new sweat from his brows, "if that woman told you that she is a ***dirty liar***."

"Yes Pastor," Kel continues, "she is a liar and so are you, because neither one of you, to this day even tried to tell me what happened between the two of you."

"So, then what are you talking about Keldrick, how could you possibly know she…" Pastor pauses and tries to hug K.C.

K.C. takes a significant step back from him. "The night before you married us on the beach," Kel says, "I flew in an hour earlier than planned. The gospel music in your hotel suit that *I paid* for was so loud, you two didn't hear me knock or walk in. I had keys to your room and ours, because again ***I paid*** for it. I walked in and turned the corner by the bathroom and I saw you, both of you… *together* Pastor."

Kel falls to his knees reaching out for Pastor White. The pastor steps back to look at him with his hands over his old quivering mouth.

"Keldrick… I'm sorry." he mumbles. "No!" Keldrick yells.

The door opens. "Keldrick are you okay?" Nancy one of the church members asks. "Get out of here now!" he yells. She does as she's told.

"Pastor, if you were any other man on this earth I swear before God I would kill you right here and now with my bare hands!" K.C. tells the old man.

"Again Keldrick, I am very sorry," Pastor White tries to hide his nerves and buy himself some more time, "and in my heart of hearts I pray one day you can forgive me."

"No Pastor," Kel repeats, "Make it right Pastor please, just make it all be a lie. Make this all go away right damn now, and tell me I didn't see what I saw, with my own eyes… because if you are just a dirty despicable sinner like me… then who do I have left to look up to?"

"God…" Pastor White says. "You look up to God, son," he

continues, "Stop making the mistake of thinking of me… your

Pastor as God in the flesh. I am just a man, just like you Keldrick. I get tempted every single day just like you. Now I could tell you some stories about your late parents God rest their souls, that I'm sure they're not proud of. But, I'm not that kind of person. My point is, none of us are perfect, nor shall any of us in good faith judge each other. You saw years ago what your father was doing to your helpless
baby brother with your own two eyes Keldrick… and what did you do?"

"What could I do, I was only a child myself?" Kel cries. "You could have said something, told somebody," Pastor continues, "anything but be quiet. You left him all alone when he tried to tell your mother what was going on, you could have confirmed his allegations. Hell, you could have told me son… I wasn't the man I am now back then; I would have killed your father myself."

"And then what…" Kel asks, "Then, I would have had no father in my life."

"Son," Pastor says, "Paul, was never really in your life anyway, and you already know this. I was more of a father to you than he ever was."

Kel continues to sob. "Stand up Keldrick," Pastor says, "and dry your face now." K.C. obeys.

"You are a good strong man," Pastor tells him, "but we live in a perfectly imperfect world. Stuff happens… stuff will always happen but you have to be strong enough to accept the things you can't change, pray about them, and then let go and let God. See Keldrick... I am not God; I never have been. God is perfect and faithful. He never changes. Take in account the sun. Every day it will rise in the East and set in the West. God will never change."

"Pastor, why does the devil just keep destroying my life?" Kel asks. "We're always so quick to blame the devil," Pastor says, "stop giving him so much credit son. And you've got to spend more time alone with God, we have to praise him, love him, and respect the gifts he gives us."

"Pastor, you don't understand," K.C. cries, "I'm all the way down at the lowest point; I've been at mentally in a long time."

"That's okay son," the Pastor smiles, "It's good to be at the bottom sometimes." "What do you mean Pastor," he asks, "How can being at the bottom be a good thing? You always say that God wants to see us happy. Why would God want me at the bottom again?"

"Because," Pastor White hugs Keldrick tightly, "Sometimes the bottom is the only place where He can reach you... and work with you. I love praising God, and I love when he shows up in my prayers. It's a very dangerous thing to have church without God present Keldrick, but son we do not have that problem here."

"No sir we don't," Kel agrees smiling at the only Pastor he has ever known, "thank you Pastor White... and I forgive you. I forgive you."

"Thank you, son," he replies, "I love you, God loves you, and we are both very, very proud of you."

"I love you too Pastor." Kel says. "I know son... now go step in my bathroom, and get yourself together, we have a wedding to attend." Pastor White tells him with a smile.

(I Do)

As Keldrick Jermaine Cole stands at the end of the aisle awaiting his bride to join him, he continues to be strong, ignoring his powerful urge to cry. He's emotional for several easily identifiable reasons. He's still not sure even now standing here at the altar, days after officially tying the knot with Megan in the Bahamas if she's the one
he should marry.

There are three women in this church today that K.C. could marry at will. He knows this, but it doesn't ease his pain. Pride, ignorance, and jealousy still cloud his decisions daily. Five and a half years is not long enough to forgive and forget the pain of

257

sudden, brutal abandonment.

Whitney and Cam both disappeared without a trace. As much hate as he holds in his heart for them both, he can't help but still love them.

As he scans the crowd full of wedding guests and family, Whit and Cam are the only two faces he's searching for. Oddly he doesn't see either one of them.

The final reason K.C. has cold feet is because he always wanted his parents to be at his wedding. For a second he thought he saw his mother and father smiling down proudly at him from the balcony of the church.

Although he wasn't close to his father, the news of his passing hit Kel hard, more so because he had just lost his mother a week before. Kel paid for the funeral and had his late father laid to rest right next to his mother.

Jamie Foxx's song, "*Wedding Vows*" begins to play. In an adorable little white sundress, with her long brown hair all in curls Jazemene appears in the doorway of the sanctuary at the top of the aisle.

Everybody stands as she begins to make her way down the aisle happily tossing soft blue and white rose petals as she goes.

After she makes it about half way down the aisle, her Uncle Love appears in the doorway dressed in an exquisite all white suit. In his arms Love is holding Jaze's handsome little brother K.J. The little Love look alike, is wearing a smaller version of the same all white suit Love himself is wearing. In K.J.'s hands is a white pillow. Atop the pillow is the blue ring box.

On their way down the aisle K.J. hands the pillow to Love, and begins to wave at all his adoring fans in the large wedding crowd as they pass by. His smile and his little green eyes are unforgettable. Every female in the crowd is in awe of the gorgeous green eyed dread head, and his adorable son.

Once they reach the groom Love puts little K.J. on the ground in front of K.C. Then Love kneels down and hands K.J. the pillow.

K.J. takes the pillow and looks up at K.C. "Here's the ring daddy." he says.

"Thank you, son..." K.C. responds, kneeling down to give his little man a fierce hug and a kiss. K.C. takes the ring. Then Love takes the pillow, and makes his way to stand beside Jay and Ty.

Now K.C. awaits his bride again, this time with his children by his comfortable side. The wedding song starts, as a dark, beautiful, china doll appears at the top of the aisle. K.C. instinctively looks over at Jay, Ty, and Love. They all nod in approval. K.C. nods back.

As his bride makes her way down the aisle, Kel can't take his eyes off of her. Out of the corner of his eye Kel sees movement. Whitney is walking into the back of the sanctuary through a side door. Kel wonders where she could be coming from, but then decides it doesn't really matter anymore. If it doesn't involve the kids, from this day forward nothing Whitney Michelle Powell does will be his concern.

No matter what Keldrick can't hide from the fact that it could have very easily been Whitney in the white dress on her way to join him at the altar. He is impressed though that she accepted Megan's invitation, and actually showed up on time and didn't even attempt to cause a scene.

Keldrick's gorgeous bride is only a few steps away from him now. The atmosphere is so perfect; from the Jasmine scented white candles everywhere, to the hundreds of people packed on the pews here just to witness this symbolic connection of two lives, two hearts, and two paths forever and always.

As his bride steps close to him the music stops and a hush falls over the church as Kel looks at his wife through her veil. With both hands, he gently lifts her veil to place it behind her head. The whispers are automatic.

For many people in attendance at this, their highly publicized wedding, this is the very first opportunity they've had to experience her unbelievable beauty in person.

She looks even better than all of the flawless pictures in the magazines. This perfect dark chocolate china doll is beauty personified, and she can't help but to glow standing so close to the man that is the reason, and architect of her happiness. She calmly reaches up to softly wipe a loan tear from rolling down K.C.'s face.

(Cam)

Lord I pray I'm not wrong in these things I have chosen to take part in as of late. But even if I have to spend all of eternity in Hell, and God you know that's not what I want, but I am here to tell you that this man, Keldrick Jermaine Cole is worth eternal damnation to me.

But surely he will not have me go that way, I know you have been working on him and through him Lord, and he will lead me and his household according to your precious word. I swear he knows it's me he's standing here face to face with and not my twin Megan. I believe that in the core of my very soul. But if not, when he finally does find out that it's me he's stuck with for life, I just pray everything goes in my favor.

Unable to withstand the emotions inside him any longer Keldrick motions for the microphone, and Pastor White gladly hands it to him. Looking deep into Cam's joyful eyes Kel clears his throat twice. *"To you my wife,"* Kel starts, *"I want to first thank you for doing me the honor of wearing my last name, and joining me on this lifelong journey towards the ideal marriage and relationship. Now I know there is no such thing as the perfect marriage, and there will be plenty of bumps and bruises along the way. So most likely we will probably never have a perfect marriage... but if ever there existed a perfect and pure love it's you and I. I would lay down my life right now for you and only you. But I would much rather live... just to ensure your every day is the archetype of blessed happiness. I love you Mrs. Cole."*

"Thank you, baby,..." Cam mouths to him taking the microphone and clearing her own throat.

"Keldrick Jermaine "Kool Hands" Cole I am so, proud of you as a person," she says, *"you know... I heard all the comparisons from when*

260

you first entered the National Football League almost six years ago. They said you would be the LeBron James of the football world and that's why they said Miami was the perfect place for you to play. They were right on so many levels. Even though you were born and raised in Orlando with the Magic, you were always the biggest Dewayne Wade and Miami Heat fan. You were nothing less than the perfect addition to so many other talented athletes who reside in our beautiful state of Florida. But you are more than an exceptional athlete to me. I know the real you. I know the man beneath the helmet and pads, the man behind the grandiose mask of physical perfection. Best of all I know and respect your heart. You are an awesome father, a fierce humanitarian, and a man who is truly trying every day to get closer to God. So, I just wanna say that in my heart and my mind, you are more than just the MVP you are the MVM. You are the most valuable man on the planet to me and so many other people. I love you baby and I'm proud to call you my one and only everything."

Cam winks at K.C. and then hands the microphone back to Pastor White.

"Well you two are a beautiful couple in my eyes and God's eyes," Pastor White says, *"I know you will be together for a very long time. Your vows to each other were heartfelt, and I think very genuine."*

"Dearly Beloved," Pastor White says, *"We are gathered here today to join this man, and this woman in holy matrimony. Through marriage, Mr. and Mrs. Cole make a commitment together; to face their disappointments, embrace their dreams, realize their hopes, and accept each other's failures. Mr. and Mrs. Cole will promise one another to aspire to these ideals throughout their lives together. They will achieve this through mutual understanding, openness, and sensitivity to each other. Marriage is a symbol of faith and a personal commitment as well as a moral and physical union between two adults. Marriage is the construction of your love and trust into a single faithful walk in your spiritual life together. It is a moral commitment that requires and deserves constant attention.*

Marriage should be a lifelong dedication of peaceful loving kindness, backed with the determination to make it last."

Pastor turns towards K.C. "Do you Keldrick Jermaine Cole take Mrs. Cole to be your lawfully wedded wife, to live together in holy matrimony? Will you love her, comfort her, honor and keep her, in sickness and in health, for richer, for poorer, for better, for worse, in sadness and in joy, to cherish and continually bestow upon her your heart's deepest devotion, forsaking all others, keep yourself only unto her as long as you both shall live?"

K.C. looks at Cam. "I do." he says.

Pastor turns towards Cam. "And do you Mrs. Cole take Keldrick to be your lawfully wedded husband, to live together in holy matrimony? Will you love him, comfort him, honor and keep him, in sickness and in health, for richer, for poorer, for better, for worse, in sadness and in joy, to cherish and continually bestow upon him your heart's deepest devotion, forsaking all others, keep yourself only unto him as long as you both shall live?"

Cam looks at her man. "I will." she confirms to the whole world. They exchange rings. Pastor looks at them both. "Now by the power vested in me by the beautiful sunny state of Florida, I pronounce you man and wife. You may kiss the bride." Pastor says.

Cam stands up on the tips of her toes to reach him. He meets her half way. Their lips combine for the first time in almost six years. The proverbial sparks are magnificent. The kiss seems to last for an eternity.

"Hey, hey, hey," Ty says, "save some of that for the honeymoon guys." The happy couple holds on a little while longer, and then they turn to face the happy applauding crowd.

As they make their way out of the church to their waiting limo, rice is flying everywhere. At the rear of the crowd Love looks on holding his sleepy baby boy in his protective arms.

"I know you're the killer Love." Someone whispers in his ear from behind him. For the first time, Love turns and faces the detective that has been chasing him since he committed his very first

murder. "What the Hell…" Love says. "Lance Orlandis Vinson a.k.a. Love, I am detective O. Blue." the detective tells him.

"Aren't you Ty's girlfriend?" he asks. "I am," she says, "I'm also detective O. Blue of the Orlando P.D."

"*Osiana Blue*." Love says, "What kind of car do you drive?" he asks.

She smiles. "Light blue 09 Camry, tiny crack in the windshield." she says. Love smiles, as he realizes just how close he was to being caught and going back to prison for the remainder of his life.

"So, what now," he says, "I can't fight you, I have my baby sleeping in my arms." "I don't' want you to fight me." Osiana says. "I can't let you arrest me either. I can't lose my son… Not now." Love tells her. "I don't want that either." she admits.

"Then what is it you want detective?" Love inquires. "It's simple," she says, "I've been watching you for weeks. I'm a fan of yours actually, and the precision of your work." "Really…" Love smiles his sadistic but handsome smile.

"Really," she tells him, "I'm curious about one thing though." "And what is that detective?" he asks. "How were you able to control the flames that burned most of the bodies of your victims?" Love smirks to himself, as he pulls out a small bottle from his pocket containing a thick blue substance.

"What is it?" Osiana asks. "Pyrotoxin," he tells her, "it's supposed to still be a German prototypical burning agent. I bought loads of it online, from some crazy chemist who got fired from the laboratory that makes this stuff. It cost me three hundred bucks a bottle. It works though so it's worth it." "Yeah, I'd say so." she replies.

"Okay, so now it's my turn to ask a question detective." Love tells her. "Shoot." she replies. "How did you figure out it was me?" he asks.

"My first clue," she starts, "was when Jay and Ty were talking

263

about Keldrick's brother getting out of jail. But what really put me onto you was the fact that the Central Florida Reception Center doesn't empty their trash cans on a daily basis."

Love smiles. "Damn, so you found my walking papers in the trash can, right?" he says. "Yep," she replies returning his smile, "I'm good at my job, but I'm not that good. Love you even had an actual hit list that you threw away in that trash can. And you have been killing everybody in the exact order from the list except your brother and Whitney. The list was *major* for me, without that huge clue, you would have been my hardest case ever. The case most likely would have gone unsolved forever, and for that fact alone, I know you can adequately help me take care of a personal problem I have."

"What personal problem?" he asks. "I have a job for you." she tells him. "What kind of job," he asks, "I don't need any money. If you've been watching me then I'm sure you know I'm very wealthy." "I know," she says, "No worries though, I'm not offering you any money." "So, then what's the deal?" he asks trying not to show the
depth of his frustration.

"The deal is," she starts, "if you take care of this job for me, you walk free." He's all ears now.

"How exactly can you promise me that?" he asks.

"All the detective work I did on your case, was done undercover I don't even have my badge right now." she tells him.

"So, you want me to do something for you and then you will forget everything I've done?" he asks.

"No," she says, "you have pulled off some amazing crimes, I'm sure they'll never escape my mind. But I'm no better than you. I could have stopped you weeks ago. I was such a fan of your work I was always purposely one step behind you. I was late so I could study your crimes after you had already committed them."

"Are you serious?" Love asks in amazement. "Yeah," she laughs to herself, "So I'm just as much to blame for your killing spree as you are. I will never forget what *we did*, but I will resign from the force,

taking with me all the evidence I have against you. Without me… the precinct has no case at all."

"Deal," Love says, "so… who do you want dead?"

Detective Osiana Blue smiles. "Smart man Mr. Cole," she says, "your target is that fat chauvinistic pig Marcel Tiago." she says.

"The Marcel Tiago," Love asks, *"the chief of the Orlando Police Department?"* "The one and only." she confirms.

"Done." he says. "Last question detective," Love says, "you seem to really love what you do. So, how are you just going to resign, and walk away from something you're obviously so passionate about?" he asks.

"Easy," she replies, "I only joined the force to impress my parents, and because I didn't know what else to do with my life. But most of all it gave me the perfect excuse for my draining, lonely, single life." she tells him.

"And what excuse was that?" Love inquires. "I told myself and others I was always too busy with the force, so I didn't have time to date, or be in a relationship," she explains, "but, now that I have Ty…"

"I get it." Love smiles. "Yeah and we're moving to Miami now anyway," Osiana continues, "to oversee Ty's new theme park that Keldrick gave him. So, I would have to leave the Orlando P.D. either way."

"Sounds like a dream," Love says, "well good luck with everything, I will take care of that job for you in the next 48 hours… and I'll uh, I'll see you around Ms. Blue." he says. "Likewise." she replies with a smile.

Love shakes the detective's hand, and then walks away staring closely at his sleepy child, as if his conversation with Osiana Blue never happened.

"Wait Lance…the child can save you. You will love the child." The old pastor's words are once again whispering in Love's head as he

makes his way to his car. Pastor White was so right about everything he said when he came to visit Love just days before his release from prison.

Love will take out Orlando Police Chief Tiago, to keep his word to Detective Blue and to secure his freedom. But that will be his last murder... at least for now.

(Just Married)

Inside the limo, the happy couple isn't wasting any time in route to their wedding reception. Its passion filled hair pulling, clothes snatching, hungry lips, and throbbing bodies. "Baby..." Kel groans between kisses. "Yeah bae..." Cam replies. "You don't think we should wait till after the reception to do this?"K.C. asks.

"Hell no." she replies climbing on top of him. She pulls him out through the slit in the front of his boxers and goes to work on him orally. She starts with the tip she knows how sensitive he can be. Slow, then fast, now with her hand she strokes him methodically. The limo rides over a huge speed bump, as a result she chokes on him. He moans.

She remembers he used to enjoy the sound of her choking on him, whenever she took him as deep in her throat as she could endure. After a deep pause due to her involuntary gag reflexes, Cam regains her composure and begins again.

She goes up and down the sides of him with her avidly skilled tongue. Her taste buds are exploding inside of her mouth at the tantalizing taste of him.

It's been years since she did this to him, but she still remembers exactly what he likes, and what's more she remembers all her little subtle tricks that used to drive him absolutely crazy.

Cam knows no one can do it like she does it, so at this point she believes Kel has to have realized she took her sister's place in the wedding and in their marriage. He grabs the back of her head forcing her down deep now.

He's so big, and deep her eyes begin to water freely. Just before she gags again he releases her head. Back in control now, Cam kisses the tip three times before engulfing him once again. Her hands, lips, and tongue, are now bringing him dangerously close to his climax.

She stops on a dime. Still positioned on top of him she sits up, unfastens her bra and then throws it on the floor of the limo. She scoots up towards his stomach so that she can ride him. She puts both of her tiny hands on his huge chest, signaling to him that's she's ready to take him on.

Kel reaches around her, gripping her behind he lifts her up with his left hand. Then with his right hand he slides her panties to the side and enters her just enough to know he's in. After placing himself in a comfortable position he lies back to let her regain control.

Cam begins to grind on him, taking more and more of him with every downward grinding motion she makes.

"Baby I miss you." Cam moans. "I'm here now." Kel replies lost completely in the moment. "Never let me go." she groans. "Never in a hundred lifetimes…" K.C. assures her.

K.C. rolls her over on her back with one swift motion. He's in her stomach now. Picking her up in his chiseled arms K.C. moves her from the back seat, to the floor of the limo. He can't restrain himself now he's too far gone into a mental state of uncontrollable passion.

With no regard for her body Kel begins to dig as deep in her as he can. Her eyes have rolled completely into the back of her head, and her toes are pointing directly towards the roof of the limo.

She can no longer scream. All she can do is whimper and moan as she takes him on.

"Baaaabby…" she groans. "Yeah bae…" he groans back. "Baby I already came, twice." she cries. "So, what…" he replies. "And I'm about to do it agaaaaaaaain…" she moans.

"Good because I think we just arrived at the reception." he tells her in the midst of his powerful strokes. "How do you know babe?" "The limo stopped and the driver is peaking in the window right now." he laughs. "Oh wow…" she moans. "Are you mad?" Kel asks while doing a slow grind inside of her.

"No let em' watch." she moans. "Oooooh," he groans as he goes as deep as he can, "bad girl. I love you so much baby." She can feel his powerful body tensing up. "Oh, baby yes." she moans as she feels him filling her body with his precious seed.

Keldrick slowly stands up, and then helps his wife to her unstable feet. As she stands up she can feel his seed dripping from her, as the excess air continues to noisily and sporadically leave her soft pink center.

(Reception)

The reception for Mr. and Mrs. Keldrick Jermaine Cole is being held at the fabulous Club of Knights, Coral Gables right here in Miami. The venue offers five-star catering, personal wedding planners, flowers, and unique gifts for the guests. The happy couple is receiving so many compliments about the building and the food. Even though their wedding coordinator had to be changed at the last second, everything still turned out well.

Everyone who's working tonight in *Fetes & Events* at the club is very easy going and extremely helpful. They're answering any questions the couple and the guests have. The reception guests seem to be very happy with the venue, food, and the D.J. Everyone is dancing, eating, drinking, and having a great time.

The dance floor begins to clear as the speakers start to play *"For You"* the super romantic ballad by the popular 90's singer Kenny Lattimore. Now the happy couple is left all alone in the center of the huge dance floor. Lost in his eyes Cameron allows Keldrick and the music to guide her in perfect hypnotic fashion.

As they sway together in harmony with the mellow tones of the song, Cameron and Keldrick feel as if they're floating on air, or dancing safely across heavenly waters. The moment is absolutely surreal to them.

Looking through her eyes to her warm soul Keldrick knows he

has found his eternal queen. Together a life of unconditional love is within their hungry deserving grasps.

To the crowd watching them move together with soul capturing precision, they look like a live scene from an epic new love movie for the ages. The two of them couldn't look or be any more perfect for one another.

After the dance ends and the reception guests are enjoying their food and beverages, Jay decides it's time to deliver his unsure Best Man speech.

With a wireless microphone in hand Jacody stands up.

"Attention everybody." he says. After everybody finally quiets down and looks in his direction he takes a deep breath before speaking.

"Okay," Jay says, *"so over the past week or so I've watched about twenty movies with weddings in them... just to try to figure out what I was gonna say about my best friend on this... his wedding day. I watched old white movies and new white movies. I watched old black movies and new black movies. And after all that man I gotta be honest... not one of those movies helped me in the slightest bit."* Everybody laughs.

"But I did enjoy watching them though." Jay tells them. Everybody laughs again. *"So then,"* Jay says, *"I picked up a pen and a note pad and I started trying to write this monumental, Martin Luther King "I have a Dream" worthy speech. But... in the end I came up with nothing. I have to admit I really did enjoy every last one of those movies I watched, especially the sweet ass chick flicks. They uh... those were the movies that were the closest replica to the unreal dream my best friend lives in every single day. Your life is a dream K.C."* Jay points at his friend with a real smile on his light brown face.

"Boy you are a black billionaire," Jay continues trying not to get emotional, *"Man, Kel you have risen up and exceeded every statistic and expectation of a black man's life in America. You are... the definition of inspiration, dedication, and loyalty. I thank you... so much for that and everything you do, and will continue to do in the future big bro."* Jay nods at him. K.C. nods back respectively.

"You know," Jay continues, *"the one thing that I did figure out from watching all of those movies is that it was never important that I write this speech... No, I needed to mean it, and make it mean something to Keldrick, and to all of you. That's what's really important. I realize that some of you don't even know him personally. And none of you know him like me and his other best friend, his little brother Tyrone know him."*

Jay looks down at Ty, who's sitting next to him, right beside his gorgeous supportive fiancé Osiana Blue. Then Jay shakes Ty's hand before continuing.

Jacody looks back at the people. *"See to most of you... he's just "Kool Hands" Cole, the Black Beast,"* Jay says, *"he's the All-Pro wide receiver who skies above all of his inferior defenders play after mind blowing play, and catches everything thrown in his vicinity. To you he's the man who breaks every record in his category, and yet still walks around just as humble as a poor man. The guy is just a class act period. He's a caring philanthropist, a worldwide super star, and also a fierce near flawless friend. But... that's not the boy Ty and I grew up with."* Jacody smiles to himself.

"We grew up," he continues, *"with Keldrick Jermaine Cole, a young boy with a head full of dreams and the talent to make them all come true. Man... let me be the first one to tell ya'll that the antics, the adventures, and ultimately the unforgettable brotherhoods that movies like The Wood, The Best Man, and The Brothers embody all pale in comparison to the journey my life has been with these two powerfully driven black men. Somebody needs to call Tyler Perry quick because the childhood I had in Orlando growing up with these two fools is screaming box office hit movie."*

"Blood of Jesus..." Ty interjects. The crowd laughs.

"We have... been through it all," Jay says, *"but through it all we always found a way to enjoy our ups and outlast our downs...together. We made it almost an art form the way we struggled together and separately, wallowed in the most painful self-pity, and then always found a way to just get by. We became*

270

masters at the art of surviving. " Everybody claps.

"Yeah, we became masters at the art of surviving," Jay says again, *"but now we are no longer just surviving... Now we're thriving. Do you know why?"* People begin to look around at each other shaking their heads, and then back at Jay.

"The three of us are thriving," Jay tells them, *"because Keldrick Cole is a man of his word. He's the kind of dreamer who doesn't mind helping other people's dreams come true alongside his own dreams."*

Tyrone stands up slowly as two real tears stream down his elegant brown face. Jay looks at his childhood friend trying hard to read his mind. Ty looks at Jay. Then with no more hesitation Jay hands Ty the microphone, hugs him and then sits down.

Ty clears his throat twice. *"Keldrick Jermaine Cole,"* Ty says, *"is my big brother and one half of my dynamic duo of best friends. I want you all to know that I haven't always been a good friend, or brother. I held onto childhood jealousy, regret, and hatred that almost destroyed some lives, including my own. I hurt Keldrick really bad..."* Ty cries.

K.C. kisses Cameron's loving hand softly before letting it go. Then he stands up and makes his way to Tyrone's side. Now face to face with him, K.C. hugs his little brother tightly.

"It's okay man..." K.C. whispers to Ty, "it's okay, we're okay now homie. No more worries or struggles... big bro is gonna always forgive you, and I will always, always, always have your back. *I promise* you that."

"I love you big bruh." Ty whispers back. After the much-needed hug, both men are now in tears. With his brother beside him Ty turns to address the people once more.

"You know," he says through his tears, *"It is my own firm belief that ninety percent of the human race would make and have made terrible wives and husbands. This is why there are more divorces than marriages today. But... one thing I know for sure is that my big brother is in that ten percent of good men and women."* Ty looks over at Cameron.

"To you," Ty smiles, *"my new sister- in- law, I want you to know*

271

that nothing in the past is relevant anymore. The past is only the past, we learn from it and we move on. To you I also say congrats, because you are one of the lucky ones. You are married to one of the rare ten percent of men left on this planet that is going to forever treat you and respect you like a real queen. Baby girl you hit the lottery in so many ways my sister. And all I ask is that you continue to love, honor, and trust my brother as he will always do the same to you." Cameron smiles at Tyrone.

(An hour later)

Jaze is sitting having a private talk about boys with her mommy, well only one boy of course, the adorable Josiah Bell. Both Whit and Jaze have dreamed about moments and talks with each other like this. "Okay so tell me all about Jojo little girl," Whit says playfully, "and leave nothing out." "Well Whit…" she starts. "Oops I mean Mommy," Jaze corrects herself, "Jojo is really cool. He can draw, paint, make those little tiny statue things I forgot what they're called… but
he can do pretty much any kind of art you can think of."

"So, he's an artist," Whit says, "now that is just too cute. Did he ever draw, sculpt, or paint you baby?" Whit asks. "Mhmm," Jaze confirms with a smile, "three times." Jaze says holding up three proud fingers. "Oh wow," Whit says, "three times? Jojo must really like you huh?"

Jaze blushes. "My daddy said the same thing." Jaze tells her mom. "When he saw one of the pictures that Jojo drew of me at the last PTA meeting we had," Jaze continues, "Daddy said Jojo took his time on the detail of the picture because he really likes the girl he was drawing. But we're just best friends Mommy. Don't worry we're not getting married."

Whitney is suddenly overpowered by jubilant laughter. This laugh feels better than anything has felt in her life for the past six years. "Who are you young lady, and what have you done with my

272

little girl?" Whit asks trying to control her own laughter.

"Besides we're too young to get married now anyway," Jaze explains to her mother, "we have to at least finish middle school first." Whit laughs again. "So, marriage is out for now for sure right…" Whitney teases her baby girl. "Uh huh," Jaze says, "Jojo and I are just best friends forever."

"Now tell me," Whit says, "What is the boy's government name? Because I know his mama didn't name him Jojo." she asks. "Josiah Bell Mama…" Jaze whines.

"Josiah Bell," Whitney thinks for a moment, "Josiah… Oh Josiah Bell. Wait, *the Josiah Bell* from Orlando? You two still communicate?" "He lives in Miami now Mama." Jaze tells her mother.

"Now how did that happen?" Whitney asks with her head tilted to the side. "I don't know Mama," Jaze tells her, "after daddy moved us here, when school started Ms. Bell was my teacher and Josiah was in my first class." "Cidra's trifling ass." Whit mumbles looking off into the distance.

"I thought that was her ass at the wedding," Whit continues, "Ms. Bell followed Keldrick to Miami. But you know what that's grown folk's business so I'm not going to corrupt your little mind with all that…" "Tell me Mama," Jaze says "I wanna know."

"Well since you asked," Whit leans in close, "I used to always catch Ms. Cidra Bell staring at your daddy in an inappropriate way, and I knew she was just waiting on the right time to make a move on him."

"Really girl…" Jaze replies. "Yes honey," Whit says, "and I'm not crazy I used to see a lot of things that your daddy thought I didn't see."

"Like what girl…" Jaze says. Whit pauses. "Look at you trying to be grown," Whit smiles, "no that is enough gossip for you tonight little girl." "Okay Mama." Jaze returns her mama's smile.

Charlie Breeze is at the bar flirting harmlessly with a cute white bar tender. Jay and Cidra Bell are on the dance floor, doing the

Electric Slide in the middle of a huge crowd including Tyrone and his new fiancé, former Orlando police detective Osiana Blue.

Love is out front playing catch with K.J... It turns out the little man is a natural at football, so Love keeps a tiny football with him everywhere he goes. This way whenever his son wants to play catch he's always ready.

Everybody at the reception seems immensely happy. Well almost everybody. Cam is all alone in one of the bathrooms in the back of the building. Inside the cold dark stall, she can't seem to stop her tears.

(Cam)

"My emotions have nothing to do with Keldrick," Cam tells God, *"I'm just sad and embarrassed that my father isn't here to have a father daughter dance with me, he didn't give me away to K.C., or walk me down the aisle. Every little girl deserves that. I'll never get this day, or this moment back and it hurts so bad. But I'll be okay I know my daddy is in a much better place. God, I swear... I don't swear, I promise that I will love this man with all of me. My path to become his wife may have been unsavory, but our life together will be nothing short of ideal in your eyes. I'm giving the rest of my life to you. Hold my hand and guide my husband and me in your way, down your perfect path."*

"Oh, bitch shut up," a voice says from outside Cam's stall, "God don't hear you, only Satan does. He can't wait to meet you in Hell. I've been there before... trust me you'll fit in perfectly."

The voice on the other side of the stall door is so eerily familiar to Cam her blood has instantly turned ice cold. Cam slowly stands up and wipes her face. On top of the back of the toilet she finds an old screwdriver, from where some maintenance man was probably in here fixing something earlier. Cam takes a couple deep breaths. Then she hears a gun cock from the other side of the door.

"Don't get quiet now bitch," the voice says, "keep talking to your false gods." Cam knows hiding in this stall can't save her.

She unlocks the door with the screwdriver held tightly behind her back. Then she slowly pushes the door open. Cam's eyes bulge at the sight through the open bathroom stall door. Her heart feels as if it has sunken to her ass, and her stomach is more than weak.

"Megan," she whispers, "I thought you were dead." "Negative." Megan says out of the side of her deformed mouth. "What did he do to you?" Cam asks stepping towards her twin sister.

"Back up bitch…" Megan tells her. "Megan, you need help." Cam says. "You helped me enough," Megan replies aiming the gun at Cam's chest, "Love attempts to murder me in the church on my wedding day, and you just happen to be right there, ready to take my place. I'm not stupid Cameron… bitch you even have my dress on."

Cam knows as long as she can keep her distraught sister talking she won't shoot her. But she smells like she's been dead for days, and she looks like a zombie who just climbed out of her own grave.

"Megan, I didn't know what happened," Cam lies, "Love just brought me the dress and told me to stand in for you. He said you were just late. I was trying to help you sissy."

"Bitch don't sissy me," Megan demands, "we are not twelve anymore."

"I'm sorry." Cam says. Cam knows that either she or Megan cannot leave this bathroom alive. Because, if Megan makes it out alive and tells what happened to her, Cam will either go to prison for life or Love will kill her before she has a chance to snitch on him. Or even worse she will lose K.C. forever. Either way her life as she knows it will
be over.

Megan is practically standing there dead. She's only hanging on by a very thin limb. Cam knows if she can get close enough she can take Megan out with the screwdriver she's hiding behind her back.

"You know Cameron," Megan points the gun directly at her twin's face, "You destroyed my childhood." "Wait… I did what?" Cam asks. "You were so fucking perfect and prude," Megan says, "nobody wanted either one of us because of how stuck up *you were*."

"Megan, I wasn't stuck up I just wasn't ready to have sex," Cam tells her, "but anytime I did have a piece of a boyfriend you didn't mind screwing him and allowing him to believe you were me. I didn't have any interest in being the school slut."

"Neither did I bitch," Megan shouts, "I had no choice. It was either fuck them or just get ignored by them all. All those extra pretty light skin bitches were always in my way." "Mine too." Cam agrees.

"You didn't mind being alone," Megan recollects, "It didn't torment you to be unwanted like it did me. I brought that unhealthy way of thinking into my adult life, and I've been stranded there ever since."

"Then what happened?" Cam asks taking a tiny step towards her ugly, foul smelling twin. "Keldrick happened," Megan says, "Keldrick *"Kool Hands"* Cole, found me at my dead-end job, thought I was you my perfect twin sister, and my sad existence changed forever."

"Megan what did Love do to you sis?" Cam asks again. "He beat me, shot me, strangled me, burned me, and then he buried me in that order." Megan cries. "But he fucked up and left me breathing." she continues.

Cam takes another step towards her sister. Just two more steps and she will be close enough to stab her right in the heart. Megan begins to cry lowering her gun to her side.

Cam realizes her identical twin is just vulnerable enough now for her to make her move with the screwdriver. She should probably take one more step but, she doesn't want to startle her sister and cause her to pull the trigger on accident.

"It's okay *sissy…*" Cam lies again. The bathroom door opens. Cam swings the screwdriver hard… Megan raises the gun quickly. ***BANG!!!***

(K.C.)

Sitting in a lone chair towards the front of the dance floor is the lucky groom. The big man is so full of love and hatred right now. No one is watching him but he feels like the entire room is staring at him. He stands up and walks towards the food. He passes it and makes his way out of the back door.

"Mama, are you watchin' me," he whispers, *"tell me Mama are you watching me up there with God? If you are I hope you're proud of me now. I'm successful and I'm already a better man than my father was. I'll be rich even after I die. Mama I could spend a million dollars every day for the rest of my life and I still couldn't spend it all. Lance told me you were making money off me Mama but it's okay. I'm not mad. I wanted you to be happy. You could have asked me for anything Mama, and I would have done everything in my power to give it to you. I swear to God I would have died for you, and... it is my fault that you're not here with me today. You died... no you were murdered on my watch. Jaze told me how Lance killed you Mama. And I would kill him now for you, but I know that's not what you would want. So, I will love him. I will love my baby brother now the way we should have when he was a lonely, confused little boy. I love you Mama and I just pray... I pray that you are proud of me."*

"She is... so proud of you baby." a soft shaky voice says from the door way. "Baby..." he says.

"Yeah..." she replies. "Are you okay, there's blood on your dress?" he asks walking towards her. "I'm fine." she insists. "Baby..." K.C. says.

"Yes Keldrick..." she replies. "K.J. is not my real son." he admits. "I know babe, but he still belongs to you," she tells him, "and soon I'm going to give you a son and another daughter."

Keldrick doesn't respond. "Forget the reception babe," she says, "let's just get the kids and go home." K.C. silently agrees, and they do just that.

Chapter 21
Life after Keldrick

(Whitney & Charlie)

I'm an adult so I have to put my childhood behind me once and for all. K.C. was my high school sweetheart, everybody knows that but I'm almost thirty now and high school ended for me over twelve years ago. And my fantasy of being his wifey officially died the second Cameron said I do.

All is not lost though I have a good man who loves me very much. My man is strong, intelligent, sexy, and he has his own massive income. Life is good, I can't complain.

Cam is Keldrick's wife but she still belongs to me. I don't go a day without speaking to her or a week without having her over to my house for a play date with Charlie and me. My overall life with him couldn't be any better.

My body feels better than ever. This is because Charlie brings me here to the Gold's Gym on Galiano Street in Coral Gables three to four times a week.

Today we're working on my thighs and buns. Not that they need any work, but I gotta keep it tight though. Charlie is in perfect shape and most days like today he doesn't workout with me, he just shows me what to do. Today he's even dressed in street clothes, so I know he has no intentions to sweat with me at all today.

Whitney looks across the gym at a tall man bending down to drink from a water fountain. She doesn't speak for at least thirty seconds. She almost forgets that Charlie is even there with her.

Charlie notices Whitney staring at the man. "Babe," he says, "you good?" Charlie asks. Whit doesn't respond. She turns around and begins to pack her gym bag. First, she puts her towels in the bag, then her water bottle, and lastly her headphones and cell phone. Then she zips her bag up.

"Whitney…" Charlie kneels down beside her. Whit turns back around to try and get another glimpse of the mysterious man. He's gone.

"Where is he?" she asks aloud. "Who…" Charlie inquires. "The guy," she says, "the guy… the, the tall guy who was just drinking from the water fountain like five seconds ago."

"Who is he?" Charlie asks. "Where, the fuck did he go!" Whit exclaims as she stands up tossing her bag over her strong shoulder.

"Whitney who is he?" Charlie asks again. "It doesn't matter," she says, "you're letting him get away." she tells him.

"The men's locker room…" Charlie mumbles. "What? I can't hear you, Charlie speak up!" she demands. "The guy from the water fountain," Charlie says, "he went inside the men's locker room. Damn are you really gonna disrespect me like this though? I mean damn Whit we do live together." he reminds her.

Whit looks up into the dreadhead's eyes. "Boy shut up." she takes off towards the men's locker room. Once she reaches the door she walks in with no remorse. Charlie follows closely behind her. She checks the bathroom stalls, and the showers, but she doesn't see the man anywhere. She hears the door open to the locker room, as she sticks her head around the corner from the showers she can see his tall frame leaving out. She walks towards the door as calmly as she possibly can. As she and Charlie step out of the locker room they're greeted by three angry gym employees.

"Excuse me sir," the short bald employee in the middle says, "your wife can't shower with you in our facilities."

"Really," Charlie smiles at the man, "did you figure that out all by yourself you short oompa loompa looking fuck?" Charlie laughs at him.

"Listen smart ass," the muscle bound Hispanic employee on the right speaks, "we're going to have to escort you both out."

"That's fine." Charlie says. Whitney rushes off towards the front door after the tall man.

"Where is that bitch going and why is she running?" the third employee yells as Whit rushes off ahead of them all.

Charlie pats his coat pocket to make sure he has his gun. "Watch your mouth, you black mother fucker!" Charlie demands.

"Yeah whatever," the brown skinned employee says to Charlie, "follow her and both of ya'll get the fuck out now!"

"I'll tell you what," Charlie steps towards all three of them as Whitney runs out of the front door, "how about all three of you pussies meet me outside and we can handle this like men?"

"After work, we can do it…" the black guy tells him. "I'm off work now." the short bald employee says.

Charlie laughs at the short man. "Yea right Sméagol," Charlie continues to laugh at him, "You ain't in my league little man." Charlie turns around and finally realizes that Whitney is long gone.

"Hold that thought." he tells the three of them before rushing outside in search of his girlfriend. Outside the front door he doesn't see her anywhere but he can hear her voice. She's yelling. Whitney is in danger. Charlie follows her voice all the way around to the back of the building.

As he turns the corner he finds Whitney up under the tall man from the water fountain. He's on top of her thrusting wildly.

"You got lucky the first-time bitch," the man says, "but this time I'm gonna make sure you get it."

Charlie runs full speed towards them. The man pulls a knife out of his pocket and cuts a whole in the crotch of Whit's workout pants. "No!" she screams.

At top speed Charlie pushes the man knocking him to the ground a few feet away from Whitney. Then he quickly picks her up off the ground.

"Baby…" he says. "Thank you, baby…" Whit cries.

"Who is this fool?" Charlie asks as the man makes his way back to his feet. Whitney doesn't respond, she just continues to use the end of her shirt to dab at the blood on her bottom lip from where he punched her twice.

"Oh, so you wanna fight huh **boy**?" the man starts to walk towards them. Charlie quickly raises his gun at the man, stopping him cold in his tracks.

"Whitney," Charlie yells, "who the fuck is he?" She doesn't respond, she just continues to stare at the man with poison in her eyes. "Girl," Charlie says, "you better tell me something because I'm
about to empty my clip in this big ass dude."

Whitney starts to walk towards the man with no obvious fear. As soon as she's close enough she slaps him hard across the face. He lifts his hand to swing back. Charlie fires a warning shot high in the air. The tall man puts his evil hand back down by his side.

"You hit women because you are weak…" Whitney pushes him. "And you're weak because no one ever showed you how to be a real man." she pushes him again harder this time. "So, for that," she tells him, "you lose at life… and you will die."

Charlie starts to approach them. "And you were really just gonna rape me in this alley," Whitney continues to hit the man, "you were going to go inside of me completely raw, knowing what you are, and what you're carrying inside of you? You tried to kill me again Corey, you son of a bitch!" Whitney yells at the man, just before spitting in his face.

281

Charlie now stands right beside Whitney with his gun still pointed directly at the tall man. "Whitney who is this…" Charlie asks one last time. Whitney looks at Charlie and then snatches his gun from him.

The tall man begins to step backwards with his hands held high in the air. "Whitney," Charlie says, "baby, what the hell are you doing?" Whitney aims the gun at the tall man's head and shoots him twice before he falls to the ground lifeless.

Standing over his limp body now, she proceeds to empty Charlie's clip in the man's head and chest.

"Baby no!" Charlie yells snatching his weapon away from her. Down on her knees now on top of the dead man's body Whit begins to try to scratch his dark eyes out of his bleeding head.

Charlie picks her up and carries her far away from the body. Then he sits her down as she begins to yell and cry hysterically. Charlie slaps her hard across the face one time. She straightens up.

"Baby…" he says. "Yes." she replies. "Are you back with me now?" he asks.

"Yes." she looks down the alley at the tall man's dead body. "Oh no," she cries, "What did I do? Everything just went black…" "It's okay." Charlie tries to comfort her.

"It was a mistake; I take it all back I didn't mean to do it..." she cries.

"Look at me baby…" Charlie pleads with her. She obeys. "Who was he?" he asks. "Corey, he was Love's ex-boyfriend," she tells him, "years ago he beat me really bad, then when I confronted him today he just tried to rape me, and he has now tried to give me AIDS more than once."

"Damn baby," Charlie says, "Look if you just do what I say everything will be fine okay?" "I don't wanna… I can't go to jail Charlie I'm not built for that lifestyle." she cries.

"Baby," he says, "you are not going to jail, if anything I'm going to jail. This is my gun okay? I shot this mother fucker, you didn't do anything wrong. Okay?" he tells her. Whit doesn't respond.

"Whitney," he shakes her hard, "Did you hear me baby?" "Yes, Charlie I heard you." she cries. Charlie reaches in his pocket, and then hands her his car keys.

"Leave," he says, "take my car and go home. Don't look for me I'll be back in a few days. Just forget this ever happened, okay baby?" he says.

Whitney looks down again at the bloody mess that used to be Corey's body. "Go," Charlie pushes her away, "run baby go now!"

Whit turns and starts running full speed. "I love you Charlie Breeze!" she yells over her fleeing shoulder. She never looks back once.

Her heart has dropped to her stomach and is beating excruciatingly fast. After jumping in Charlie's Phantom, she cranks up and speeds back to the house to burn her clothes and take a hot shower.

Chapter 22
Father Daughter Retreat

"**W**ake up baby girl, today's the day." K.C. yells through Jaze's door. "Okay Dad," she yells back, "I'm getting up." Six months ago, K.C. and Jaze received an invitation to a father-daughter retreat at the Miami, Winton Woods Park. The retreat is only two days, but the entire weekend's itinerary is filled with activities that are designed to strengthen the bond between each father-daughter couple at the retreat.

Kel and Jaze arrive early for the bus that is taking them to the campgrounds. They sit on a bench near another father and daughter who appear to be waiting on the same bus. "Hi, my name is Ricky Brown Sr., and this beautiful angel next to me is my ten-year-old baby girl Katrice." the man says in a delightful New York accent.

"Nice to meet you both," Kel shakes the nice man's hand, "My name is…" "Are you kidding me," Mr. Brown interjects, "I know who you are. Hell, the whole world knows who you are." Kel smiles to himself. "The question is Keldrick do you know yourself?" Brown asks. "What do you mean Mr. Brown?" Kel asks.

"Well son," he says, "it seems to me that sometimes when people are given so much at one time, they tend to lose sight of what really matters."

"Maybe you're right sir." Keldrick replies. "I'm right there's no doubt about that," Mr. Brown chuckles to himself, "now of course I'm not perfect by a long shot. I've made plenty of mistakes but I love my wife and all of my kids with a fierce passion that not even death could destroy."

"That's beautiful." Mr. Brown. "It really is," Brown agrees, "even if God forbid, I pass away my love for my family will live on. Do you know why that is Keldrick..." "No sir," Kel admits, "Why is that?"

"Well now it's simple son," he explains, "I have four kids and a good-looking wife. I try to make sure as much as possible, I show them all how much I love and care for them now, while I'm still here. True love like that never dies. It lives on through a lifetime of lessons, memories, and mistakes."

"You're a very wise man Mr. Brown." K.C. admits. "Thanks son," he replies, "call me Ricky. By the way I'm the retreat leader. The bus is parked on the backside of the gym, has been since seven this morning." The two men and their daughters all share a good laugh together.

"Then why are we sitting here?" K.C. asks smiling at Mr. Brown. "Well we've all been here for over an hour waiting on you, superstar," Brown says, "but I couldn't leave without you. God has a plan for you, and your beautiful daughter. He has a plan for your entire family in fact, and this weekend I'm going to help show you exactly
what that is."

"I'm ready and willing." K.C. stands up to grab his and Jaze's bags. "You ready to ride Tricey?" Mr. Brown asks his adorable shy daughter. "Yeah Daddy, I'm ready." Katrice replies. "Then up we go..." Brown picks Katrice up high in the air as she screams joyfully. Brown places his princess on his shoulders so he can carry her to the bus.

Katrice wishes she could freeze this moment in time and ride on her dad's shoulders like this forever. Jaze and K.C. can tell how close Katrice, and her loving father Ricky Brown Sr. are, and they know with his guidance, and wisdom they can get to that point as well.

On the bus, all of the father daughter couples are lost in conversation except Keldrick and his baby girl. He stares down at his daughter wishing he knew what to say to her. She's looking out of the bus window probably lost in some childish daydream. He doesn't want to disturb her, but he also knows that this trip was designed to bring them closer together. He thinks long and hard on what to say to her.

"So princess, are you still wetting the bed?" Kel asks, knowing he just asked the worst possible question. She looks up at him with a sad face. She quickly looks through the crack of their seat to see if the people behind them heard her dad's embarrassing question. "I'm sorry baby," he whispers, "nobody heard me though." "Daddy," she whines quietly, "why would you ask me that… here?"

"I was just trying to start a conversation with you honey." he admits. "Not a good topic Daddy." she says.

"Well, talk to me Jazzy he pleads with her," "tell me what's on your mind." "I don't know Daddy," she responds, "nothing, really I guess."

"No, I know there's something on your mind Jazzy, tell Daddy." he prods. Jaze doesn't respond. "It doesn't matter what it is," he continues, "boys, basketball, your mom…"

"Okay first off dad I will never talk to you about boys," she confirms, "that's just weird. And I don't like boys, I just like Jojo." she tells him. K.C. smiles at her.

"I thought you didn't want to talk about boys, baby girl?" he asks. "I don't," she tells him, "Josiah is not a boy Daddy he's my best friend."

"Okay," Kel agrees, "well what about basketball? Can we talk about that?" "Oh, basketball is cool right now," Jaze says, "we got this new point guard named Dominique. She's from California, and she can really dribble the ball well. Her crossover is deadly Daddy."

"Is she better than you princess?" K.C. asks. "I don't know." she replies.

"Did the coach give her your starting position?" he asks. "No, not yet..." Jaze tells him.

"Wait, wait, wait," Kel says, "what do you mean not yet?" K.C. asks. "Not yet Daddy," Jaze repeats, "coach didn't give Dominique my starting position yet."

"What is your last name little girl?" Kel turns towards her. Jaze stares up at him with her little brows wrinkled tightly.

"Um Daddy," she says, "do you have amnesia again, or is this some kind of joke?" she asks. "I know exactly who you are," he tells her, "Now like I said before, what is your last name?"

"Cole..." she replies. "That's right," he says, "you are a Cole, and we do not fail. You have been the starting point guard on the **Florida Fire** traveling youth basketball team since the day you joined the team. That is not going to change unless you allow it to."

"But Daddy..." she says. "No buts Jaze," he interjects, "we do not fail." "Her crossover is sick Dad," Jaze reminds him, "I can't guard her so how can I expect to play over her?"

"Defense," he says, "we just need to work on your defense. What else?" he asks. "Well she's also taller than me, and her dad is the coach's brother." Jaze tells him. "Well we can't do anything about the last part," Kel tells her, "but defensively, that's a plus for you Jaze." "Being shorter than her?" she asks. "Yes," he tells her, "that means your closer to the ground than she is."

"Yeah so what..." Jaze says. "So," K.C. explains, "when you guard her you break all the way down into your defensive stance that I taught you, and when she puts the ball on the floor you swipe it away."

"I can try." Jaze says. "Just study her tendencies," Kel says, "do you know what tendencies are baby?" "Yeah that's something someone does most of the time." Jaze replies.

287

"You are so smart for an eleven-year-old." he tells her through a proud smile. "So, you watch her," he continues, "and you learn her tendencies. Whatever side she goes to most times when she drives to the basket, you just start forcing her to go the opposite direction." "Okay Dad." she says.

"Thanks Daddy," she smiles up at him, "I thought you didn't care about how I played anymore."

"Jazemene Argelle Cole," he takes her tiny hand in his and kisses it, "as long as you live you will always be on my mind. And everything you do will always matter to me. Okay?"

"Daddy…" she says. "Yeah babe." he replies. "Can I live with Mommy and Uncle Charlie?" she asks. Keldrick can feel his very heart sinking to his stomach.

"Why Jazemene?" he asks. "I don't know," she replies, "I keep trying to fight it… but I really miss her Daddy." "Wow," he says, "Okay…"

"I don't want to live with them forever Daddy," she tells him, "just for the summer." "If that's what you want Jazemene," he looks out of the window, "I will speak to your mother and your step mother about it." "Yes!" she gushes in triumph.

Not really sure how to feel about this new development, Keldrick can't help but to smile at his daughter's obvious joy. He knows Jazemene is not choosing Whitney over him, but it still feels like she is. Deep down K.C. knows just how great this is that Jaze wants her mother to be in her life going forward.

The bond between mother and daughter can make or break a young girl's future. So, for that reason alone Keldrick is going to find it inside himself to not stand in the way of what his daughter is asking for.

"Alright campers," Mr. Brown says from the front of the bus, "the campsite is just up the road here. After we park, we will leave everything on the bus and go down to the lake to eat some barbecue and take some time to get to know one another."

"Good," Jaze whispers to her dad, "because I'm starving. Since *somebody* didn't feed me this morning."

"I'm sorry babe we got a late start." K.C. reminds her. "I know Dad," she smiles, "I'm glad we came on this trip. I really missed you Daddy." "I missed you too pumpkin." he admits.

The retreat was a complete success. As Jaze and K.C. head back home their relationship has new life, meaning, and most importantly a new understanding. They owe it all to the wise and comical Mr. Ricky Brown Sr.

(R.I.P. Mr. Brown)

Chapter 23
We will follow God...

(Pastor White's final appeal)

P astor White has so much on his heart and mind this Sunday morning. As he finishes his sermon, and prepares to leave the pulpit he offers his final appeal.

"I have loved you with an everlasting love. Before... time began, I knew you. For years you swam around in a sea of meaningless, searching for love, hoping for hope. All that time I was pursuing you, aching to pursue you in My compassionate arms. I lifted you out of the sea of despair and set you down on a firm foundation. Sometimes you felt naked... exposed to the revealing Light of My Presence. I wrapped an ermine robe around you: My robe of righteousness. I sang you a love song, whose beginning and end are veiled in eternity. I infused meaning into your mind and harmony in your heart. Join Me in singing My song. Together we will draw others out of darkness into My Marvelous Light."

Pastor White steps down out of the pulpit and walks down onto the floor directly in front of his congregation. *"Jesus... is calling you people of God. He is calling you right now, and he wants to hold you and wash all your painful tears and sins away."*

Pastor White pauses briefly to smile comfortingly at little

Jazemene on the second row, and now he smiles and nods to the rest of her family.

"*Some are called*" Pastor says, "*some are sent, and some just packed up and went.*" he laughs comfortingly.

"**We are all ministers in some shape form or fashion,**" he continues, "*But if you want it... you may not be the one. Let me say that again. If you want it... you may not be the one. See God... often times, calls people who don't want to be called. We come here to church to worship, praise, and glorify Him. We don't come in here to be seen, and glorify ourselves or each other. We, People of God... are not in show business... we are in the soul business. And now together we all have a Goal to go home with Jesus. In Heaven... there is no Westside or Eastside of Heaven. There is no white or black side of Heaven... no racial or economical barriers between us. All of the blood is red and its purity will make us all as white as snow. God is calling you right now... The ball is in your court. Make your move People of God. I love you all, be eternally blessed.*"

Epilogue

Jaze is living with Whitney and Charlie Breeze for the summer. Her baby brother K.J. is in Brazil with his father Love, on an amazing two-month South American excursion. Tyrone's theme park is doing very well to say the least. He and Osiana have a huge new house together in Miami, and they plan to get married in a few months at Pastor White's church. Jay has released several successful mix tapes. And now that his fan base has gotten freakishly big, he is considering releasing his first full length album later this year. His main focus now though musically is producing and managing new young talent in the Miami and Orlando area. He and Jaze's teacher Cidra Bell are still dating but nothing too serious.

(Cam)

Lying here in his arms, in our bed I finally know what true happiness is. I will never in my life forget that I owe every ounce of my joy to my handsome brother in law, Lance Orlandis Vinson, B.K.A. Love. The moment my dead twin lifted her gun and aimed it at me that last time, my entire life flashed before my eyes. Love walked in a second before she tried to shoot me, and when I swung that old rusty screwdriver at that bitch, he shot her in the back of her head. Luckily not much blood got on me or my gorgeous dress. After he shot her, he told me to go find my husband and he would take care of everything else.

Cam rolls over and passionately kisses her husband's big soft lips. "Goodnight Mr. Keldrick Jermaine Cole Sr." she says.

He smiles knowingly at her. "I don't know exactly what happened, and I probably never will," K.C. admits, "but know that I know exactly who you are. I can tell the difference. Goodnight... Mrs. *Cameron* Jiles Cole." Cam's heart stops... and then she smiles with her flushed face dug deep into his strong chest.

THE END

Bonus Chapter

*H*e rarely comes here anymore. In fact, the city itself rarely crosses his mind ever. Jet-setting around the world has become common place to him. Being gone is his only comfort zone now. The unknown is the only welcomed constant component in his life at this point.

Nothing can stand in the way of the level of freedom his mind, body, and soul know now. He has been to each end of the spiritual spectrum and back again. He has been the deepest darkest demon the world has ever known, and he has been a saver and protector of the weak, a loving brother and uncle, as well as the primary care giver to his beautiful son.

None-the-less he's back in the city now. This could very well be his last time in Orlando, Florida ever. He didn't want to come back at all but a promise is a promise, and a deal is a deal.

One thing that comforts him is the fact that the only people that know he's the "Florida Finisher" are all dead. Well, all except for his family members of course, and they would never tell a soul. The Florida Finisher, they actually gave him a name and everything.

After Osiana Blue left the force the chief eventually dropped the case completely. Chief Tiago knows the only person he had who was capable of finding a killer of Love's magnitude was Detective Blue. The day she resigned, he already decided in his mind that the case of the Florida Finisher would never be solved.

A bright red Camaro pulls up in front of the Orlando police station. "I'll be right back." he says looking over his shoulders. He checks his large pants pocket, to make sure his silencer is already attached and ready to go.

He says a short mental prayer, and then takes a deep breath before stepping out of his gorgeous car adorned with brand new gold rims and a matching gold grill in the front.

He's dressed in a black loose-fitting polo collar shirt, designer jeans, and concord 11 retro Jordan shoes laced tightly. His long dreads are pulled back into a rigid ponytail, and he has dark tinted black Ray Bans on his face.

Even as he gets closer and closer to the front door he realizes just how insane this last mission is, even for him. But for some reason that makes it all the more exciting to him. His adrenaline is pumping fiercely and maintaining an all-time high now.

As he grabs the handle to the front door he feels so powerful. He feels as if he could pull the entire door completely off its hinges.

As he walks in he's greeted by several friendly officers who speak and keep walking as if he's not the monumental threat that he is to all of them. Looking around Love tries to decide which way he thinks the Chief's office is.

"May I help you?" an ugly young clerk asks him from behind. Love spins around quickly trying not to make his panic, and surprise too obvious. "Excuse me…" he says to her, as he wipes the new sweat from his brown brows.

"Wow," she smiles an unpleasant toothy smile, "you are pretty, aren't you?" Love returns an uncomfortable smile. "Um yeah… thanks." he replies.

"May we help you with something," she's blushing now, "do you need to file a report, or do you need to report a *Florida Finisher* sighting maybe? We've been getting them all week." she laughs.

Love wrinkles his brows, crosses his arms, and settles into a comfortable posture. "What's funny miss…" he asks.

"Well," she explains, "the whole *Florida Finisher* case, right? The reason they can't find him… and the reason nobody really knows what he looks like is because the mother fucker doesn't really exist." she tells him. "Is that so?" Love inquires.

"You're damn right it's so," she confirms, "and what a weak name right? The *Florida Finisher,* like that's the best they could come up with?" she laughs.

"But you think this guy doesn't exist at all though?" Love asks. "If he does exist he's definitely *a gay*." she says.

Lance feels his blood beginning to boil rapidly. As the ugly young woman continues to unknowingly bash him to his face he can no longer hear a word she's saying. Her lips are moving but absolutely no sound is reaching Love's yellow ears.

"Where is Chief Tiago's office?" he interjects coldly. "It's… right down that hall, third door on the left," she turns around to point, "he's in there now. I actually just left his office moments ago. Do you have an appointment with him?"

"Yeah," Love replies blankly, "hey can you uh show me where the bathroom is?" he asks. "Sure, it's right over…" she starts.

"No, I want you to take me…" he interjects with a sick sexy smile. "Oh… Oh my," she returns his smile, "you wanna have random hot sex with me at my job, don't you?" She blushes bright red.

"I work at the police station," she whispers, "that would be *so epic*… and *so wrong*. Oh, to hell with it, you only live once right? And you are just too gorgeous to turn down. Come on…" she takes him by the hand.

As they walk Love notices that no one seems to be paying them any attention. When they reach the door, she turns around to see if anybody is watching. Love quickly grabs her by the head and pushes her inside.

After stepping inside the bathroom himself, he walks her into an empty stall. She immediately drops down to her knees and opens his zipper. After she licks his shiny head twice, Love pulls his gun out, pushes her back hard towards the toilet stool behind her, and shoots her twice in the face.

The blood on his dark shirt is barely noticeable. He quickly exits the bathroom and makes his way to the Chief 's office. He walks in without knocking.

"Who the hell are you?" Chief Tiago demands. "I'm Love," he says, "well technically I'm Lance right now but…"

"Love," Tiago repeats, "so you're the sorry son of a bitch that's been playing on my phone all damn day… trying to meet me somewhere?"

"You know," Love smirks, "I am actually *the son of a bitch*, but she's dead now and I killed her. Wow… it feels so good to admit that." Love looks all around him trapped inside his own new amazement. "And in a police station none-the-less," Love continues, "I killed Patterson the correctional officer, Ligetti my old scumbag landlord, my brother's father Paul, my childhood shrink, Bruce Granger. Man, the list just goes on and on." Love's smile is growing larger.

Tiago stands up on two shaky feet, with his eyes as wide open as they have ever been before. "You… you're the *Finisher*?" the chief stutters.

"In the flesh; you fat, sexist, son of a bitch," Love says," and if I knew who your mom was… I'd kill that ugly, old, brown bitch too sir." Love laughs in perfect rendition of an evil genius.

"Why me?" the chief asks. "All your victims were connected," Tiago continues, "everybody you killed wronged you in some way. I've done my research, there was always a connection. I don't even know you, hell I never even met you." the chief reminds Love.

"You sir," Love smiles as he pulls out his loaded weapon, "Owe your dark fate to a pretty young lady by the name of Osiana Blue.

297

Oh, and you also stopped answering my phone calls Chief Tiago...
see that's my biggest pet peeve."

"Detective Blue," the chief asks, "so you're working for a bitch?
You little faggot..." he says. Love lifts his gun.

"And that sir," Love says, "is my other huge pet peeve. Gay is a
sexual act that I have never willingly participated in."

With supreme satisfaction Love shoots the chief twice, once
in the head, and once in the chest. Walking around the desk Love
kneels down close to his limp body.

Chief Tiago's cold eyes are staring up into Love's eyes as he
devours his soul. With gloved hands, he locks the chief's door
from the inside and walks out as calmly as possible.

After jumping back in his car Love drives off slowly. "What took
you so long Daddy?" a voice says from the back seat. Love turns
around as he drives off to gaze at his handsome little boy.

"It's over now son," Love tells K.J. "Daddy is never gonna leave
you like that ever again. I promise..."

Characters

Jazemene Argelle Cole
Keldrick Jermaine Cole Jr. "K.J."
Cameron Candice Jiles "Cam"
Keldrick Jermaine "K.C." Cole
Whitney Michelle Powell "Suga Mama"
Lance Orlandis Vinson "Love"
Carlos Luis Sanchez "Dr. Sanchez"
Jacody "Jay" Miller
Tyrone "Tyboonie"
Linda Cole "Mama Cole"
Detective Blue
Megan
Josiah "JB" Bell
Cidra Denise Bell
Paul
Dr. Bruce Granger
Osiana

"MY PRAYER"

I pray that you all love and enjoy my characters as well as their stories. Know that all things are possible through Christ who strengthens us, and we can do nothing that matters without Him.

In Jesus name, I pray Amen.

M. De'Lure

If you enjoyed this novel you should check out these other *AMAZING* titles by De'Lure

Onyx Cielo: Book 1 -The Tree of Transformation- (Fantasy)
Take My Breath Away 1: Orlando Nights (Realistic Romance/ Drama/ Erotica)
Take My Breath Away 3: Moments (Realistic Romance/ Drama/ Erotica)
Passion Absolute –Radicon's Princess- (Realistic Romance/ Drama/Erotica)
De'Lure Shorts & Poem (Poetry/Drama/Short Stories)
De'Lure Shorts & Poems 2 (Poetry/Drama/Short Stories)
He Without Sin (Realistic/Romance/Drama)
Kissed (Realistic/ Drama/ Murder/ Mystery)
Mental Apex -Invisible Pyramids- (Poetic Perfection)

About the Author

De'Lure is a dreamer who writes with his heart and a very realistic imagination. His first passion was acting, but from that love spawned an even deeper passion for the art of writing. The imagery he uses to create stories is packed with all the components of legendary writing careers. Expect great things from De'Lure.

Love me, because I love you… or hate me because I love you. Either way I will continue to do what my God has created me to do until he calls me home.

Facebook: Published De'Lure
Email: ceom.love@gmail.com

www.ingramcontent.com/pod-product-compliance
Lightning Source LLC
Chambersburg PA
CBHW060516180626
46817CB00002B/378